CULTURAL VALUES
IN POLITICAL ECONOMY

CULTURAL VALUES IN POLITICAL ECONOMY

Edited by J. P. Singh

Foreword by Arjun Appadurai

Stanford University Press
Stanford, California

Stanford University Press
Stanford, California

Printed in the United States of America on acid-free, archival-quality paper

Library of Congress Cataloging-in-Publication Data

Names: Singh, J. P., editor.
Title: Cultural values in political economy / edited by J. P. Singh.
Description: Stanford, California : Stanford University Press, 2020. |
    Includes bibliographical references and index.
Identifiers: LCCN 2019053658 (print) | LCCN 2019053659 (ebook) |
    ISBN 9781503612686 (cloth) | ISBN 9781503612693 (paperback) |
    ISBN 9781503612709 (ebook)
Subjects: LCSH: Politics and culture. | Economics—Political aspects. | Culture—
    Economic aspects.
Classification: LCC JA75.7 .C854 2020 (print) | LCC JA75.7 (ebook) | DDC 306.2—
    dc23
LC record available at https://lccn.loc.gov/2019053658
LC ebook record available at https://lccn.loc.gov/2019053659

Cover photos (clockwise from lower left): Container ship *Aadrian*; San Francisco Museum of Modern Art; Emanuel African Methodist Church, Charleston, SC; factory building, Zlin, Czech Republic. All images from Wikimedia Commons.

Typeset by Newgen in 10/14 Minion

Contents

Tables and Figures

Tables

Figures

Foreword

Cultural Mediations and Political Economy

THERE IS A SHORT WAY TO STATE THE MESSAGE I GET FROM THIS wonderful set of chapters: *culture mediates between economy and politics.* But every term in this short statement could be debated and refined, and the authors do that carefully and thoughtfully. Especially in regard to culture, this book brings together various traditions of definition and recognizes that culture is simultaneously a horizon, a map, and a resource for actors seeking to define their political and economic goals. I appreciate the authors' opening up of key terms such as agency, interest, rationality, and collectivity. They have motivated me to think further about these terms, and rather than gloss over what the authors say about them, I add here some thoughts on these terms.

Agency has a complex and contested history in the social sciences. There is wide agreement that it implies the capacity to act on the world or, as Hannah Arendt (1958) taught us, to make something new in the world, thus making action different from mere behavior. Action in this Arendtian sense is thus always political, insofar as it seeks to make a nontrivial change in the way things appear to be. Arendt was not much concerned with culture in its disciplinary sense, but it does not take much discernment to see that her idea of action, as the initiation of something new in the world, has to do with creativity, vision, and change. It is thus deeply cultural, but it has little to do with habit, routine, or custom. It is about newness, innovation, and hope. Thus, Arendt's idea of action opens up a deep justification for thinking about culture as oriented as much to the future as to the past. As the authors in this book show in various contexts, culture is not the inert ballast against which economic or political action is undertaken. It is also a scheme for action, a map of possibilities, and a tool for making new arrangements in the world. Culture has everything to do with agency, since it is the broad cosmological canvas that informs and underwrites action, both individual and collective, and provides a repertoire of values to imagine or constrain action. Even if interest can be seen as informing individual action, politics is always a matter of collective action, and collective action is not possible without the navigational apparatus of culture.

Several of the chapters also take up the matter of interest, a term that is closely tied to ideas about choice, preference, and utility in neoclassical economics. It is no exaggeration to say that rational choice theory, the dominant paradigm for much recent work in political economy, is grounded in a certain idea of interest. This approach to interest ties it closely to calculation, choice, and utility maximization as motives for rational action. This is also the view that has allowed a certain kind of economic analysis to colonize many aspects of human behavior in areas as varied as marriage, suicide, segregation, crime, and more. This is a style of explanation that aims to explain everything worth explaining. And it eliminates culture by translating it into the language of preferences. Preferences are in turn seen as essential to market rationality, and market rationality is seen as the only form of rationality worth discussing. At best, culture in this view is a mechanism for bounding rationality. Through a remarkable conceptual sleight of hand, value is treated as reducible to interest, interest is made the basis of preference, and preference is treated as the explanatory key to choice. In this view, culture enriches our understanding of interest formation or preferences, but we learn nothing about culture as a generative factor, and we are not enabled to question the linear transformation of cultural values into interests. This view of interest more or less trivializes culture as an autonomous and collective system of meanings, values, and dispositions. It also dilutes the idea of collectivity.

The authors and the editor of this collection are deeply concerned about collectivity, solidarity, and community. This orientation accounts for their skepticism toward many brands of rational choice theory and their endorsement of the role of culture in economics and politics. I share their inclinations and have also worried over the years about how to define the social, the collective, and the solidarity as foundational concerns of the social sciences. What they have now prompted me to see is that in our world today, the populist right has largely captured the terrain of the social by mobilizing various fears, anxieties, resentments, and angers among populations that are close enough to cosmopolitan life to see its benefits but far enough from it to fear and resent it. This special focal distance from the globalized good life is a key to the followers of Donald Trump, Narendra Modi, Recep Tayyip Erdoğan, Marine Le Pen, and many other new authoritarians. This emerging global right has rewritten politics as exclusion by creating a compelling narrative of the wounds, harms, and humiliations of an imagined (often racialized) majority and by targeting various kinds of others (ethnic, religious, sexual, and racial) as the sources of their humiliation. Thus, sexual policing, moral censorship, immigration barriers, and racial superiority become a key to the cultural mobilization of the popular vote, and that vote becomes the basis for electing antidemocratic leaders. This is the death of democracy by democratic means. What this book points to is a new way of connecting value, interest, community, and inclusion by restoring the role of culture in accounting for political economy. The book goes beyond our current politics to bring in historical precedents from global commerce, the role of the Tea Party in eliminating export subsidies to firms, or the links between material and cultural values for evangelical Christians.

This approach to culture demands a rereading of the relationship between such terms as value, interest, collectivity, and agency in just the ways that the authors assembled here propose. Their chapters join the work of other scholars who argue that culture is the crucial mediator between economics and politics. But these authors also recognize that for such mediation to gain analytic and ethical traction, culture itself needs to be revisioned. As an anthropologist, I am especially receptive to this mandate. The future is as cultural as the past. And any approach to global transactions in the domain of state or market that confines culture to the past will lose the distinctive assets of the idea of culture. In this perspective, culture is the common ground for action as defined by Arendt, the creation of something new in the world.

Arjun Appadurai

Preface

RECENT POPULIST POLITICAL OUTCOMES AND THE PERVASIVE cultural anxieties about the global economy and its flows motivated this book. Periods of cultural turbulence can expose the compact between political interests, economic conditions, and human conduct. Existing explanations often address the material and distributional impact of the global economy, but cultural factors—dealing with sediments of socialization and ways of life—are now increasingly mobilized to explain interests and outcomes. To note that cultural anxieties explain the turbulence of our times is a useful starting point but somewhat tautological; we need to investigate the causes of this cultural turbulence.

This book analyzes the links between culture and political economy theoretically, historically, methodologically, and empirically. We start with recent events but seek to provide explanations that cover periods of both cultural turbulence and stability. The interdisciplinary scholarship offered in this book questions the widely held assumption in many social science analyses that holds culture constant, which in practice has sometimes meant keeping it out or marginalizing culture in the explanation.

We build on analyses across the social sciences that engage in the origins and impacts of cultural factors. The authors come from many disciplines, including anthropology, communication, economics, international relations, philosophy, political science, and sociology. Each of them enlists interdisciplinary literatures on culture. Many have published well-known studies dealing with culture and political economy.

Theoretically, most of the authors conceptualize culture as a set of values and alternatives—"cultural repertoires" or "tool kits," as sociologist Ann Swidler (1986, 273, 284) calls them—that are differentially mobilized but also shared across groups. Cultural repertoires are a capacity and a constraint for human conduct and, depending on the context, both shape and are shaped through material conditions. The intersection of cultural and material interests explains both the dynamism of the past and possibilities for the future.

Exploring the underlying cultural values in human interests does not make strategic or instrumental calculations of interests redundant. To use a term from anthropologist Clifford Geertz (1973, 27), the authors examine contexts in which cultural explanations provide "thick descriptions" of instrumental interests. They also go beyond instrumental interests and strategic calculations to analyze how cultural values constitute interests, including those contributing to cultural anxiety. A few trace the workings of culture through socially informed or sociotropic preferences. We avoid the language of cultural identity as it often assumes the dominance of a single cultural value or trait.

These theoretical moorings allow the authors to usefully operationalize culture through a variety of methods. The book includes historical, ethnographic, case study, and quantitative evidence for a variety of outcomes in which cultural factors mattered. Our intent is to examine theoretical and methodological ways in which culture may be examined as an explanation. Empirically, it would be impossible to examine a majority of relevant puzzles and outcomes in a single text. Nevertheless, we offer a mix of recent and historical examples as evidence.

This book developed from a two-day workshop at the University of Edinburgh where I was professor and chair of culture and political economy (2016–2018). The motivating events for the workshop were the Brexit referendum results and the election of Donald Trump as president of the United States. At the workshop, the authors presented short preliminary papers, and the discussions led to a collaborative endeavor over the next two years to develop the papers fully. The authors received extensive feedback at the workshop from at least two discussants for each paper, and there were also overall discussants at the workshop to suggest theoretical coherence and linkages among papers. We were careful to bring in discussants from various social studies ranging from anthropology to theology and religion. We thank the following scholars for their careful commentaries on the chapters presented in this book: Cora Lacatus, Faith Liddell, L. H. M. Ling, Dave O'Brien, John Odell, Nicholas Phillipson, Paolo Quattrone, Joshua Ralston, Laura Roselle, Michal Rozynek, Jo Shaw, and Oliver Turner. We are also immensely grateful to the University of Edinburgh for its financial and administrative support. In particular, Charlie Jeffrey, Fiona Mackay, and Dorothy Miell contributed both their support and scholarly insights toward this endeavor. Over the course of the year following the workshop, the authors continued to receive feedback from each other, and several colleagues are thanked individually in their chapters. Many authors also presented their papers at other workshops and conferences. Stanford University Press took an eager interest in this book and obtained two excellent and timely anonymous reviews for it. Apart from the reviewers, we thank Alan Harvey and his team for being careful and kind shepherds for our book. This includes Stephanie Adams, Sunna Juhn, Rebecca Logan, Caroline McKusick, Leah Pennywark, and Emily Smith.

On a personal note, I have gained immensely from living in three places over the last three years as this project crystalized from a workshop idea to an edited book. Numerous conversations with colleagues in Edinburgh; Washington, DC; and Berlin helped refine ideas about cultural values that I foreground in Chapter 1 along with empirical or historical examples from each place. Research in Germany during summer 2019 as a Richard von Weizsäcker Fellow with the Robert Bosch Academy provided a firsthand perspective on the rise of populist pressures in that country. My graduate students in the Technology, Culture, and Commerce seminar in the Schar School at George Mason University eagerly debated perspectives on cultural anxiety and political economy during the 2018–2019 academic year. More than ever (and as always!), my partner, Chuck Johnson, was ready to provide feedback on successive drafts and deliberate ideas. I am indebted to my colleagues, my students, and my wonderful partner. It is a great privilege to be part of intense and intellectually stimulating conversations in different places.

Finally, the authors hope that the chapters provide useful explanations of cultural stability and change and motivate scholars and students to undertake further studies of the links between culture and political economy. More than just culture is at stake: the stability of our political and economic systems depends on the cultural values that sustain them.

Contributors

Arjun Appadurai is professor of anthropology and globalization at the Hertie School of Governance in Berlin. He is also Paulette Goddard Professor of Media, Culture, and Communication at New York University. He is an internationally recognized scholar of globalization, the cultural dimensions of economic development, and struggles over national and transnational identity. He specializes in South Asia. Appadurai is the author of numerous books and articles on migration, transnational dynamics, sovereignty, and media. The most recent is *Banking on Words: The Failure of Language in the Age of Derivative Finance* (2015).

Daniel M. Hausman grew up in the Chicago suburbs and then attended Harvard College, where he first majored in biochemistry and then received his BA in 1969 in English history and literature. After teaching intermediate school in the Bronx and earning an MA in teaching at New York University, he spent two years studying moral sciences at Gonville and Caius College, Cambridge, before earning his PhD in philosophy in 1978 at Columbia University. He has taught at the University of Maryland at College Park, Carnegie Mellon University, and, since 1988, the University of Wisconsin–Madison, and he has visited at the Institute for Advanced Studies and the London School of Economics. Most of his research has focused on methodological, metaphysical, and ethical issues at the boundaries between economics and philosophy, and in collaboration with Michael McPherson, he founded the journal *Economics* *and Philosophy* and edited it for its first ten years. He is also the editor of *The Philosophy of Economics: An Anthology* (2007). His most important books are *Capital, Profits, and Prices: An Essay in the Philosophy of Economics* (1981), *The Inexact and Separate Science of Economics* (1992), *Economic Analysis and Moral Philosophy* (coauthored with Michael McPherson, 1996), *Causal Asymmetries* (1998), *Economic Analysis, Moral Philosophy, and Public Policy* (coauthored with Michael McPherson, 2006), and *Preference, Value, Choice and Welfare* (2011). His most recent books are *Valuing Health: Well-Being, Freedom, and Suffering* (2015) and a third edition of *Economic Analysis, Moral Philosophy and Public Policy* (coauthored with Michael McPherson and Debra Satz, 2017). In 2009, Hausman was elected to the American Academy of Arts and Sciences.

Kristen Hopewell is an associate professor at the University of British Columbia. Her research and teaching interests are in international political economy and global governance and development, with a focus on emerging powers. Her first book, *Breaking the WTO: How Emerging Powers Disrupted the Neoliberal Project* (2016), analyzes the rising power of Brazil, India, and China at the World Trade Organization (WTO) and their impact on the multilateral trading system. This research was supported by a Fulbright Fellowship, the National Science Foundation (NSF), and the Social Science and Humanities Research Council of Canada (SSHRC). Her current research examines the changing global dynamics of export credit in the context of contemporary power shifts. This research has been supported by an Economic and Social Research Council (ESRC) Future Research Leaders grant. Hopewell has been a visiting fellow at Peking University in Beijing, the Graduate Institute of International and Development Studies (HEID) in Geneva, and the Lyndon B. Johnson School of Public Affairs at the University of Texas at Austin. Before entering academia, she worked as a trade official for the Canadian government and as an investment banker for Morgan Stanley.

Miles Kahler is Distinguished Professor at the School of International Service, American University, and senior fellow for Global Governance at the Council on Foreign Relations in Washington, DC. Previously, he was Rohr Professor of Pacific International Relations and Distinguished Professor of Political Science at the School of Global Policy and Strategy and the Political Science Department, University of California, San Diego (UCSD). He is a member of the editorial boards of *International Organization, Global Gov-*

ernance, and *Global Summitry* and an associate editor of the Cambridge Elements Series in International Relations. Kahler has been a distinguished fellow at the Munk School of Global Affairs and Public Policy at the University of Toronto (2018) and a fellow at the Woodrow Wilson International Center for Scholars (2012–2013) and the Center for Advanced Study in the Behavioral Sciences at Stanford University (2007–2008). He has published widely in the fields of international politics and international political economy, including articles and books on global governance, international financial institutions, and Asia-Pacific regionalism. His current research projects include the development of institutions of complex governance, the changing role of emerging economies in world politics and global governance, and the sources of cosmopolitanism and parochialism in contemporary politics.

Sharon R. Krause is William R. Kenan, Jr. University Professor of Political Science at Brown University. She is the author of *Liberalism with Honor* (2002), *Civil Passions: Moral Sentiment and Democratic Deliberation* (2008), and *Freedom Beyond Sovereignty: Reconstructing Liberal Individualism* (2015). She has also published numerous articles on topics in classical and contemporary liberalism and democratic theory, ranging from David Hume and Montesquieu to Simone de Beauvoir; freedom and social inequality; contemporary theories of justice; and environmental domination. Her book *Civil Passions* won the 2010 Spitz Prize for best book in liberal or democratic theory from the Conference for the Study of Political Thought and the 2009 Alexander George Book Award for best book in political psychology from the International Society of Political Psychology. Her work has appeared in such journals as *Political Theory, The Review of Politics, Politics and Gender, Contemporary Political Theory, Philosophy and Social Criticism, Polity,* and *History of Political Thought.* She received her BA from Wellesley College, an MTS from Harvard Divinity School, and a PhD in political theory from Harvard University.

Steven Livingston is the director of the Institute for Data, Democracy, and Politics (IDDP) and professor of media and public affairs at George Washington University. His research centers on technology and politics, including the use of various digital technologies in open-source investigations of war crimes and human rights abuse. In his role as director of IDDP, he oversees a multidisciplinary team of researchers who identify and track distorted digital content on social media platforms. Livingston is coauthor (with W. Lance

Bennett and Regina Lawrence) of *When the Press Fails: Political Power and the News Media from Iraq to Katrina* (2007). He is coeditor (with Gregor Walter-Drop) of *Bits and Atoms: Information and Communication Technology in Areas of Limited Statehood* (2014) and (with W. Lance Bennett) of *The Disinformation Age: Politics, Technology and Disruptive Communication in the United States* (forthcoming). He is author of *Africa's Evolving Infosystems: A Pathway to Security and Stability* (2011) and *Africa's Information Revolution: Implications for Crime, Policing, and Citizen Security* (2013). Since 2010, Livingston has worked and traveled to more than fifty-five countries, including Iraq and Afghanistan on several occasions. Most of these efforts have involved what he calls humanitarian work by way of governance capacity building.

Mark J. Rozell is dean of the Schar School of Policy and Government and the Ruth D. and John T. Hazel Chair in Public Policy at George Mason University. He is a political scientist and author of nine books and editor of twenty books on various topics in US government and politics including the presidency, religion and politics, media and politics, and interest groups in elections. He has testified before Congress several times regarding separation of powers issues and has lectured extensively in the United States and abroad on similar topics. He writes columns for major news dailies and is consulted frequently by media for his expertise in US national and state politics. Rozell received his PhD in politics from the University of Virginia. He has served as acting dean and then dean of the Schar School since 2013 and previously as director of the Master of Public Policy program. He came to Mason in 2004 from The Catholic University of America, where he was Ordinary Professor and chair of the Department of Politics.

J. P. Singh is professor of international commerce and policy at the Schar School of Policy and Government, George Mason University, and Richard von Weizsäcker Fellow with the Robert Bosch Academy in Berlin. From 2016–2018, he was chair of culture and political economy and director of the Institute for International Cultural Relations at the University of Edinburgh. Singh has authored five monographs, edited four books, and published dozens of scholarly articles. His single-authored books include *Sweet Talk: Paternalism and Collective Action in North-South Trade Negotiations* (2017), *Negotiation and the Global Information Economy* (2008), and *Globalized Arts: The Entertainment Economy and Cultural Identity* (2011), which won the American Political Science Association's award for best book in information technology and politics in 2012. His current book project is *Development 2.0: How Technologies Can Foster Inclusivity in the Developing World*. Singh is editor of the journal *Arts and International Affairs* and Stanford's book series on emerging frontiers in the global economy; he is *Global Perspectives'* section editor for Political Economy, Markets, and Institutions. He served as editor from 2006–2009 and dramatically increased the impact of *Review of Policy Research*, the journal specializing in the politics and policy of science and technology.

David Throsby is Distinguished Professor in the Department of Economics at Macquarie University. He is known internationally for his work as an economist with specialist interests in the economics of the arts and culture. He holds a BA and master's degree from the University of Sydney and a PhD in economics from the London School of Economics. Throsby's research interests include the role of culture in economic development, the economic situation of individual artists, the economics of the performing arts, the creative industries, and the economics of heritage and the relationship between cultural and economic policy. He has published several books and a large number of reports and journal articles in these areas, as well as in the economics of education and of the environment. His book *Economics and Culture* (2001) has been translated into eight languages. Recent research-related publications include *Handbook of the Economics of Art and Culture*, vol. 2 (2014), coedited with Victor Ginsburgh. He is also coeditor (with Michael Hutter) of *Beyond Price: Value in Culture, Economics and the Arts* (2008). His latest book is *The Economics of Cultural Policy* (2010). Throsby has been a fellow of the Academy of the Social Sciences in Australia since 1987 and was elected Distinguished Fellow of the Association for Cultural Economics International in 2008. He is a member of several editorial boards, including the *Journal of Cultural Economics*, the *International Journal of Cultural Policy*, *Poetics*, the *Asia Pacific Journal of Arts and Cultural Management*, and the *Journal of Cultural Property*.

Irene S. Wu is senior analyst in the Office of Economic Analysis of the Federal Communications Commission (FCC). She is also an adjunct professor at the Communication, Culture, and Technology Program at Georgetown University. Wu was a 2017–2018 fellow at the Woodrow Wilson Center for International Scholars and is an expert on the international history and politics of communications technology. Her book *Forging Trust Communities: How*

Technology Changes Politics (2015) tells the story of how activists and governments around the world use the new technologies of the day—from the telegraph to social media—to get people to work together. She also authored *From Iron Fist to Invisible Hand: The Uneven Path of Telecommunications Policy Reform in China* (2009) and several articles on communications policy and regulation. Her current research is to measure soft power in the international system, a project she launched while a fellow at the Wilson Center for International Scholars. In 2007–2008, she was the first Yahoo! Fellow in Residence at Georgetown University's School of Foreign Service, where her research focused on change in global values and information technology in Brazil, Russia, India, and China. She received her BA from Harvard University and PhD in international relations from Johns Hopkins School of Advanced International Studies, with additional studies undertaken at the National Taiwan Normal University, the University of Puerto Rico, and the Chinese Academy of Social Sciences in Beijing, China.

CULTURAL VALUES
IN POLITICAL ECONOMY

1 Introduction

Cultural Values in Political Economy

J. P. Singh

THE PUZZLING RELATIONSHIP BETWEEN ECONOMIC CONDITIONS and cultural anxieties is now front and center in global debates. From the headlines about rural-urban economic divides to the effects of trade and migration, the distance between values and beliefs that constitute culture and the material and political conditions of economics has closed. The blurring of these boundaries should not be surprising: culture underlies all human action. Terry Eagleton describes culture as the "social unconscious" that shapes human conduct and is, therefore, present and implicit even when unnoticeable in material conditions (2016, viii). Allen Patten terms culture a "precipitate" of socialization (2011, 741). The difference from the past is that the "unconscious" and the "precipitate" of culture have come to the fore in our global political-economic outcomes. Trade, immigration, and rural-urban demographics are now increasingly understood as cultural phenomena. Cultural politics seem ubiquitous.

The coexistence of seemingly stable economic conditions and the turbulent cultural anxieties of recent times further complicates how we understand their relationship (Eichengreen 2018; Sunstein 2018; Rodrik 2018). A few examples from current cultural political economy, before the COVID-19 pandemic, are illustrative. The US unemployment rate held around 3.7 percent during 2018–2019, the lowest since 1969, along with a healthy 2–3 percent growth rate for the economy (US Bureau of Labor Statistics 2020; Badkar, Fleming, and Rennison 2018; *Financial Times* 2019). The economic indicators hardly produced any widespread satisfaction: they arrived in the midst of "deep and boiling anger" revealed in public opinion polls (Dann 2019). Germany's Bavaria, the country's most populated state with thirteen million people, headed into provincial elections in October 2018 with a 2.8 percent unemployment rate and surpluses in most city governments. Instead of rewarding the incumbents, voters ensured that the Christian Social Union lost its majority electoral share in the regional parliament that it had held for sixty years (Chazan 2018; Buck 2018). During the June 2019 European Parliamentary elections, Christian and Social Democrats, who have dominated EU politics since its inception, decreased their share of elected members to 44.7 percent of the total from 53.5 percent in the last election in 2014. The EU growth rate hovered above 2 percent in 2017–2018, and the unemployment rate was at 6.3 percent by mid-2019, the lowest since 2000 when EU monthly unemployment statistics began to be reported (Eurostat 2019). A mix of material and cultural factors are cited in the media for electoral shifts from the majority incumbents toward rising shares of liberal, green, and far-right parties. These statistics raise further questions about cultural anxieties and economic conditions.

How can we analyze the perplexing links between cultural and material factors in recent (or historical) political-economy outcomes? This book locates human interests in cultural contexts to understand both their origins and impact on outcomes. An intrinsic part of culture is its history. However, at any given time, different cultural values are sifted through this history and mobilized or instrumentalized for collective action. Values are the core traits of any culture; their variability through space and time, synchronically or diachronically, endows cultures with uniqueness and collective meanings. Values also intersect with other cultures. They include belief systems, symbols, and principles of everyday life. In Adam Smith's ([1759] 1976) terms, they are moral sentiments both intrinsic to and negotiated for human conduct. Methodologically and empirically, we suggest ways to operationalize cultural values that underlie political interests to explain outcomes. As many chapters show, not all outcomes involving values are beneficial, despite the strategic calculations of political players. Cultural values shape outcomes that can make groups worse or better off through times of instability and stability and help with understanding cultural contradictions when they do arise.

This chapter provides a context for understanding the role of cultural values in political economy examined in this book. It analyzes the understandings of cultural values as everyday life with socialization experiences that include both symbolic representations and group inclusions and exclusions. The relevant literatures come from social sciences, especially anthropology and economics, but also from cultural studies and art. For reasons explained later, this book avoids the language of cultural identity around singular values or traits. Instead, culture is conceived of as a set of alternatives and values that are mobilized—strategically, instrumentally, cognitively, or habitually—through varying political economies. Our current global politics have brought cultural anxieties and values to the fore. However, the latent invisibility of cultural values and interests does not mean that they did not exist earlier.

Conceptually, the book attempts to provide an interdisciplinary and comprehensive understanding of the ways cultural values are imbricated in political economy—whether they are implicit or explicit, utilitarian or symbolic, constant or changing—and the way to move from collective to individual interests, and vice versa. We are especially cognizant of cultural values in times of stability versus instability. The chapters include references to many of our current cultural moments, but we have also included historical examples to increase the scope of our queries and examine issues such as environmental change, international trade and development, cultural economies of class and religion, and international cultural relations. This chapter concludes with an illustrative historical example from North-South trade relations to describe how colonial and postcolonial cultural values embedded in racism and paternalism intersect with trade specialization to explain the lack of trade reciprocity toward the developing world.

The Motivation and Plan

The current cultural politics and the questions they engender provide the immediate motivation for this book. Cultural fallouts and anger—expressed through populism, nationalism, political rallies and marches, "alt-right" or "radical left" ideologies, and tumultuous voting results—are often linked in the media to cultural perceptions regarding economic processes: international trade and its institutions, concerns about immigrants and refugees, income inequalities and shrinking of the middle class, loss of manufacturing jobs, and the claims on government-provided public goods such as education and health care. However, until recently, dominant scholarship on these processes and institutions tended to exclude cultural explanations.

The Brexit vote in the United Kingdom in June 2016 and President Donald Trump's victory in the United States in November 2016 coincided with and, arguably, further encouraged the rise of economic nationalism and populism in the world. In Germany, the extreme right-wing Alternative for Germany (Alternative für Deutschland [AfD]) now controls 92 of the 709 seats in the Bundestag following the October 2017 elections.[1] The AfD is the biggest opposition party to the government, though it polled lower than expected at 10.7 percent in the subsequent October 2018 Bavarian election. The September–October state elections in Germany reduced the shares of incumbent Christian Democrats in Saxony and Thuringia and of Social Democrats in Brandenburg. Although its vote share was not enough to form the government, the AfD received 27.5 percent of the vote share in Saxony, 23.5 percent in Brandenburg, and 23.4 percent in Thuringia. In Brazil, the right-wing populist Jair Bolsonaro won elections for the presidency at the end of October 2018. In Mexico, the left-wing president, populist Andrés Manuel López Obrador, was inaugurated in December 2018. The de facto heads of state in Austria, the Philippines, Hungary, India, Italy, Poland, Turkey, the United Kingdom, and the United States have often stoked cultural tensions through populist rhetoric and policies, including shoring up the extremist right wing in their country.[2]

What happens when underlying cultural values that inform political interests, as evidenced in the cultural anxieties previously referenced, are no longer dormant but begin exercising greater political influence? Or when the explicit equilibrium of material interests rests precariously on the underlying support from shared cultural beliefs and values? Periods of cultural turbulence can expose the compact between cultural values, economic conditions, and human conduct that stable cultures take for granted.

The links between culture and political economy are complicated and important, but in social sciences such as economics and political science, they have until recently been marginalized. The intellectual legacy from Homer to David Hume, or from the Upanishads to Mohandas Karamchand Gandhi, links people's habits and interests to their social and culture sentiments. Culture became marginalized during the behavioral revolution of the postwar era when rational and strategic calculations, contingent on payoffs or incentives but devoid of cultural content, began to explain human endeavor. Cultural analyses continued, albeit in a secondary position. One early analysis in international relations traced the strategies of great powers such as the

United States and the USSR to Greco-Roman and Byzantine cultural ideas, respectively (Bozeman 1960). In the present day, economic sociologists show that the self, rational or otherwise, rests on socialization experiences (Smelser 2013; Granovetter 1985). Constructivists in international relations point out that willingness to be open (or closed) to each other and the world rests on cultural understandings, as do norms of cooperation and anarchy (Klotz 1995; Finnemore and Sikkink 1998; Wendt 1999). Even the legitimacy of law at national or international levels rests on cultural congruence (Focarelli 2012). Political-economic institutions can be traced back to cultural understandings (North 1994). Despite this formidable intellectual history, cultural interests have been taken for granted or held constant in most economic and political analyses while material interests and strategic calculations are used to explain outcomes.

The current cultural politics and the questions they foreground provide the immediate motivation for this book. However, we attempt to provide conceptual tools and empirical examples to examine varied and changing cultural political economies in general over time. Part I provides the conceptual foundations that engender the cultural assumptions held implicit or constant in a few analyses and explain the contexts under which cultures transform interests. The interplay of deeply held cultural values and instrumental interests is important in this section. These include the cultural context of individual interests (Chapter 2), the distinction between formative and functional cultural values (Chapter 3), the fixity and evolution of cultural values and interests (Chapter 4), and the links between parochial and cosmopolitan interests arising culturally from an interplay of globalization, demographies, and other political economies (Chapter 5).

Part II examines the processes of cultural interaction, which expand or close the cultural stratifications referenced in Part I. While Chapter 5 briefly references the way education shapes group interests, Chapter 6 outlines how cultural boundary work from classes produces inequalities, including disparities in access to higher education. Chapter 7 points out the deeper cultural ideologies that shape trade politics (as does this chapter's last section, which gives a brief example taken from North-South trade relations). Chapter 8 shows how the rise of the religious right in the United States may be linked to an underlying political economy and ways that religious values have adapted to this political economy. Chapter 9 examines intercultural interactions through the realm of soft power and cultural diplomacy and takes up the question of global access to higher education. The focus on education in three chapters is not coincidental; it is a major explanatory factor for our current political economy outcomes. The authors, nevertheless, analyze education as culturally shaped and produced before explaining outcomes.

All chapters have a theoretical and empirical component, though Part I strives for conceptualization, while Part II leans toward praxis. Collectively, as anthropologist Arjun Appadurai instructs us in the foreword, culture is not just "inert ballast" but also "a scheme for action, a map of possibilities, and a tool for making new arrangements in the world."

To summarize, cultures are understood as repertoires of values, distributed (and shared) differentially across and within groups. To state it crudely, values can be linked to culture as prices to markets. They provide the signals and incentives for collective action. Given varying values, cultural interests can be instrumentally rallied to influence outcomes. During times of cultural instability, there is a great need for mobilizing values through ideologies that simplify reality. Education serves as a counterpoint to this simplification. Methodologically, cultural values provide a vocabulary for operationalizing culture without arresting it in static categories of cultural identity.

Collectively, the book forwards the following worldview with each author contributing to one or more of the propositions:

1. Preferences and interests are always embedded in cultural values.

2. Cultural values emerge over the long run and influence transformations of cultural meanings.

3. Cultural values narrow or broaden the set of possible political economy outcomes through their distributional and meaning-making effects. This proposition links cultural and material or economic explanations.

4. Cultures replenish and evolve through interactions across bundles of values, but there are different levels of interaction ranging from observation to immersion.

5. Ideological arguments become salient in unstable cultural times.

6. Cultural identity is a valid political category but a fraught concept that lacks operational measures.

7. Cultures and cultural identities often contain contradictory values. Therefore, an instrumental view of culture, based on transitivity

of preferences, will always be insufficient to explain cultural evolution. Even in times of stability, people will cite values that sound contradictory.

Toward Cultural Repertoires

The term "culture" generally connotes collective experiences, practices, and identities—and their symbolic representations through various texts and art that present cultural discourses or narratives. Following Clifford Geertz (1973), these are public meanings—understood through observable cultural values, traits, and narratives—that allow people to make sense of their lives. Socialization processes shape, rank, and embed the public meanings of culture in everyday life through institutionalization that can lead to reification (Berger and Luckmann 1966). A culture and its values are both constant and dynamic: a processual view of culture emphasizes this point. In the words of social anthropologist Riall Nolan, "Cultures are flexible, resilient, and able to change, but they are remarkably enduring" (2001, 25).

It is hard to operationalize a social phenomenon that is at once resilient and dynamic and cuts across social groups and identity markers in numerous ways with multiple values. Public meanings, after all, are often confusing. The singularity or linearity imposed on them from analysts is useful for research but can simplify a cultural understanding to the point of essentialism or empirical uselessness. To identify a culture along a single axis of value—as in a notion of cultural identity—that remains unchanging also invites charges of primordialism and inability to account for change. Nevertheless, social scientists have attended to critiques that culture is a slippery concept. Building on these responses, three issues are paramount for the definition and operationalization of culture in this book. The following sections address in turn the processes of cultural dynamics, cultural tool kits, and the evolution of values in culture.

Cultural Dynamics

Culture becomes a variable process when treated as a social lineage or precipitate. It reveals patterns of public meanings that are always contested and shared differentially among groups, including in intergenerational transfer (Patten 2011). Thus, we can speak of American culture, as well as its overlap with African American or teenage American culture, as ensuring compatibility with "internal variations and external overlap of beliefs, values and meanings" (742). The key to understanding these shared meanings is socialization.

Most empirical work in global politics avoids the problem of static cultures through an examination of cultural values that can be operationalized for the weightage attached to behavioral and normative aspects of a culture. Examining cultural values and traits implicitly acknowledges overlapping and variable characteristics of culture without having to essentialize cultures or to hold them as mutually distinct. The method of multivariate analysis, for example, is instructive in that it can include shared but differential rates of values across groups. Pippa Norris's (2018) analysis of the June 2016 Brexit referendum vote in the United Kingdom provides a composite index of cultural values—specifically values leaning toward authoritarianism and populism—that explain the Brexit vote. Interestingly, Norris's (2018) and Inglehart and Norris's (2016) cultural models fare better than the economic models (including income, occupational, and left-right ideological statistics) in explaining the Brexit outcome. Similarly, Diana Mutz (2018) analyzes panel data for the 2012 and 2016 presidential elections in the United States to show that a decline in perceived social dominance among white Christian men, along with xenophobia, motivated the vote for Trump. The social dominance scale provides empirical verification for the widely cited cultural anxiety thesis for Trump's election. These studies are consistent with previous analyses of sociotropic preferences. Edward Mansfield and Mutz (2009) empirically demonstrate the prevalence of xenophobic preferences among groups of people as possible determinants of protectionist trade policy even as traditional theories of comparative advantage explain why trade should take place.[3] Jens Hainmueller and Daniel Hopkins (2014) find that European attitudes toward immigrants in Europe are not related to the Europeans' economic or material standing.

Cultural Tool Kits

Culture can be viewed as a tool kit or a repertoire of options that assists in specifying causal mechanisms inherent in culture rather than as traits that are too nebulous to explain anything at all (Swidler 1986; Kymlicka 1995; Patten 2011). Ann Swidler analyzes the kinds of cultural values—understood as an assemblage of "diverse often conflicting symbols, rituals, stories, and guides to action"—that are likely to be mobilized through times of cultural stability and instability (1986, 277). Unstable times feature periods of social transformation and the ascendance of ideological explanations as strategies of action. Seen through a Swidlerian lens, Norris's (2018) or Mutz's (2018) explanations for the rise of populism in the context of cultural anxiety may be viewed as ideologies of latent or explicit cultural traits mobilized for turbulent times rather than an unchanging cultural condition in the United Kingdom or the United States. As Swidler notes, "Coherent ideologies emerge when new ways of organizing action are being developed" (1986, 280). In contrast, settled lives feature sedimented habits of action that are often not traceable to culture. Mary Douglas (1986) similarly argues that the stability of preferences in economics assumes an institutional and cultural context that hides the processes through which the institutions develop: in exercising their preferences, individuals internalize social cues from the environment.

Linking cultural options to political or policy action provides a dynamic model with explanatory factors and outcomes (Rao and Walton 2004). In important ways, this causality relates to economist Amartya Sen's (1999) entitlement or capabilities approach and anthropologist Arjun Appadurai's (2004) notion of the capacity to aspire. In the former case, a woman's entitlement to a dignified way of life is constrained through a cultural repertoire or distribution of choices for nutrition, education, marriage partner, job, and even where to sit or serve in a place of worship. The social inclusions and exclusions shape economic and material action. Similarly, Appadurai (2004) speaks of aspiration or the future orientation of people as strongly determined by Sen's capabilities approach, both of which he traces back to culture. Appadurai revisits these issues in the foreword with his discussion of human agency and collectives. "The future is as cultural as the past," he notes.

Cultural values link the past with possibilities for the future. According to Mary Douglas and Aaron Wildavsky (1982), people operate through cultural repertoires in making sense of technological and environmental risks and their future, and even seemingly contradictory guides to action are resolved through cultural values. Douglas and Wildavsky note that people accept the scientific data on climate change but may be culturally constrained from taking action, making it seem as if they do not believe in climate change. Similarly, Will Kymlicka (1995) writes of culture as a set of options with values attached to them. Swidler (2001) shows how individuals resolve a mythic (Hollywood-like) conception of falling in love with the more mundane and ambiguous everyday reality by resolving these cultural repertoires chiefly in favor of a mythic narrative through the unsettled experience of falling in love.[4] At a broader level, consider the observance of scientific and religious beliefs among individuals and groups regardless of their seeming contradiction with each other. Individuals can be both scientific and religious depending on the values being mobilized, although some may choose to be predominantly one or the other.

Resolving or maintaining contradictions requires cultural work. Irving Goffman's classic treatment of cultural cues being understood by the participants as a dramaturgical performance shows how societies accommodate themselves to contradictory narratives: "The maintenance of this surface of agreement, this veneer of consensus, is facilitated by each participant concealing his own wants behind statements which assert values to which everyone present feels obliged to pay lip service" (1959, 9). Nevertheless, these narratives can break down when the actors or audiences ignore dramaturgical devices. The mask of hypocrites can ensure the integrity of performance only if the actor does not conflate acting with reality. Olga Taxidou (2018) notes that the tragedy of Trump's performance lies in forgetting that acting is an illusion or interpretation, related to the Greek word *hupokrités*, that the actor creates. Once the stability of performance breaks down—to extend the previous discussion from Douglas (1986)—the cultural narrative or illusion begins to fall apart. Swidler (1986) invokes Kuhnian epistemology to argue that, much like scientific paradigms, cultures break down when they can no longer allow people to address processes in their daily life.

Evolution of Values

It follows from the preceding discussion that the notion of cultural values is not static: new cultural values can arise and old values can be shared among cultures or recalled to provide an impetus to preference formation. James Whitman (2017) writes that Nazi Germany held the United States as a model for its own racialized Nuremburg Laws. This finding has received attention in light of historical and current propagation of racist values: "In the early Twentieth century the United States was not just a country with racism. It was *the* leading racist jurisdiction—so much so that even Nazi Germany looked to America for inspiration" (2017, 138; emphasis in original).

The new and old values that groups hold or share also provide the way to make causal connections with action, both in emancipatory and binding ways. Sharon Krause notes in Chapter 4 that values can also arise over time and allow individuals to constitute new types of action, in her case that of the rise of environmental norms. Krause distinguishes between realized and unrealized alternatives in a culture; whatever values constitute a culture can thus change over time. For cultures to remain static, boundary work is necessary. Steven Livingston, in Chapter 6, attends to the type of boundary work performed through increasingly limited access to higher education to hinder class mobility in the United States. Mark Rozell, in Chapter 8, shows how the role of religion in the United States has shifted with the bundle of values that politicians can mobilize.

In the often-critiqued model of homo economicus, the rationality calculus of humans breaks down when trying to show how a group decides to be rational about X in time period 1 but Y in time period 2. While rational choice is not the only predicate for human action examined in this book, many authors explain how different values can shape a utilitarian calculation of interests. Daniel Hausman notes in Chapter 2 how accounting for the cultural origins of values moves us toward a constitutive understanding of preference maximization, but his model accommodates a rational calculation of interests. Similarly, in Chapter 5, Miles Kahler brings in socioeconomic, cultural, and psychological factors from an individual's environment to fully account for the way interests are calculated, in this case the Brexit vote and the election of Trump.

Cultural Interests and Values

Dominant accounts in political economy seldom venture beyond material factors in explaining interests. In the iconic version, variabilities in price can explain differential rational calculations of producers and consumers.[5] Political economy changes its variables but not the logic of the calculus of interests in moving from markets to account for other institutions: calculations of utility maximization extend beyond producers and consumers to include voters, politicians, social movements, class, business and industry groups, nations, regions, and international organizations. Using a mathematical additive, individuals are transposed into collective formations.

Society and culture are not mere additive conditions. They shape human conduct and interests. This is obvious in Ernest Gellner's famous thesis that "nations maketh man" (1983, 6), which borrows from Karl Marx when he wrote, "Man makes religion, religion does not make man" ([1843] 1970, 1) or the dictum that "religion is the opiate of the masses." Similarly, David Hume and Adam Smith counsel paying attention to both reason and moral sentiments in understanding human conduct. Max Weber's notion of ethos explains human rationality as being furthered through bureaucracy and industrialization but developing out of cultural contexts such as puritanical values related to discipline and self-control (Kim 2017). In each of the preceding cases, an individual's calculation is intimately bound up in social customs or ideology. As long as nations or their moral sentiments are stable and religions are not turbulent, the social or the political unit can function predictably. The previous section notes that calculations of interest in stable cultures take place within a relatively well-defined repertoire of alternatives or values. Herein the microeconomist's prescription of *ceterus paribus* also applies. While George Akerlof and Rachel Kranton give heed to the short run of economics "where consumers and firms make decisions, given a fixed technology and a fixed market structure," they also note that in the long run, "people can change norms and ideals and the very nature of the social categories" (2010, 18, 19). In other words, the basket of values can change, in turn changing the interests, even if the format for specifying those interests remains the same (e.g., a utility calculation or a heuristic).

The chapters in Part I explain how to account for stability of interests in the short run but also for changes in the environment in the long run through periods of transformation. In both cases, the authors bring cultural value to the fore rather than assuming it to be constant. Holding culture constant in social science has in the past often meant omitting it altogether from analysis. A statistical analogy reveals the problem: holding something constant in multiple variable analysis often means including it as a vector of variables (in this case specifying cultural values) and then showing how other factors account for an outcome. The obverse also applies: not holding it constant would mean including vectors for both cultural and other categories of variables. In the analysis mentioned earlier, Mutz (2018) and Norris (2018) demonstrate that sociotropic preferences and populist cultures veering toward authoritarianism, respectively, explain voting outcomes over and above economic factors in various iterations of their models. This is ideally what it would mean to hold (or not hold) culture constant. Of course, this assumption can be relaxed and cultural factors assumed away and kept out of the explanation if cultural environments are stable, and, in practice, this is often the case for most economists and political scientists. Unfortunately, this condition has applied even when there was no reason to keep cultural variables out.

Holding culture constant (out) has important implications. The short-run calculations can account for interests but not values and in doing so specify an artificial constraint on the explanation. The mathematical precision of economic or political signals can tell us whether a product would be successful in the market or an electoral candidate will win or lose in the elections. But this precision tells us little about the moral sentiments, collective beliefs, or sociotropic preferences being mobilized in a market. A Grecian urn of the type lauded in a Keats poem is fundamentally different from a vase sold at Walmart. In both cases, pricing signals matter but they say nothing of the aesthetics, social orders, or individuals who demand or supply them—or the cultural values that result from them. "What do we mean when we say Monteverdi's operas or Giotto's frescoes are valuable in the history of art? In neither case does an appeal to individual utility or to price seem appropriate" (Throsby 2001, 26; see also Goodwin 2006).

The first task of operationalizing culture is to show how preferences arise out of a cultural milieu. Strategic or instrumental utility calculations provide one way of specifying preferences. Given price as a value, preferences can be specified for different quantities of demand or supply. But what if the price is not right as a valuation exercise? In critiquing economists' notion of interests, Dani Rodrik admonishes them for not realizing that "self-interest is empty and useless" without paying attention to the underlying ideas that produce this self-interest (2018, 159). "Identities, norms, values, worldviews, opportunities, and constraints are all shaped by ideas in the air—and not just those of economists!" (159). Rodrik's use of the word "ideas" is close to that of culture. But Rodrik avoids that term to argue that there are other ideas that can and should guide trade policies than just economists' notions of comparative advantage or strategic trade theory. Other economists such as Akerlof and Kranton (2010) analyze the distributional impact of values that make up a culture. Cultural beliefs influence labor markets and employment practices, and these can be validated through ethnographic evidence. This might explain why in nursing, an occupation traditionally seen as appropriate for women, only 7 percent of the nurses in the United States are men (2010, chap. 7). Similarly, cultural values can inform racism in job discrimination (2010, chap. 8).

Hausman, an economic philosopher, both deepens and questions such utility calculations in Chapter 2. Consistent with this book's focus, Hausman defines culture as a "historically received set of alternatives from which actual preferences may be drawn." Economists speak mostly of choice rather than preference formation, which depends on internalization of cultural norms. Preferences are subjective states that change when the underlying belief or feelings change. In a departure from neoclassical economics, Hausman notes that "people's preferences among alternatives are often not accurate indicators of what is good for them." He also lists factors other than utility calculation in preference formation such as imitation, habit, and cognitive dissonance.

Economist David Throsby, in Chapter 3, distinguishes between culture in a constitutive and functional sense; both shape values in economics (and beyond). The constitutive understanding of culture is always plural and arises out of shared epistemes and beliefs including those embedded in trust. These may be "religious beliefs, ethical values, ethnic origins, linguistic in-heritance, and group allegiances of various sorts." The functional notion of culture can be seen in creative expressions, often termed "cultural goods." Price can provide a valuation, but such goods also contain other valuations such as aesthetic, historical, intrinsic, religious, and spiritual values. Empiri-cally, Throsby discusses the debate over cultural trade and diversity that arose in international economic relations at the World Trade Organization (WTO) and the United Nations Educational, Scientific, and Cultural Organization (UNESCO); a full understanding of the various registers of this debate in dif-ferent places demand an understanding of both the constitutive and func-tional values in culture.

While Hausman and Throsby show how preferences reflect an available set of values, Chapters 4 and 5 outline factors that broaden or constrain the meanings of values in culture. In Chapter 4, Krause further expands the notion of human interests and the interplay with the cultural background. Prefacing philosophical traditions from Scottish Enlightenment's Hume to political theorist Iris Marion Young in the present, Krause advances an un-derstanding of social connections to argue that transformations in interests are possible as the underlying cultural values evolve. She then argues for an emergent culture (and values thereof) of responsibility toward the environ-ment. Broadening the notion of responsibility as arising out of social connec-tions, she notes that it can also address the lack of control people feel about their lives, in this case with uncertainty about the environment.

In Chapter 5, Kahler, an international relations scholar, brings in the in-terplay between distributive impact of material factors and their subsequent perception through cultural and geographic lenses to understand outcomes such as the Brexit vote and Trump's election. The relative gains of global-ization are filtered culturally and explain the preferences of parochials, who express their interests through ethnonationalism, versus cosmopolitans, who advocate economic and cultural openness. The filters include factors such as psychological and cultural attitudes about authority, location (urban-rural divides), and education. He recalls the scholarship on sociotropic preferences as mediating between distributional impact of globalization among groups and their voting preferences.

This book veers toward the distributional and constitutive impact of ma-terial and cultural factors (or values), and a processual (functional) view of culture to account for human interests. As noted earlier, it avoids the language of cultural identity. Cultural identities are attractive labels, but as concep-tual or operational categories, they are tremendously slippery and static. Sen (2006, 178) notes the "solitarist illusion" in thinking that a singular trait in cultural identity can explain behavior or outcomes. Solitarist traits miniatur-ize human beings. Identity is almost always plural and context dependent. For example, poverty is often linked with violence, but Indian cities feature low levels of violent crime compared to the relatively high levels of poor in these cities. Further, Kolkata, although poorer than Mumbai, features lower levels of violence of the two and the lowest level of violent crimes among Indian cities. Sen (2008) attributes this to the intermixing of ethnicities and plural identities in Kolkata, whereas the poor may be segregated along ethnic lines in other cities such as Mumbai. As opposed to the safety of a singular identity, it is the intermixing and sharing of identities that leads to lack of violence in Kolkata. More importantly, the lack of violence lies in the values being mobi-lized and shared rather than attributing it to a singular trait (such as poverty).

Accounts of culture on a singular identity dimension such as religion, eth-nicity, or nationality break down in different spatial and temporal constructs. The Protestant ethic produces the outward-oriented spirit of capitalism in Weber but, in the present day, produces many of the ethnonationalist paro-chials identified in Chapter 5 and a version of evangelicals supporting Trump in Chapter 8. Revisions to history show that Catholic monks developed laws of motion underlying astronomy in the so-called Dark Ages when scientific enquiry was supposed to be limited (Jaki 1993). Robert Putnam (1993) shows how social capital and trust developed in Italian city-states that encour-aged enterprise. European renaissance also burgeoned from places that were chiefly Catholic, a religion that Weber did not posit as particularly progressive

(Cohen 1980). Yesterday's Hindu rate of growth (Rodrik and Subramaniam 2005) or the Hindu equilibrium (Lal 1988–1989, 2001) is now discarded in favor of India's culture of aspiration. Similarly, communist China, which at one time killed economic incentives, is now applauded for its Confucian work ethic and economic growth (Kahn 1979; Harrison and Huntington 2000). Two chapters in this book (Chapters 6 and 8) that can be understood as cultural identities of class and religion are, in effect, about the varying values and politics of their constitution.

It is easy to locate progressive values in a culture, and many go on to associate these values to identify the sum total of nations, ethnicity, or religion (Harrison and Huntington 2000). But often scholars substitute identity for values for operational convenience. After a discussion of cultural values and beliefs, Luigi Guiso, Paola Sapienza, and Luigi Zingales (2006) settle for instrumental variables such as ethnicity and religion to measure the impact of cultural values on economic factors such as entrepreneurship. If identities are plural and context dependent, then it may be better to show how a basket of values achieves valence and institutionalization at one time but not another. Deirdre McCloskey's (2010) account of the rise of bourgeois culture with a set of values in Europe does a far better job than solitarist narratives in showing how a pro-commerce but context- and location-specific culture came about in Europe as a result of factors such the Industrial Revolution, the Protestant Reformation, and the growth of cities.

Cultural Interactions and Praxis

This book forwards a dialogue between economic and cultural determinants of human behavior and through their praxis shows that it is often hard to distinguish between the functional and constitutive elements of culture. The boundaries of market and nonmarket allocation and those leading toward culture have always been blurred, though, in an academic division of labor, economics has traditionally examined distributional issues (functional in Throsby's terms), while anthropologists emphasize constitutive effects. In a similar sense, sociologist Anthony Giddens (1984) writes of routinized practical (functional) consciousness versus a discursive consciousness, which accounts for the constitution of meanings. However, as economic or political actors adopt strategies, the functional and the constitutive merge. For example, in economic analyses, individuals and firms adopt various strategies to maximize their utilities and profits. Equally, they need to minimize risk and uncertainty (Knight 1921; Chamberlain 1933) and may seek to constitute an environment that fosters these goals through networks and learning (Granovetter 2005). Ronald Coase's (1960) theory of the social cost introduced a non-market and organizational dynamic into firm decision making and paved the way toward transactions costs and institutional economics. Economic historian Avner Greif's (1993) analysis of the trusted coalition among medieval Maghribi traders shows how they reduced transaction costs and uncertainty of cheating from their agents. Similarly, Chinese economic networks (*guanxi*) serve as a proxy for commitments to property rights (Wang 2001). The networks are similar to the social connections referenced in Chapter 4, except that economists are generally at a loss to explain how new values arise or old ones are constrained.

The distinction between experience values and decision values, relating to utility and broader social norms or values in behavioral economics, tries to bridge the gap between different forms of decision making (Kahneman and Tversky 1984). Utility values take people's beliefs and preferences as given, but decision values lead people toward subjective or normative logics of decision making, including rational decisions. Daniel Kahneman (2011) is careful to point out that people are more or less rational even when institutions assist people in making decisions through filtering or reducing risk and uncertainty. In general, it is easier to account for instrumental or rational decision making in choosing a course of action within a defined distribution of values than it is to show how values arise in the first place (Friedman 1996). Dennis Chong rescues rational choice in noting that in most circumstances norms are created, maintained, and eventually transformed for strategic reasons: social change comes from "*psychological resistance* to social and cultural change, and the *economic responsiveness* of individuals to changes in incentives" (2000, 189; emphasis in original). This model of motivation and incentives does not explain how new ideas or values develop in the first place (in Chong's case pro-human rights values, from the chapter where the quote is drawn). Philosopher Jon Elster, who once ascribed to rational choice to explain cultural change and maintenance, is less sure in his later writings. Norms are beneficial and induce cooperation and moderation: "Civilization as we know it would not exist without them. But that is not to say that people act to maintain civilization when they follow these norms" (Elster 1989, 117). A broader critique comes from cultural theorists. Eagleton's (2016) precept on ideology as culture sees instrumental or practical reasoning and strategy only at the level of disguising the cultural contradictions of capitalism and its materials conditions, especially for hiding its contradictions. Eagleton notes that our current culture will allow debates on cultural diversity as acceptable, but those on class are ruled out; his book appeared before the Brexit vote or Trump's election, when questions of inequality, exclusion, and class began to be debated again—especially in the diminishing incomes of the white working class.

This book is not agnostic between instrumental versus intrinsic logics of culture in maintaining or creating cultural values. Most authors acknowledge the latter—Hausman, Krause, and Throsby provide the conceptual foundations—but they also note that instrumental logic follows a social context and a distribution of cultural values and that other forms of decision making that are not rational do exist. Following Hausman, the authors are also considerably unsure that preferences are always beneficial. Certainly, three chapters in Part II (Chapters 6, 7, and 8) provide a view of outcomes that can hardly be seen as beneficial despite the strategic calculations of the political actors. What they do reveal is that cultural interactions lead to the praxis of cultural maintenance and multiplication. Chapter 8 also points out the cultural contradictions that are smoothed over in the religious right's support for Trump.

Cultural interactions and praxis are important for examining evolution. A distribution of values shapes the capabilities of actors through periods of stability, but transformation of those values with new meanings can be seen as antecedent to the distributional impact. Figure 1.1 captures the logic of cultural change through human interactions including the sequence of both a transformational (constitutive) and instrumental (functional) logic to the creation of new values. I have called these transformations of meanings meta-power since the late 1990s, but there are other analogous concepts (see Krasner 1985; Lukes 2005; Barnett and Duvall 2005; Burns and Hall 2013). As an

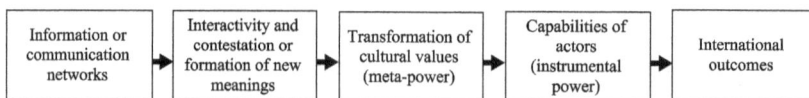

| Information or communication networks | → | Interactivity and contestation or formation of new meanings | → | Transformation of cultural values (meta-power) | → | Capabilities of actors (instrumental power) | → | International outcomes |

FIGURE 1.1 Information networks and power.
SOURCE: Adapted from Singh 2013, 7.

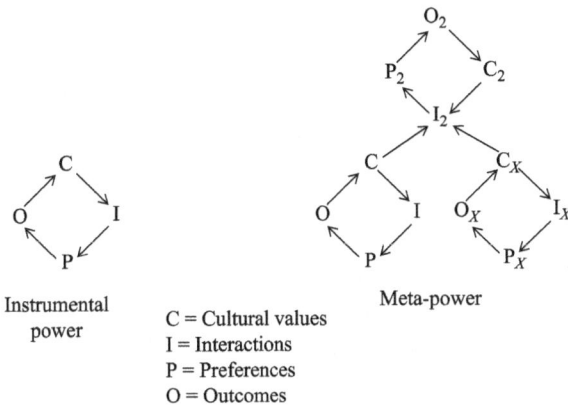

FIGURE 1.2 The logic of cultural change through instrumental and meta-power.

SOURCE: Adapted from Singh 2013, 8.

example, the notion of international security assumes a culture of security among nation-states, but notions of human security about capabilities and entitlements for individuals are fundamentally different. These different cultural values and public meanings arise from human interactions through acts of communication and persuasion (Risse 2000).

Figure 1.2 tries to capture this logic of cultural change. The instrumental version of human interactions assumes a fixity of meanings, and preferences can stay constant. However, other possibilities of interaction exist in Cx cultural groups, especially as they interact with each other. In fact, as culture groups C and Cx interact, new forms of preferences, outcomes, and eventually a new hybrid culture (C_2) appears. In Part II, two communications theorists—Steve Livingston and Irene Wu—take up issues of interaction in cultures to show how cultural interactions lead to making boundaries of meanings (Chapter 6) and defining different ways in which human beings understand each other (Chapter 9).

Sociology, anthropology, and historical political economy, as noted earlier, have posited human behavior as a product of socialization, leading to customs, habits, and norms. More recently, anthropologies of globalization have dealt with the breakdown, changes, and transformation in cultures as a result of global flows. Appadurai's (1996) ethnographies of globalization have attended to the social imaginaries in global cultures through his notion of "scapes," which are suffixes for factors—techno, ideo, finance, media, and ethno—that change the character of globalization. Scapes embody networked interactions that include existing meanings and production systems around the world while facilitating new imaginary capacities. Culture then becomes "a dialogue between aspirations and sedimented traditions" (2004, 84). While media, migration, and technologies accelerate the imaginaries of cultural globalization, Appadurai leaves the effects somewhat open-ended.

Anthropologists examining cultural globalization have been attuned to human anxiety with changes in culture, and their analyses are useful for examining the current times. Social anthropologist Ulf Hannerz writes of "information overload" and "information anxiety" as processes of disruption that make it hard for people to "manage the relationship between the entire cultural inventory and their reasonable personal share in it" (1992, 32). The notion of inventory is not far from that of cultural repertoires mentioned earlier. Ronald Niezen writes that cultural globalization can be understood as "a permanent state of uncertainty" between universal and particular values (2004, 36). Interestingly, even those challenging cultural globalizations do so at a global level: antiglobalization has a global character (48). Certainly, the populism of the Far Right in recent times has crossed frontiers: Steve Bannon, former Trump staffer and cofounder of the far-right online publication *Breitbart*, advises European right-wing movements; Nigel Farage, leader of the right-wing United Kingdom Independence Party (UKIP), campaigned for Trump. The progressive antiglobalization Left is also organized globally. Examples include the 1999 protests against the WTO in Seattle or those against the 1 percent (of top income groups) following the 2008 financial crisis. The 2018 *gilets jaunes*, or yellow jacket, protests against economic hardship in France and Belgium, but later other European countries including the United Kingdom, included both right- and left-wing protesters.

That past cultures influence present ones is an aphorism. But we also need to locate departures from the past. For every one of the previous examples, a past precedent can be cited. The roots of AfD can be traced to rural areas in Germany, especially conservative Bavaria, in the postwar era when the rest of Germany moved toward an accommodational social democracy. Similar parallels can be drawn with the recent focus on rural areas elsewhere. A plethora of accounts have also dealt with their cultural and economic marginalization (Vance 2016; Bageant 2007; Gaventa 1982). However, cultural pasts cannot always provide a coherent narrative or resolve contradictions through cultural repertoires or values, leading to anomalies in cultural processes in the present. As noted earlier, Swidler (1986) argues that cultures, like scientific paradigms, fall apart when people can no longer recall their cultural repertoires to resolve issues in their daily life. Goffman (1959, 251) also notes that the possibility of misrepresentation is inherent in the collective dramaturgies that make up social and culturally cued performances. Ideological narratives may hide contradictions—be they benign or evil—but sometimes the contradictions come to the fore and depart from history. In 2019, to mark the eightieth anniversary of the outbreak of World War II in Warsaw, while Polish president Andrzej Duda bemoaned that the West should have never allowed Nazism to grow, German president Frank Walter-Steinmeier apologized for an ideology that in its time captured the hearts and minds of Germany: "I ask for forgiveness for Germany's historical guilt and I recognise our enduring responsibility" (Walker 2019).

Part II examines how cultural values and institutions shape human behavior through change and uncertainty. Two chapters (Chapters 7 and 8) deal with cultural contradictions and the way they are resolved through ideology. Another two (Chapters 6 and 9) deal with processes where the past spills into the present but in unexpected ways. Both Kristen Hopewell (Chapter 7) and Rozell (Chapter 8) attend to the rise of cultural ideologies in political-economic life to resolve anomalies and contradictions. Hopewell describes the rise of Tea-Party conservatism in the midst of the United States' strategic trade policies to improve its competitive advantage. A minority ideology, well-funded through the billionaire Koch brothers in the United States, stood in opposition to the Export-Import Bank that is favored among a broad intersection of business interests. However, "the ultra-free-market ideology of the Tea Party" overrode other business interests. She concludes, "Culture—specifically the antistate ideology of the Tea Party—plays a critical role in explaining American exceptionalism."

Similarly, Rozell, in Chapter 8, describes how the evangelical right and sections of the Catholic population in the United States began to support Trump, whose knowledge and practice of Christianity has always been questionable. This cultural contradiction was resolved through a confluence of social-cultural values and material factors that brought together the religious right: "Economic factors are filtered through a cultural lens for socially conservative, religious right voters." The linkage between economic and cultural factors appealed to Protestant evangelicals and Catholics in different ways:

Trump's economic populism appealed to working-class Catholic voters, while his anti-immigrant rhetoric appealed to evangelicals. The expectation galvanizing both groups was that Trump's Supreme Court appointments would overturn the pro-abortion legislation in the United States.

Two chapters on communication interactions deal with past trends but with new insights, and the lessons of both extend far beyond education. Livingston writes in Chapter 6 that cultural values are maintained through boundary work. He describes this work in the context of working-class America: "Boundaries of economic class are policed by cultural norms. Class is cultural and culture is policed." He then goes on to describe various communication and pedagogic mechanisms, including access to higher education, that have maintained class boundaries in the United States.

In Chapter 9, Wu examines the communication and cultural dimensions of soft power that, according to its proponent Joseph Nye (2004), is the ability to get others to do what you want through the force of culture, values, and foreign policies. In the soft power strategy of winning over people's hearts and minds without direct use of force, Wu examines different forms of interactions and attractions for people: "People create and perform culture as they interact with each other." A decision to watch a foreign film or eat foreign foods are long-distance interactions, while that of tourism, study abroad, and emigration are close interactions, leading, in the case of emigration, to changing one's place of residence and integration with another culture. She then presents an in-depth case of study abroad with quantitative indicators to outline the decisions that a student makes in the context of push and pull factors for a geographic location. In examining the possibilities of soft power and intercultural understanding, Wu notes, "An underlying principle of the Soft Power Rubric is that interaction is necessary to understanding and that empathy is an essential precursor to foreigners thinking of *us* as 'we' rather than as 'they.'"

North-South Trade Relations: An Example

I now provide a brief example to demonstrate the latent influence of historically generated cultural values on economic outcomes even though this influence is not obvious at first glance. North-South trade relations outcomes can illustrate the influence of latent and historical cultural values and the extent to which the colonial past shaped trade relations in the postwar era through General Agreements on Tariffs and Trade (GATT) until 1995 when the WTO took over that role.

The main outcome to be explained here is the lack of reciprocal trade concessions toward the developing world. The chief form of trade concessions to the developing world through the GATT era was unilateral trade concessions from the developed world, known as special and differential treatment (SDT). SDT's Generalized System of Preferences (GSP) allowed tariff-free access for fixed quantities of exports—most of which were agricultural—from the developing world. Starting in the 1960s, another system of quantitative measures was applied to textiles and garments, products in which the developing world could claim comparative advantage, through a system that evolved into the Multifiber Arrangement (MFA).

The standard economic or material explanation for the lack of reciprocal concession toward the developing world is that we can expect prosperous states in the Global North to negotiate reciprocal concessions with Global South countries with large markets in seeking increasing returns and benevolently offer reciprocal or nonreciprocal trade access, as needed, only to those with small markets (Krugman 1987; Bagwell and Staiger 2002). Without going into details, first, it is hard to show that the developed world makes reciprocal trade concessions to developing countries with large markets—Brazil or India in the GATT period—on products that are of interest to them. Second, the developed world has squeezed out extranormal concessions from small countries in preferential trade agreements (PTAs) with them, showing that even the so-called generosity of unilateral concessions such as the GSP are only available at the multilateral level. Finally, it is hard to show empirically that even small countries may not have economies of scale in products that they produce in large volumes. Examples include cotton and sugarcane, in which the developed countries have some of the highest amounts of protections against efficient and potentially high levels of exports from the developing world.

The alternative explanation explored here is located in historically received cultural values, in this case paternalistic values derived from a colonial history of racism in the Global North. In a recent study employing mixed methods, I demonstrate that postwar North-South trade relations were embedded in the North's culturally paternalistic preferences that thwarted trade reciprocity—the giving and taking of tariff and nontariff concessions—toward the Global South and an understanding of its development concerns (Singh 2017). Paternalism is defined "as a patronizing discourse resulting from a position of economic and political strength and cultural distance from the Global South" (1).

Two brief pieces of evidence may illustrate the effects of paternalism. A content analysis of twelve years of press releases from the United States Trade Representative's office for the 1982–1993 period—roughly corresponding to the multilateral Uruguay Round of trade negotiations from its agenda-setting stage to its conclusion—demonstrates that 93 percent of all paternalistic references made in these press releases were toward the developing world.[6] In other words, these references included statements that were moralistic, preachy, or patronizing toward the trade partner. By contrast, less than 3 percent of the total paternalistic references were toward the developed economies operationalized as members of the Organization for Economic Cooperation and Development (OECD).

Next, I examined how paternalism affects trade reciprocity. Figure 1.3 shows the nearly perfect hyperbolic relationship between official development assistance as a percentage of gross national product (GNP) (taken here to be a manifestation of paternalism) and trade reciprocity in agriculture. This graph provides an intuitive idea: countries that receive foreign aid do not receive trade concessions in agriculture. The rest of my 2017 study provides further

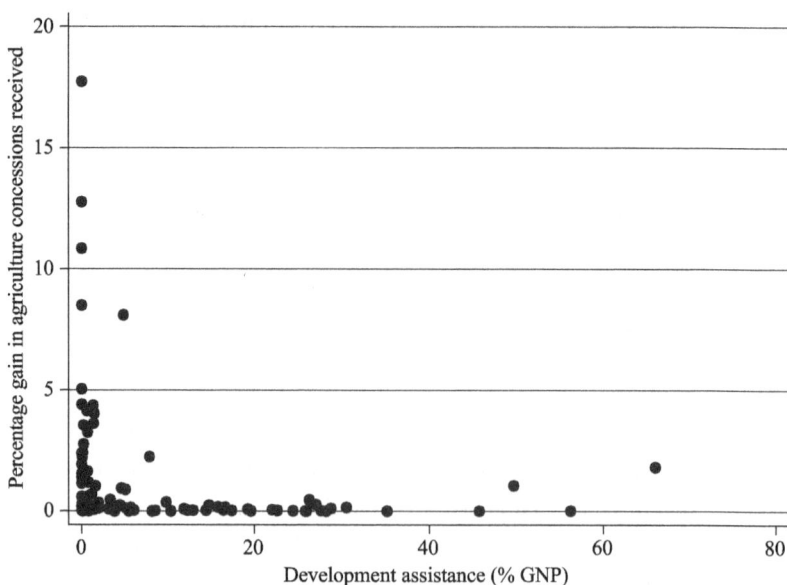

FIGURE 1.3 Percentage gain in agriculture concessions received and official development assistance as percentage of GNP.
SOURCE: Singh 2017, 12.

TABLE 1.1 Paternalism strength index

Paternalistic countries	Paternalistic strength	Less paternalistic countries	Paternalistic strength
United States	3.17	China	−0.083
France	2.48	Brazil	−0.248
United Kingdom	2.34	India	−0.307
Japan	1.16	Singapore	−0.47
Canada	0.936	Kenya	−0.50
Sweden	0.497	Mexico	−0.55

historical and quantitative evidence for the negative effects of paternalism on trade reciprocity. This includes the development of a paternalism strength index through factor analysis that captures the influence of latent and related factors in other economic, political, and cultural indexes to provide a basis for measuring variable amounts of paternalism (see Table 1.1 for a partial listing of this index). Almost in all issue areas of trade—manufacturing, agriculture, services, and intellectual property—high degrees of paternalistic strength were found to be negatively related to trade reciprocity toward the developing world in dozens of models employing multiple regression. As with the cultural models mentioned earlier in this chapter, the paternalism strength index predicted the lack of trade concessions toward the developing world over and above the standard political economy explanations.

A historical cultural lens shows that values of colonial racism evolved into postcolonial paternalism and provide a counterpoint to findings that (1) regard paternalism in a positive light (Barnett 2011, 2012, albeit in the context of humanitarian efforts) or (2) specify positive effects of international hierarchies (Lake 2009a). These analyses offer a thin understanding of the workings of the cultural structures and processes that contain paternalistic values. My analysis—quantitative, historical, case study based—does not confirm positive suppositions about hierarchy for those at the bottom in international trade relations hierarchies. Further, a paternalistic explanation of trade reciprocity outcomes tends to do better than tests for several alternative noncultural explanations drawn from strategic trade theory in economics or power-based theories in international relations.[7]

This example of North-South trade relations also illustrates a larger point: cultural factors provide a deeper examination of international trade relations than standard economic models, and they can be usefully operationalized and examined with empirical evidence. Cultural factors also point out that the stability of any given political order is predicated on a set of underlying cultural values. Given the history of paternalism from the Global North and the history of resentment against paternalism from the Global South, it is not surprising that the Doha Development Round of multilateral trade talks is now defunct. The rise of emerging powers continues to be perceived in resentful and xenophobic ways in the Global North. In this sense, Trump's often incendiary statements about the developing worlds are less of a deviation and more of an intensification of the historically racist and paternalistic rhetoric that has always been directed toward the Global South. The trade war against China is equally a cultural war: economists frequently point out that the cost of the trade war or tariffs on China—that in December 2019 totaled more than 90 percent of the nearly $600 billion US trade with China—are being borne by consumers in the United States.

Conclusion

The language of social science is often uncomfortable with notions of culture: various paradigms within social science either dismiss cultural origins of interests or acknowledge that ultimately it is hard to link (or operationalize) culture to account for specific sets of outcomes. Even in anthropology, with culture as its primary subject of study, one of the historical debates concerns the usefulness of constructing theories to account for generalizable outcomes that are not context or ethnographically specific (Geertz 1973; Ortner 1984; Barnard 2000).

The discomfort with culture in current scholarship notwithstanding, observing or accounting for the formation of values and interests is hardly new in social studies. The Scottish Enlightenment of Hume and Smith emphasized the social context of economic action (McCloskey 2010). In the present time, economist Douglass North notes that culture as "the cumulative experience of past generations" and learning are important to understand the formation of institutions such as markets (1994, 364). Institutional economics, therefore, often ventures into the noneconomic bottom or the long run that neoclassical economists avoid. In addition, sociologist Mark Granovetter (1985) argues that neoclassical economics assumes an under- or oversocialized homo economicus that neglects the underlying social relations of economic agents.

The work in this book is consistent with sociological and institutionalist accounts in political economy. Most of that literature has concentrated on how norms or values arise in international relations through socialization and subsequent internalization (Finnemore and Sikkink 1998). Ned Lebow (2008) offers an expansive theory of culture in international relations. His concept of the collective "spirit" of the people provides both a constant and a dynamic that changes through time. The so-called cultural turn in international relations also responds to recent changes in group experiences and learning induced through accelerated human interactions (Onuf 2012). These interactions and changing meanings include the rise of the internet and the ways that groups tend toward homophily, the complex functioning of value chains around the world making moot the cultural meaning of national comparative advantage, or the new cultural vocabularies of international development that have veered toward a human development and participatory approach (Singh 2013). Culture also provides a deeper look into the formation of political institutions. Turning to nonmarket institutions, historian Eric Mazower (2009) has shown that the formation of post–World War II institutions such as the United Nations disguised the imperialistic and "civilizational" values of the Western cultural elite who crafted these institutions. Therefore, the postwar cooperation in these institutions auto-excluded countries and peoples that this elite held to be culturally inferior.

This book contributes to the literature on culture and political economy in three ways. Theoretically, it conceptualizes cultures as repertoires of values or alternatives that can be shared across cultural groups. As noted before, values may be to culture as prices are to markets or, one might add, power to politics: they are the building blocks for understanding human agency and collective action. In this conceptualization of culture, values provide a dynamic sense of cultures rather than one arrested through solitarist identities, as Amartya Sen (2006) calls them. Values can also be shared across cultures and time. Concurrently, boundary making work and ideologies help distinguish unique cultures with particular sets of values (see Chapters 6, 7, and 9). Similarly, cultural interactions can lead to new values and understandings (see Chapters 3, 4, and 9).

Methodologically, our contribution rests on showing how cultural beliefs and cultural values may be usefully operationalized in political economy with various techniques. By studying values, we avoid cultural stereotypes and provide a variable and dynamic language to empirically analyze cultures. A set of values may be identified with a culture or a subset of it. The authors present both qualitative and quantitative analyses in examining these cultures. More importantly, operationalizing culture does not mean specifying it as an antecedent condition or a secondary or residual variable. A complex relationship exists between culture and political economy in functional and constitutive ways. This chapter argues for an approach that shows how both materialist and cultural factors determine values and interests. Most authors in this book attend to a discussion of cultural values. In doing so, they implicitly endorse multiple and mixed methods. We present or borrow cultural analyses rooted in ethnography, history, case studies, process tracing, and quantitative techniques. These are suggestive of the kinds of conceptual and methodological criteria that can be employed to understand culture. This is not an attempt to paper over differences: we are not convinced that the intersection of culture and political economy can only be studied through inferential techniques (King, Keohane, and Verba 1994) or historically rich theories (Puchala 2003). Finally, we contribute through our empirical examples. They are by no means exhaustive of culture and political economy analyses, but their geographic, temporal, and issue coverage explores the work of cultural values and alternatives at multiple levels.

The chapters seek to provide thick descriptions of cultural stability and change, useful for analyzing the puzzles arising from the links between culture and political economy. Political economy can often appear abstract and ambiguous in a world of reified strategic or rational calculations that seem devoid of origins and unable to explain complex cultural interactions. The acculturations infused in this book provide both a historical and humanized view of the world, albeit one that accords human agency a repertoire of options.

Notes

1. Interestingly, several economists helped start AfD in 2013 as an anti-euro party following the Greek debt crisis. AfD gained popularity after Chancellor Angela Merkel's decision to allow one million refugees into the country in 2015. AfD includes former Christian Democratic Union (CDU) politicians.

2. Leaders such as Bernie Sanders and Elizabeth Warren in the United States and Jeremy Corbyn and Boris Johnson in the United Kingdom are also often viewed as populist.

3. For a materialist questioning of the sociotropic preferences model, see Schaffer and Spilker 2019. The authors argue that whether an individual employs strategic or sociotropic consideration depends on the information in the system. Nevertheless, they conflate sociotropic frames with information about "country-level gains and losses from trade" thereby reducing Mansfield and Mutz's seminal contribution about culture to a materialist and distributive conception of interests consistent with other noncultural explanations in political economy.

4. Swidler and Watkins (2015) ethnographically contrast the ways in which rural Malawians resolve the indigenous structures of deliberation, which allow them agency and voice at an individual level, with hierarchical and (supposedly) communal colonial or foreign structures that promise them status but less voice through formalized and policed hierarchies.

5. This chapter returns to moral sentiments to locate the origins of interests. However, classical political economy—with its emphasis on the labor theory of value and exchange value—also sets in place a spiral that increasingly removes moral sentiments from questions of value and interest formation.

6. The press releases were obtained through a Freedom of Information Act request. A typical statement of paternalism is the following pertaining in this case to the announcement of the signing of a bilateral investment treaty with Bangladesh on March 12, 1986, in which US trade representative Clayton Yeutter is quoted: "Developing countries such as Bangladesh, which recognize the importance of direct investment to their long-term economic development plans, now are taking actions to attract such investment. I hope that more countries follow the leadership Bangladesh has shown" (Office of the US Trade Representative 1986). Another instance is preferential access granted to Andean countries under the Andean Trade Preference Act (ATPA). A 1992 release admitting Bolivia and Colombia to ATPA notes, "The ATPA fulfills the U.S. commitment to improve access to the U.S. market for exports from the Andean nations. It is designed to help the beneficiary nations encourage their people to export legitimate products instead of illicit drugs" (Office of the US Trade Representative 1992).

7. For example, David Lake (2009a) provides a positive reading, particularly of realism, to posit beneficial effects of hierarchy. Economic analyses do not support Lake's theory. In strategic trade theory, Kyle Bagwell and Robert Staiger (1997) find that unilateral rather than reciprocal preferences granted to the developing world in trade negotiations are trade-distorting and inefficient. My analysis of North-South relations, rooted in paternalistic trade preferences, shows not only why culturally the developing world does not receive reciprocal trade concessions but how it negatively affects the South's growth prospects (Singh 2017).

I CULTURAL INTERESTS AND VALUES

2 Culture and Preference Formation

Daniel M. Hausman

IT IS OBVIOUS THAT CULTURE AFFECTS ECONOMIC OUTCOMES and that economic outcomes influence culture. Cultural anthropologists and other social commentators have been concerned with these interactions. But economists have had much less to say about them. Many economists maintain that economics starts where culture leaves off—that is, with people's beliefs and preferences—and that economics stops short of commenting on culture when it derives prices and quantities exchanged on markets from people's beliefs, preferences, and their initial endowments with resources. This chapter argues that economists who exclude cultural influences from their models are wrong to do so, both because including cultural influences can contribute to economic theory and applications and because economics can contribute to the understanding of culture. Culture and rational choice are not incompatible: culture provides the broad, historically received set of alternatives from which actual preferences may be drawn.

Please note that I am not maintaining that economics can or should supplant theories of culture, and I offer no detailed practical proposals concerning how economic models should incorporate cultural variables. In arguing that economic modeling can and should encompass cultural factors, I am not supposing that economics can supplant cultural studies; nor am I endorsing any sort of economic imperialism.

Preferences and the Standard Model of Choice

Economists explain, predict, and interpret behavior in terms of preferences and beliefs (or, more formally, subjective probabilities). Their simplest model, which I call the standard model, like more complex models, is continuous with so-called folk psychology, which takes people's actions to depend on their beliefs and desires. Economists similarly maintain that among those alternatives that the agent correctly believes to be feasible, the agent chooses an alternative he or she most prefers and that an agent's preferences among actions depend on beliefs about the consequences and characteristics of actions and on evaluations of those consequences and characteristics.

In everyday usage, considerations such as duties compete with preferences to determine behavior, and a rational individual, Q, who heeds duty's demand that action x be chosen may well have preferred to do something else. Not so in economic modeling. While not denying that many different factors, including duties, are relevant to choices, economists stipulate that every factor that influences choices other than constraints and beliefs does so via influencing preferences. This is not a disagreement about what Q does or what explains what Q does. It is instead a disagreement about how to categorize the explanatory factors. The economist places duties among the factors determining preferences rather than regarding them as factors that compete with preferences in influencing choices. In the economist's view, once rational agents know which actions are feasible and what are the properties and consequences of those actions, the agents' preferences completely determine their choices.

Economists rarely define preferences. Instead, they specify formal conditions that preferences must satisfy. Although some of these are purely technical, others are interpreted both as conditions of rationality and as features that characterize, albeit only approximately, people's actual preferences. The two most important of these conditions take the preferences of rational agents to be complete and transitive. Q's preferences are complete if for all alternatives x and y, Q prefers x to y, Q prefers y to x, or Q is indifferent between x and y. Q's preferences are transitive if and only if, for any three alternatives x, y, and z, Q prefers x to y and y to z and, thus, prefers x to z.[1] Although not formally specified, economists also suppose that the preferences of rational agents are stable (that for the most part, they change slowly, if at all) and that any relevant features of context are already built into the individuation of the objects of preference. If when faced with a choice between x, y, and z, individuals choose x, they will not choose y when faced with a choice between x, y, and w. If one individuates alternatives as, for example, drinking a glass of white wine or drinking a glass of red wine, then those who prefer white wine with fish and red with meat will violate this condition. To avoid this context dependence, economists suppose that features of context, such as whether one is eating meat or fish, are built into the alternatives.

Although some economists, defenders of so-called revealed preference theory, attempt to relate preferences directly to choices, it is impossible without premises concerning beliefs to make inferences concerning preferences from data concerning choices or to make predictions concerning choices from premises concerning preferences. Moreover, preferences extend far beyond those alternatives among which agents actually choose. Preferences, as they figure in economics, cannot be defined in terms of choices.

Because preferences rank alternatives, they are necessarily comparative. To say of Isidore that he prefers asparagus is elliptical. What is meant is that he prefers asparagus to something else. Because preferences influence choices only via beliefs, they are subjective states. Because preferences encompass all the factors that the agent regards as relevant to choice, they are "total" rankings. Hence, as I have elsewhere argued (Hausman 2012), economists take preferences to be total subjective comparative evaluations. They are judgments concerning how states of affairs or actions rank with respect to every consideration that the agent considers to be relevant. In some cases, such as an uninformed preference for the Rolling Stones over Rachmaninoff, the only consideration the agent finds relevant might be the enjoyment the agent experiences, but our preferences are always subject to revision as our feelings and beliefs change. Moreover, as comparisons of the value of alternatives, preferences motivate choices and expressions of sentiments (see Chapter 1 for a discussion of cultural alternatives).

Choices depend on constraints and beliefs as well as preferences, although in different ways. Constraints sometimes prevent choices without the interposition of beliefs. Those who attempt to fly unassisted do not succeed. Notice that the constraint prevents the flight, not the attempt to fly. More typically, individuals learn about constraints and do not attempt what they cannot accomplish. People's beliefs about constraints limit what they attempt to do, while constraints and causal facts in general determine the outcomes of attempts to bring things about. We explain why a young Superman fan ties on a cape and jumps off his back porch by that child's false beliefs, and we explain the bruises (both to his knees and to his pride) by physical, biological, and psychological facts.

One can thus interpret beliefs about constraints either as determining which actions lie within the subjectively determined feasible set (without affecting their evaluation) or as determining preferences among basic actions or among those things that the agent attempts. When Janet, despite her thirst, refuses to drink a glass of water because she falsely believes it is poisoned, one can take her belief that the water is poisoned as influencing her ranking of the alternatives *drink* or *do not drink* or as removing the alternative of drinking *a glass of unpoisoned water* from what she takes to be the set of feasible actions. Either way, to explain what she is doing, one invokes her beliefs.

This view of rational choice clearly allows culture to play a role in explaining choices and economic outcomes. Where did the child's idea of putting on a cape and jumping off the porch or the possibility of listening to Rachmaninoff or the Rolling Stones come from? Rational choice (or even not-so-rational choice) is fully compatible with the fact that culture so often sets the alternatives among which individuals choose. But in limiting the factors that influence choices to constraints, beliefs, and preferences, the economist's model of rational choice maintains that when culture influences choices it does so mainly by imposing constraints and affecting beliefs.

Of course, culture influences preferences as well, but economists typically claim that they take preferences as givens and leave accounts of their formation and modification to psychologists and other social scientists. On this view, economics is concerned exclusively with preferences over alternative actions and the relationship of preferences to choices. Let us call preferences over alternative actions—that is, preferences over the immediate objects of choice—"final preferences." In any given context, some actions are feasible, and others are not, regardless of what the agent believes. If economists suppose, as they often quite reasonably do, that people have true beliefs about these constraints and hence about which actions are feasible, then choice is completely determined by final preferences. On this view, economists have nothing to say about how preferences are formed or revised and thus have nothing to say about cultural influences on preferences. Moreover, if economists forget about the crucial, but often trivial, role of belief, then it is easy for them to be tempted by revealed preference theory, which treats final preferences and choices as standing in a one-to-one relationship.

If economists proceed in this way and consider only final preferences, then they have trivialized their theory of choice. To the question "Why did Isidore choose x rather than some other feasible action y?" the answer, for all x and y, is "Isidore prefers x to y."[2] Those who are interested in individual choice no longer need to study textbooks or indeed to know anything about Isidore or his circumstances. What explains why Isidore chose x rather than y is Isidore's preference for x rather than y. That is the total content of this very uninteresting story.

This implication might not distress those economists who maintain (1) that economics aims only at prediction, not at explanation, or (2) that economics does not attempt to predict or to explain individual choices, as opposed to their aggregate ramifications. One can find views like these in Faruk Gul and Wolfgang Pesendorfer's influential 2008 essay, "The Case for Mindless Economics." But the trivialization entailed by treating individuals as having complete final preferences is a serious matter. Even if the ultimate goals of economics are, as some would maintain, purely predictive, explanation is a crucial task, because diagnosing the causes of certain phenomena (which is a form of explanation) contributes to the ability to make accurate predictions. An exclusive focus on aggregate outcomes also would not render the trivialization harmless, because individual choice is usually an essential intermediary between outcomes and shocks, whether they be harvest failures, new legislation, or election results. To predict the results of shocks, economists must invoke the expectations of economic agents concerning what the consequences of choices will be in the wake of the shocks and their preferences over those consequences.

For just one example showing the importance of preferences over alternatives that are not immediate objects of choice, consider the fact that, according to CNN, by the end of February 2017, the price of stocks in private prison companies was double their price at the time of the November 2016 American presidential election (Long 2017). Many economists earn their keep by predicting phenomena such as this. To make accurate predictions, they need to determine what factors lead agents to change their final preferences among different investment options. It is unhelpful simply to say that shares increased in value because people preferred to pay more for them. To say something informative requires attributing beliefs and nonfinal preferences to individual investors. Before the 2016 election, investors believed that

Hillary Clinton was likely to be elected, and they anticipated that private prisons would not be profitable. When Donald Trump was elected, they expected that private prisons would become very profitable and that shares in private prison companies would yield larger returns. Add to these beliefs the preference for larger as opposed to smaller returns on investments, and it is easy to predict that private prison stocks would increase in value. Notice that the preference of investors for larger returns over smaller returns is not a final preference. It does not directly rank actions. In buying or selling particular stocks, I can hope that I will earn larger returns, but because I do not know what the returns will be, the returns are not an immediate object of choice.

These simple observations reveal a tension in the basic explanatory and predictive model of individual choice that economists employ. To avoid triviality, agents must have preferences among states of affairs that are not immediate objects of choice, and for those preferences to have any role to play, it must not be the case that agents have complete final preferences prior to deliberation. On pain of triviality, there must be a space in which final preferences are derived from other preferences and beliefs. It is because of that space and the process of traversing it that I call preferences over the immediate objects of choice "final."

This conclusion has an important corollary. It is a mistake to claim, as economists often do, that economics has nothing to say about preference formation or revision. The preceding example shows how an event that changes expectations (in this case, Trump's election) leads to a change in final preferences. To be sure, this story relies on the unchanging "given" preferences of investors for larger returns rather than smaller. It might thus be possible to defend a qualified version of economists' claims that they have nothing to say about preference formation, limiting it to underlying preferences, such as the preference for larger returns over smaller.

Nevertheless, a very large part of economics consists of models of preference formation and modification. No significant theory of choice can avoid making claims about how preferences are formed and modified. Consider, for example, a standard derivation of a firm's demand for inputs and its level of output. Preferences for larger net returns explain and predict a relationship between changes in the prices of a firm's inputs and outputs and final preferences among production techniques and levels of output. Similarly, from a specification of a player's preferences among the possible outcomes of a game, economists derive—that is, explain and predict—the player's final preferences among strategies. Economists hide this ubiquitous theorizing concerning preference formation by speaking only of preferences over outcomes of games, not preferences among strategies and by not speaking of prices as changing preferences among input mixtures or levels of output in the theory of production. But the terminology determines nothing. Economists theorize extensively about preference formation and modification—a theme taken up in Chapter 3.

This conclusion opens the door to considering the relationships between culture and preferences. Once it becomes clear that economists are concerned with the factors that determine final preferences among actions, there is no sensible reason not to study how cultures influence preferences and ultimately economic outcomes.

Culture and Preferences

I have said nothing so far about culture except to note that economists have had little to say about it. As we have just seen, on pain of triviality, economists cannot justify their disinterest in culture by disavowing any interest in preference formation (or, for that matter, the formation of popular beliefs). I suspect that economists fear that admitting cultural variables opens the way to ad hoc attributions of every outcome to some cultural variable or other. Unlike well-specified theories of preference formation, such as expected utility theory, which derive preferences for actions from beliefs about their consequences and preferences over their consequences, it seems that there are few constraints on claims about the relations between culture and preferences. But these thoughts seem to me to be more of a reason to explore the influence of culture on preferences than grounds for ignoring it. The absence of models is no reason not to create them.

Culture matters to economic outcomes. Consider, for example, attitudes toward women's employment. There can be no doubt that these attitudes have had enormously important consequences for the American economy, and, at the same time, they have been influenced by changes in the economy. The shift in attitudes is not simply an exogenous shock like an earthquake that, as it were, rattles people's preferences. There are complex interactions between changes in the economy and changes in culture. Only arbitrary fiat would maintain that economics has nothing to contribute to the study of these interactions.

Culture manifests itself in patterns of behavior, in beliefs, in sentiments, in social norms, in people's characters, in artifacts and architecture, and in the environment. As noted in Chapter 1, culture provides a repertoire of values for each of these patterns. The different manifestations of culture are interdependent. They sustain one another and are reinforced by social norms and institutions. Yet at the same time, they allow for change, which is sometimes rapid. Culturally specific social norms require or prohibit behavior and expressions of sentiments. Some of the social norms that define and sustain aspects of cultures are moral. For example, cultures have social norms governing the expression of gratitude for gifts and assistance, which are also moral norms. Other norms concern aesthetics or etiquette and have no moral content. Nonmoral norms may be as stringent as moral norms, but they are not as stable. For example, by violating the etiquette norm requiring that men wear hats in public, President John F. Kennedy undermined the norm almost overnight (and caused great distress to hatters). In contrast, Trump's many violations of norms of courtesy and truth telling will only slowly, if at all (one hopes), undermine those norms. By means of social norms, in conjunction with ideals and exemplars, cultures also define social roles. Consider, for example, the differences in what it is to be a parent or a teacher in different cultures. Cultures also inevitably encompass some history and myth and are defined in part by the depiction of villains and heroes. Horatio Alger is a very different cultural icon than is Ivanhoe, Napoleon, or Mao.

How then might one attempt to employ the economist's model of choice, including its fragmentary account of the mechanisms of preference change, to understand the influence of culture on preferences, beliefs, and economic outcomes? Some of the effects of cultures on beliefs is unproblematic. Although economists typically have little to say about belief acquisition, they take for granted standard sources of belief, such as the testimony of others. People in a given culture read many of the same history books, watch similar news programs, use the same artifacts, attend similar schools, and talk with others who reinforce their beliefs. They evidently share many beliefs. My guess is that the influence of culture on belief runs much deeper, as cultures also shape emotions and reactions. Recall the murder trial of O. J. Simpson in 1995. Presented with the same evidence, cultural identification strongly influenced people's beliefs. Economists will have a hard time modeling cultural influences on beliefs such as these. But at least part of the story concerning how cultures influence preferences fits comfortably into models in which preferences depend on beliefs about the properties and consequences of actions.

Clearly, this is not the only mechanism whereby cultures shape preferences. A second route, which the standard model of choice also encompasses, relies on the sanctions that reward those who comply with social norms and punish those who violate them. A male Wall Street lawyer who decides to wear shorts, nylon stockings, and women's high heels to work can expect looks of surprise and disapproval or perhaps even a pink slip. To the amazement of many who laughed at laws requiring that owners pick up after their dogs and were sure that crusty urbanites would never conform, the laws quickly gave rise to stringent social norms. The standard model can explain why individuals conform to the social norms implicit in cultures by citing the sanctions attached to norms.

But people conform to cultural norms even when there are no sanctions attached to violating them, and they enforce cultural norms even when doing so is costly. They come to embrace culturally sensitive attitudes, and they express appropriate sentiments even when they do not fear punishment. People internalize cultural norms and ideals: Chapter 4 shows how new cultural norms and ideals develop. The standard model of choice should show how norms and ideals are internalized. The challenge for economists is to broaden the standard model while retaining its ability to make specific predictions.

Moreover, economic actions have cultural consequences as well as cultural antecedents. Just as culture influences preferences, so the economic choices of individuals and models of those choices influence cultures. Although cultural changes made it easier in the last decades of the twentieth century for women to go to work, women also went to work because their families needed their incomes; in choosing to work, they changed the norms governing their choices. At the same time that economists model ways in which cultures shape preferences, they should model ways in which economic choices influence aspects of culture.

Extending Economic Modeling: Some Speculations

How can economists expand their models to encompass the influence of culture without undermining their basic approach to explaining and predicting economic phenomena? We have already seen two possibilities: by more explicit and subtle treatment of belief formation and by acknowledging the sanctions that enforce cultural norms.

Some possible additions that retain the basic structure of the standard model are simple. One can crudely model imitation by treating the probability of a choice as a function of the proportion of relevant others who are making a similar choice, and one can crudely model habit by treating the probability of a choice as a function of how often an individual has previously made it. Habit and imitation may give rise to widespread preferences for culturally favored alternatives. We do not like to disagree with our neighbors. In addition to habit and invitation, when cultural norms rule out certain alternatives, the "sour grapes" mechanism that Jon Elster (1983) discusses may lead people to prefer other alternatives over the ones that are prohibited.

Of course, there are also countervailing mechanisms. The grass is greener on the other side of the fence: people can come to value what they are told they cannot have, and they may assert themselves by defying social norms rather than complying with them willingly (even when such defiance is not itself a cultural tradition). Admitting further mechanisms of preference modification, as one must, raises the specter that choice theory will have a mechanism for every possible result and hence predict nothing. This worry does not, however, forbid models that recognize a multiplicity of causes; it insists, rather, that they must nail down the effects.

Cultures may also shape preferences via controlling the environment in which individuals choose. For example, those who drive to work inhabit a different cultural environment than those who commute via public transit. Choosing a job puts one in contact with some individuals and groups and divorces one from contact with others. It establishes a rhythm in one's life and a relationship to the product or service to which one's employment contributes. The need to avoid cognitive dissonance—to regard our activities as worthy and our past choices as wise—then shapes our preferences. For example, those who work in the coal or oil industry typically develop both a distinctive culture and a distinctive set of preferences, both of which arise from the conditions of their lives much more than from one another. One's job shapes one's skills and character. Indeed, it often determines one's identity, which is bound up with one's culture and arguably the deepest source of one's preferences.

The mechanisms I have sketched—imitation, habit, sour grapes, the greener grass, and cognitive dissonance coupled with the circumstances of one's life—could permit economists to model some of the ways in which cultures govern people's beliefs, preferences, and choices. One's job, one's church and other social group affiliations, one's recreations, the responsibilities one takes on to care for others, and where one lives and travels define social roles and make certain activities easily accessible and initially attractive while discouraging others. Through such life choices, cultures influence the attitudes of their members. Expanded economic models could help clarify how, in shaping people's lives, cultures shape their identities and hence their preferences and beliefs. (See Chapters 5 and 6 for how they shape our politics and educational alternatives.)

At the same time, because this influence of cultures on people's preferences is mediated by people's life experiences, cultures have the potential to transform. If circumstances in society change, owing perhaps to changes in technology, exterior threats, more travel, greater immigration, some new policy or fad, or changes in the media, how people live will change, and if cultural identification and preferences depend on life's activities and experiences, both culture and preferences may change rapidly. Moreover, there may be no new equilibrium in the short run between cultural values and the preferences individuals acquire by attempting to live in the way that cultural values direct. I think that one sees something like this in the chaotic, rapid, yet halting changes in American attitudes toward family life and women's work over the last two generations.

Economic modeling has limits, and I do not suppose that by incorporating additional mechanisms of preference modification, economic models will illuminate all the many aspects of the ways in which culture influences economic choices, institutions, and outcomes. Furthermore, no satisfactory extension of the standard model of choice to incorporate the influences of cultures on preferences can be created in a philosopher's armchair. I have offered no more than speculations about how economic models can be extended to help us understand how the circumstances of people's lives, which are shaped by culture and individual preference, determine people's cultural identification and preferences.

Integrating Cultural Influence into Applied Economics

I have thus far discussed cultural change and the influence of culture on preferences as if they had no particular relevance to the nitty-gritty practical tasks of economists. But that is not the case. Consider, for example, the economic assessment of policies to limit automobile pollution. Cost-benefit analyses of important policies such as those regulating fuel efficiency are required by US law and are highly sophisticated. Parts of these are uncontroversial. For example, imposing a gasoline tax leads people with existing cars to drive them less by increasing the cost of doing so, unlike a stricter fuel efficiency standard on new cars, which could lower the marginal cost of additional driving if it leads to lower fuel prices.

One alleged strike against both increased fuel efficiency standards and a gasoline tax is that they will frustrate consumer preferences for heavier and more powerful vehicles. In a 2003 analysis, the Congressional Budget Office (CBO) points out that the remarkable improvements in engine design over the previous generation, which could have led to much greater fuel efficiency, resulted almost entirely in increases in horsepower and in the size and weight of vehicles. Inferring consumer's preferences from this fact, and assuming that the preferences of car buyers will not change, the CBO finds that both increases in the gasoline tax and higher fuel economy standards impose large costs on consumers in the form of disappointment with smaller and less powerful vehicles.

Nicolas Loris and Derrick Morgan of the Heritage Foundation take this fact to be an argument against interference with the market:

> Consumers have other preferences as well, including weight and engine power, for safety, enjoyment, and practical reasons. . . . In fact, a 2011 paper from the Massachusetts Institute of Technology found that if weight, horsepower, and torque were held constant at 1980 levels, fuel efficiency would have increased 60 percent from 1980 to 2006 instead of the 15 percent increase that did occur. . . .
>
> Consumers consider these trade-offs and place higher or lower values on different vehicle features depending on what they want. . . . Whether the preference is for safety, performance, or fuel efficiency, the market—not the federal government—is in the best position to meet that demand. (2012, 3)

Both the CBO analysis and Loris and Morgan's argument depend crucially on three assumptions: (1) that willingness to pay, which is inferred from market behavior, is a reasonable (albeit imperfect) indicator of people's preferences, (2) that people's preferences are reliable indicators of what is good for them, and (3) that the preferences of drivers will not change in response to fuel economy standards or increases in fuel costs.[3] Clearly, willingness to pay is a problematic indicator of preferences, if for no other reason than the differences in how much people have to spend. However, as a first approximation, the first assumption may be reasonable in this context.

With respect to the second assumption, people's preferences among alternatives are often not accurate indicators of what is good for them because people may have false beliefs or inadequate information, because preferences may not be self-interested, or because, for one reason or another, people are not good judges of what is in their interests. In some applications of cost-benefit analysis, these reasons to question whether preferences are a good guide to welfare are much stronger than others. There are obviously some reasons to hesitate in this context. Consumers may be unable to estimate the future costs of gasoline or the benefits to them or to others of driving less, or consumers may be misled by advertising into fantasizing that powerful automobiles will win them attractive spouses or children who do not fuss on car trips. Let us pass over these qualms and suppose (somewhat heroically) that preferences are in this context reasonable indicators of well-being.

The third assumption is the crucial one for the purposes of this chapter. Clearly, American consumers have demanded very large, heavy, and powerful vehicles. Fuel efficiency standards may make such vehicles impossible to obtain, and gasoline taxes will make such vehicles more expensive to operate. Standard cost-benefit analysis requires that one monetize these preferences for large, heavy, and powerful vehicles and take the frustration of these preferences as among the costs of policies designed to limit automobile emissions.

But these preferences are not universal or unchanging, and if they change in response to the policy, then their frustration should not be counted as among its costs. If in response to higher fuel prices people drive smaller cars, they will not need a large car to be able to see over other big cars or to survive crashes with them. The benefits of large cars and hence the preferences for them depend on the size of the other cars on the road. Moreover, small and lightweight cars are (other things being equal) more nimble and able to stop more quickly and thus better able to avoid collisions. The successful implementation of a policy that greatly reduced the number of large vehicles on the road would thus undermine one of the reasons for purchasing large vehicles. If there is less reason to want a large vehicle, there should be a shift in preferences away from larger and heavier vehicles.[4]

The desires for big and powerful vehicles reflect alterable features of American culture rather than invariant aspects of human psychology. As evidence, notice that these desires are far weaker in Europe. An orthodox economist might argue that the difference reflects merely the difference in costs of driving a large SUV in the United States compared to driving it in Europe (and the physical difficulties of driving large vehicles in some of the older parts of European cities). But there are also social norms at work and shared values concerning what one wants in a car. The culture of driving is different. (How else can one explain why most cars in Europe have manual transmissions, while most cars in the United States have automatic transmissions?) It is a cultural fact that European drivers pride themselves on the agility of their driving rather than on the size and power of their cars, and there is no evidence that they are any less satisfied with their cars than Americans (R. Frank 2009).

Standard economic modeling fails at the task of estimating the costs and benefits of policies requiring greater fuel economy because it fails to model the ways in which preferences respond to policies and cultural norms. Driving is such an important feature of contemporary society and car ownership such an important part of people's identities that estimations of the effects of policies need to take into account how they may change preferences. There are bound to be multiple mechanisms. On the one hand, increases in fuel economy standards, which will make large and heavy vehicles much more expensive, may make the purchase of those vehicles a way to demonstrate one's wealth and thus increase rather than decrease the demand for those vehicles. On the other hand, driving smaller vehicles may provide drivers with more, rather than less, enjoyment, quite apart from lower prices, as drivers discover the pleasures of nimble handling or ease of parking. If large and heavy vehicles become unaffordable, individuals may be resentful and unhappy, or they may instead come not to want what they cannot have. If improved fuel economy is part of a collective effort to combat the environmental threat that automobile pollution poses, people may take pride in their smaller and more efficient cars and make a virtue out of being unable to afford to purchase or operate large, heavy vehicles.

I am not a marketer, and I cannot assess the plausibility of these stories. But the example suggests that the influence of culture on preferences matters to applied economic analysis. Understanding how culture, preferences, and what people actually do interact with one another is—or should be—as important to economists as it is to anthropologists or sociologists.

Notes

Acknowledgments: For many useful comments and criticisms, I am indebted to Natalia Carrillo, Luis Mireles-Flores, Wade Hands, Aki Lehtinen, Uskali Mäki, Caterina

Marchionni, Paolo Quattrone, J. P. Singh, David Throsby, and the other participants at the Cultural Values and Interests conference.

1. In addition, if Q prefers x to y and is indifferent between y and z, then Q prefers x to z. Transitivity can be stated more compactly in terms of the relation (R) of weak preference, where $xR_Q y$ if and only if Q prefers x to y or is indifferent between x and y. Transitivity says that if $xR_Q y$, and $yR_Q z$, then $xR_Q z$.

2. To allow for the possibility that Isidore is indifferent between x and y and simply picks x, the formulation in the text needs to be revised, but complicating the exposition makes no substantive difference to the point I am making.

3. The quotation from Loris and Morgan also apparently ignores the externalities of driving and the absence of a market for clean air. There is no way to determine from examining only the choices of car buyers what the net benefits would be of policies to limit air pollution that results from driving.

4. Similarly, if a driver's preference is for a faster car than others (as opposed to some absolute rate of acceleration), then the driver's preference among cars depends on the distribution of cars, which in turn depends on policies such as gasoline taxes or fuel efficiency standards. "A car that is experienced subjectively as fast is simply one that accelerates more briskly than other cars in the same local environment. So when all purchase cars with more powerful engines, the same car that once seemed fast no longer does" (R. Frank 2009). Once again, we see that preferences among cars will change with changes in policies.

3   Value and Values in Economics and Culture
David Throsby

THE DISTINCTION COMMON IN THE SOCIAL SCIENCES BETWEEN a functional and a constituent sense in which culture is defined is reflected in economics in two divergent lines of theory and analysis, each with its own interpretation of value. On the one hand, when culture is considered in its constituent sense, referring to the shared knowledge and belief systems that serve to identify a group, it is values in the plural that are of concern. Economists have been interested in the extent to which cultural characteristics and values of people affect their economic behavior and contribute to determining economic outcomes. On the other hand, the functional sense of culture in economics is seen in the material manifestations of human action, represented in economic discourse by cultural goods and services. The economist's interest in value in this latter context lies in understanding the processes by which the value of art comes to be expressed in monetary terms and in ascertaining whether it is possible or necessary to identify a distinctive form of cultural value that stands apart from conventional notions of economic value in providing a full account of the value of cultural phenomena. If the concept of cultural value is accepted, the economist's concern is with investigating the relationships between these two value concepts in affecting individual and collective decision making.

In this chapter, I consider both of these approaches as they relate to fundamental questions of value and valuation in the economics of art and culture. The chapter is structured as follows. In the first section, I ask how it is that economists deal with the relationships between culture and economics: Are these two areas of intellectual and policy discourse oppositional or integrative? At a macro level, a response to this question is framed in terms of the constituent interpretation of culture previously noted; accordingly, the second section considers the relationship between culture and economic performance at the international, national, and subnational levels. In a micro context, where the functional representation of culture is appropriate, the concept of cultural value as referred to earlier lies at the heart of efforts by economists to interpret the value of art and culture in circumstances where the primary models of use in their discipline are instrumental in nature. Thus, the third section considers how a nonutilitarian notion of the value of art can be rationalized in such models, with illustrations drawn from studies of the value of visual art, literature, and music. In the fourth section, the chapter introduces an international dimension, in which both constituent and functional senses of culture are in play. In this section, I discuss questions of value and valuation in the areas of intercultural dialogue, cultural diversity, and sustainable development. The chapter concludes with a plea for more dialogue at the interdisciplinary level.

How Do Economists Deal with Culture?

Culture is not a matter that troubles the minds of many economists. Much of what they learned as students of economics concerns individual and collective behavior that takes place in a culture-free environment, or at least in a context where culture, whatever it is, is considered to be given, exogenous, and largely irrelevant to the behavioral models that are useful in understanding economic decision making. Such a caricature of economics describes the way the discipline has developed through the twentieth century. But in earlier periods in the history of economic thought, the situation was very different.[1] Before Adam Smith, art was regarded by economists as an inessential luxury, even if trade in art could be seen as an important economic activity. Smith, however, developed a different line of analysis, particularly in *The Theory of Moral Sentiments* ([1759] 1976), in which he considered the role of fashion in influencing the demand for art and the motivations of artists in affecting supply. Some elements of his analysis of aesthetics were carried through into *An Inquiry into the Nature and Causes of the Wealth of Nations* ([1776] 1976).

But the great nineteenth-century political economists—Thomas Robert Malthus, David Ricardo, J. S. Mill, and Jeremy Bentham—were not so much concerned with art and culture specifically as with the wider social and cultural context within which economic activity occurs. Even so, debate about cultural factors in relation to the nineteenth-century economy flourished, carried on not so much by political economists as by humanist writers such as Matthew Arnold, William Morris, Charles Dickens, and others who drew attention to the adverse social and cultural impacts of industrialization. A lone exception among the political economists was John Ruskin; in his 1857 lectures titled "The Political Economy of Art," he brought together his prodigious experience of art and architecture with his often quirky theories of economics in ways that to some extent prefigure the concerns of modern cultural economists.[2]

In the radical political economy of the current era, culture is generally viewed from the disciplinary perspective of cultural studies, in which class relationships and the operations of contemporary capitalism are of central concern. Within this tradition, it is the exercise of power—for example by a dominant class or by corporate interests—that is seen to determine outcomes. Thus, for instance, corporate culture is interpreted as having a pervasive influence on many aspects of economic life, ranging from the operation of labor markets to the cultural choices of consumers.

The marginal revolution of the late nineteenth century produced an intellectually beautiful and theoretically complete model of an economic system and in so doing relegated art and culture even further onto the periphery of economic thinking. It was not until half a century later that some broader ideas about the significance of art and culture in human affairs resurfaced in economics, notably in the life and work of John Maynard Keynes, the most important economist of the twentieth century. Keynes's life was intimately connected with art and artists, and although he wrote little on the subject himself, his views and his experience in cohabiting in the worlds of art and the economy were influential in the discussions within the Bloomsbury Group on matters including the place of art in economic life, the role of artists, the working of the arts market, and the possibilities for cultural policy (Moggridge 2005).

Developments in thinking about the relationship between economics and culture in the history of economic thought, sketched briefly in this section, have all had issues of value as an explicit or implicit concern: How is the value of art and culture to society to be interpreted and expressed, and how is economic activity influenced, if at all, by cultural considerations? These questions continue to be of interest today, not only in economics but also in the other social sciences and the humanities. Indeed, the relationship between economics as a scholarly tradition and other disciplines such as philosophy, sociology, and anthropology is called into question by these very issues. To take but one example, there has been a long debate about the theoretical and methodological differences between anthropology and economics in which some economists, including Frank Knight (1941) and Richard Posner (1980), have at different times argued that anthropologists fail to appreciate the explanatory power of economic models of human behavior. Such opinions have prompted accusations that economists are guilty of intellectual imperialism, a charge that continues to be discussed today in one way or another (Fine 2000). Contributors to this debate from a variety of perspectives within the social sciences have opened up a more productive discourse. In regard to anthropology, for example, it has been suggested that there are three dichotomies that separate the two fields (Bardhan and Ray 2006): economics is concerned with individualism, outcomes, and parsimony in model building, whereas anthropology is concerned with the embeddedness of behavior in societal norms, processes, and complexity. Although this distinction between the two fields is essentially methodological, it is possible that it may overlook more fundamental epistemological issues that cannot be avoided (Appadurai 1989).

Despite differences between disciplines in their approaches to questions of value and valuation in relation to art and culture, there appears to be some concordance across disciplinary boundaries on the fundamental question of defining culture, a task that has been described as "trying to encage the wind" (Borofsky 1998, 64). The constituent versus functional interpretation of culture referred to at the beginning of this chapter is reflected, if not always explicitly, in the way the subject is treated in different approaches and serves as an appropriate basis on which to carry forward our consideration of value in the relationship between economics and culture in the remainder of this chapter.

Culture in the Constituent Sense

Conventional neoclassical macro models of economic growth seek to explain the performance of an economy by reference to such variables as levels of investment in physical and human capital, population, technology, and so on. In such models, the role of culture is taken as exogenous. However, these models have proved inadequate in explaining differential rates of development over time between rich and poor countries and the persistence of differences in intercountry income distribution. Thus, economists have looked for more fundamental factors that might underpin development processes. One of the most important of such factors is culture. In this context, culture is interpreted in its constituent sense as the values, beliefs, customs, and traditions that identify a group and provide it with a recognizable identity. Such factors, which in some interpretations might be regarded more as sociological than cultural in nature, include religious beliefs, ethical values, ethnic origins, linguistic inheritance, and group allegiances of various sorts. In cross-country analyses of these effects, the "culture" referred to can often be broadly interpreted as "national culture."

Not surprisingly, one of the most prominent cultural traits that has attracted attention is religious belief, following the original contribution of Max Weber. As is well known, Weber (1930) argued that the Protestant values of honesty, thrift, and espousal of a work ethic provided the foundation for a productive economy and were the reasons for the success of capitalism. Empirical economic evidence derived from intercountry studies supports the proposition that strong religious beliefs stimulate economic growth because they underpin individual behavioral patterns that tend to improve productivity (Barro and McCleary 2003).

More general interpretations of cultural values have also been explored as determinants of economic performance. For instance, an influential line of enquiry into the relationships between cultural factors and economic behavior has flowed from the original work of James Coleman (1988) and Robert Putnam, Robert Leonardi, and Raffaella Nonetti (1993) on social capital. Central to these efforts has been an emphasis on trust as a behavioral trait that facilitates social interaction, encourages investment in human capital, enhances productivity, and generates the social cohesion that characterizes well-integrated societies. It is argued that cultural characteristics such as trust are reflected in social norms, which act as constraints on individual action and which foster the development of institutional structures that regulate society in ways consistent with these norms.[3]

It can also be suggested that there is a staged process here. To unravel the influence of culture on economic performance, a more productive approach might be to look at relationships between measures of life satisfaction and economic outcomes. In this context, the focus might shift to investigating the prior link in the chain connecting culture and economic performance—that is, the effect of cultural factors on levels of subjective well-being. There has been interest in examining this relationship across a range of countries (Kenny 2005); in such a situation, cultural values that affect how happy people are can take their place alongside other influences on well-being.[4] Once that connection has been established, the onward linkage through to economic performance can be investigated. In a situation such as this, the impact of cultural factors on growth or on other economic variables is somewhat less direct than postulated earlier, and it implies that attributing outcomes specifically to culture in an empirical estimation may not be easy.

In studies of the relationship between culture and economic performance, there remains a question over the causal direction. Reverse causation is a possibility familiar in areas such as analyses of the effect of education on economic growth: Does education improve productivity and hence growth, or do faster-growing economies allocate more resources to education? Similarly with culture, it is quite plausible to propose that the cultural factors that we have been discussing affect economic growth in some way, but the causation may in some situations run in the reverse direction—it may be that patterns of economic development have some effect on cultural values. For example, there has been some interest in the persistence of traditional cultural values—those that are assumed to be acquired by individuals as a result of intergenerational transmission. It can be argued that if different cultural traditions around the world are resistant to change, those traditions may contain elements that influence the rate of economic development in different ways. If so, there may be at least a partial explanation of continued disparities in the level of development between countries (Inglehart and Baker 2000).

Reference to intergenerational transmission raises the question of long-term processes of cultural change. Cultures are not static but subject to constant evolution over time. In this context, for example, Ronald Inglehart (1990) has studied the effects of system-level changes such as technological development, rising levels of education, and expansion of communications on individual values and skills. Changes in these characteristics of people lead to system-level consequences that affect economic outcomes. Such effects work through society and the economy over time as younger generations grow older and the overall cultural values shared by the population change.

Culture in the Functional Sense

Turning from the macro to the micro, we move to the interpretation of culture as the tangible and intangible manifestations of cultural activity and creative expression. In this sense, we refer to the ways in which culture is practiced rather than to culture as a set of characteristics. The application of economic theory and analysis to such cultural manifestations comprises the field of cultural economics, now referred to more generally as the economics of art and culture. The field has grown over the last half-century, starting with initial contributions from well-known economists including John Kenneth Galbraith (1960), William Baumol (Baumol and Bowen 1966), Tibor Scitovsky (1972), and Mark Blaug (1976) and expanding into a wide range of areas including production, distribution and demand for cultural goods and services, art markets, artistic labor supply, arts and cultural policy, trade in cultural goods, culture in sustainable development, and many more. The field has its own journal, international scholarly association, and biennial conference and has generated an enormous literature that is constantly growing in sophistication and reach.[5]

A fundamental element in an economic approach to art is the concept of a cultural good. An essential initial question is to ask whether such goods have unique characteristics that distinguish them as a commodity class from other goods and services in the economy. A reasonable definition of cultural goods attributes to them three necessary features: they require some input of human creativity in their manufacture; they possess or convey some symbolic meaning or messages; and they contain, at least potentially, some form of intellectual property. This definition extends to include a wide range of arts- and culture-related products, some of which have only minor cultural content such as fashion design, some forms of advertising, and some architectural services. The definition also serves as a basis for defining cultural industries and the cultural sector of the economy.

The second characteristic noted—namely, the generation of some symbolic meaning or message—raises the question of value, leading to an alternative definitional approach in economics that involves portraying cultural goods as embodying or giving rise to a form of value that lies beyond the reach of conventional economic assessment and is not expressible (or is only imperfectly expressible) in market prices or in individual willingness-to-pay judgments. In the case of artworks, for example, such cultural value might derive from ineffable aesthetic or spiritual qualities that such works of art are known to possess and to convey to those who experience them. While some such value characteristics may be translatable into financial terms, some may not; existence of the latter underlies the distinction between economic value and cultural value.

Interpretation of the value of artistic and cultural phenomena as comprising these two elements is not confined to economics. Indeed, a certain duality in the value of art was strongly argued by Barbara Herrnstein Smith in the late 1980s. She suggested that it is possible to observe two discursive domains:

> On the one hand there is the discourse of economic theory: money, commerce, technology, industry, production and consumption, workers and consumers; on the other hand, there is the discourse of aesthetic axiology: culture, art, genius, creation and appreciation, artists and connoisseurs. In the first discourse, events are explained in terms of calculation, preferences, costs, benefits, profits, prices, and utility. In the second, events are explained—or, rather . . . "justified"—in terms of inspiration, discrimination, taste . . . , the test of time, intrinsic value, and transcendent value. (1988, 127)

Such a duality in ascribing value to artistic phenomena finds resonances across the humanities and the social sciences. This is illustrated in a collection of essays published in 2008 exploring the conjunction of economic and cultural value in fields as disparate as philosophy, art history, sociology, anthropology, ethnomusicology, and cultural studies (Hutter and Throsby 2008).

Returning to the economics of art and culture, we can observe that discussion about the value of cultural goods and services has sharpened the distinction between the concepts of economic value and cultural value as descriptors of the value embodied in or yielded by such commodities. Economic value in this discourse is defined as the aggregate market and nonmarket valuation of a cultural good or service as measured in monetary terms by the conventional methods of economic analysis. The relevant market value can be assessed from price data or other indicators of direct user benefits, possibly supplemented by estimates of consumers' surplus, while nonmarket value can be measured using revealed- or stated-preference methods. Nonmarket value in this context arises because the arts can be assumed to give rise to diffused community benefits, or nonrival, nonexcludable public goods. For example, in considering the collection of any major art museum—the Louvre, the Uffizi, the Tate, the Metropolitan, the Hermitage—individuals are likely to recognize existence, option, and bequest values attributable to the collections in these institutions, meaning that they value the fact that the collections are there, potentially accessible, and important to be preserved.[6]

Cultural value can be deconstructed into identifiable components that might include aesthetic value, symbolic value, spiritual value, historical value, and so on (see Throsby 2001, 26–31).[7] The application of these attributes to any of the aforementioned museum collections is obvious. Given its multidimensional nature and lack of a common unit of account, cultural value within this paradigm can be assessed for a given cultural manifestation and for specific value components by applying various ranking or rating procedures to yield ordinal or cardinal scores; such scores can be determined by individuals through their considered judgments and can be aggregated, weighted if appropriate, to reach a mean rating for a group with respect to any given dimension of value for the cultural item in question. These procedures could be applied, for example, to any of the collections referred to earlier, or to individual works contained in them.

If the concepts of economic and cultural value for cultural goods are defined separately as in the previous paragraphs, it can be suggested that the total value of these commodities could be represented as some combination of these two distinct forms of value. Such a proposition moves the analysis outside the neoclassical framework of economics because in conventional economic theory, as noted earlier, all sources of cultural value for a particular good would be expected to be captured in its economic value, making the need for a separate concept of cultural value redundant.

The argument motivating this broadening of scope of the value concept for cultural commodities in economics has turned on the adequacy of money as a value metric. Individuals, it is argued, may find it inappropriate or impossible to express their valuation of some cultural phenomena in terms of willingness to pay; for example, they may have difficulty articulating in financial terms the value they place on their cultural identity or on their spiritual experiences. If it is true that a purely financial assessment of the value of cultural phenomena is incapable of capturing all the variables that affect choice, it will be inadequate as a basis for individual or collective decision making on resource allocation in the cultural arena.[8] Such an outcome would have implications that ramify into a wide area of public and private action, including the functioning of art markets, trade in cultural goods and services, public support for cultural institutions, production of art, the conservation of heritage, and so on.

To conclude this discussion on the value of culture in the functional sense, let us consider some examples from the creative arts. First, artworks such as paintings are cultural goods to which the dual concepts of economic and cultural value can be readily applied. Paintings have an economic value that can be indicated in the first instance by the market price at which they can be bought and sold. They are also likely to demonstrate some artistic or interpretive intention that could be taken to represent their cultural value or their significance as cultural objects. In an empirical study investigating these concepts, Throsby and Anita Zednik (2013) set out to discover whether the economic and cultural values of a group of paintings hanging in a public gallery gave rise to different and incommensurable value assessments among a sample of individual observers. The cultural value of the paintings was measured by seeking the respondents' level of agreement with a series of statements about the aesthetic, spiritual, social, and educational value of each painting and transforming the judgments into a cardinal measure using Likert-style procedures. The economic value was assessed by asking respondents how much they would pay to rent a particular painting for one month (a flow value) and how much they thought a public gallery should pay for the painting (a stock value). The study analyzed the extent to which economic valuations were determined by the various cultural valuations. The results showed that individuals' cultural valuations of the works provided some explanation of the works' economic value but that this explanation was incomplete. So, for example, a strong relationship emerged between economic value and aesthetic value (people think beautiful paintings are worth more financially, *cet. par.*); however, some cultural dimensions that were recognized by respondents as important to themselves and others, such as the spiritual value of the paintings, were found to have no significant influence on economic value.

A second example can be drawn from literature. Like artworks, books can be classified as cultural goods with both an economic price, on the one hand, and a cultural value in the symbolic meaning that they convey, on the other. This duality in value can be seen in both fiction and nonfiction literary works. In the former case, the cultural value as perceived by the reader is experienced via engagement with narrative, character, and so on, bringing the reader's moral imagination into play and stimulating creative thinking (see, e.g., Attridge 2004; Bromwich 2014). In the case of literary nonfiction, the cultural value may lie in the way in which books contribute to public debate about contemporary issues, in illuminating the past, in providing insight into the characters of public figures past and present, and so on. In all of these respects, books can be seen as having a value to the individual and to society that goes beyond their price. Indeed, in a national survey of Australian readers, this very proposition was put to respondents; two-thirds agreed with it (Throsby, Zwar, and Morgan 2017).

Finally, we turn to classical music, a genre whose relative position in the musical landscape has suffered a secular decline as new musical forms emerge, new technologies for music consumption are developed, and shifts in cultural tastes occur. Both supply and demand sides of the market for classical music have been profoundly affected by these changes. Ultimately, however, it can be argued that the survival of classical music is dependent not so much on the economics of music supply and demand as it is on the fundamental significance of the intrinsic aesthetic qualities of this genre. Such an argument interprets the cultural value of classical music as relating to the importance of music as a repository of meaning, a purveyor of civilizing values, and a vehicle for cultural transmission through time. It reflects the distinction between economic and cultural value that we have been discussing, and it points to the different imperatives conveyed by each form of value. History suggests that, despite the vagaries of the marketplace, the essential nature of art that classical music embodies will, in the long term, prevail.[9]

Cultural Value in International Economic Relations

In this section, we expand questions of value and values in economics and culture to the sphere of international relations. Both interpretations of culture and both forms of value that we have been discussing come into play in this arena. Areas of concern include cultural trade, cultural diplomacy and the exercise of soft power, international movement of artists, cultural diversity, and the role of culture in sustainable development.

International economic relations in the contemporary world take place in the context of the major economic transformation that has affected all aspects of human interaction—the phenomenon of globalization, a process driven by the digital revolution, the explosion in computational power, the growth of the internet, and the invention of new devices for communication and data transmission. The expansion of globalization has been facilitated by a wide-spread acceptance of neoliberal economic principles as the basis for national and international policy making. In these circumstances, the development agenda that drives international relations is relentlessly economic in orientation, exemplified in the sorts of global forums in which world leaders regularly gather. Culture rarely rates a mention at these meetings, except insofar as the cultural industries may perhaps figure in discussions about creativity and innovation. The issues listed for consideration at the G20 meeting in Osaka in 2019, for example, contained little that could be seen to recognize culture in either the constituent or the functional sense. The situation is somewhat different at regional levels, where shared notions of cultural identity may be stronger; for instance, the Association of Southeast Asian Nations (ASEAN) has as its motto, "One Vision, One Identity, One Community," and although its conferences place strong emphasis on economic and development issues, they do also include meetings of ministers for arts and culture, with clear references across the board to both interpretations of culture.

Even though culture may not be prominent in the concerns of global economic summits, there are other international arenas in which cultural issues are especially important, such as in trade negotiations. Cultural goods and services have always proved a contentious issue in multilateral and bilateral trade negotiations for precisely the reason that has been a focus throughout this chapter—that is, that cultural goods can be considered to be more than just commercial merchandise whose trade can be subject to the usual precepts of free markets and comparative advantage. The argument rests again on the concept of the cultural value of such goods that transcends their economic value; if the argument is accepted, it implies that cultural goods require an alternative mechanism governing their international exchange.[10] Such a mechanism has been found over the years in the possibility of invoking the so-called cultural exception (or cultural exemption) provision in trade negotiations, which effectively excludes cultural products from the negotiations. Over the last ten years or so there has been an increase in the use of cultural exception measures to exclude some cultural products from trade agreements. Moreover, some new trade instruments have emerged in this time to recognize the specificity of cultural goods and services and to promote cultural cooperation (Guèvremont 2015).

Of course, it is not only in the field of trade that economics and culture intersect at an international level. Cultural diplomacy, or the exercise of soft power, may be ostensibly about the promulgation of cultural values, particularly those espoused by the hegemonic powers of the industrialized West, but such efforts generally have a strategic purpose linked directly to economic interest. Cultural diplomacy may, for example, be implemented with one eye on the old adage, "culture leads, trade follows." This proposition may be an expression of faith rather than fact, but it is at least plausible to propose that the improved understanding and better communication that is expected to flow from cultural exchange between countries is likely to facilitate rather than hinder the development of future trading relationships (see Chapter 9).

Artists are an important means through which intercultural dialogue is initiated and carried forward at an international level. Creative artists have a long history of moving independently between countries in search of artistic stimulus and income-earning opportunities, and in so doing they promote cultural understanding—usually, this is a two-way process. Moreover, artists frequently travel with the support of their home government, either as individuals or as members of an ensemble or company, in pursuit of some diplomatic purpose or simply to showcase their national culture abroad. A range of economic obstacles as well as incentives affect the mobility of artistic labor, including difficulties in obtaining visas, increasing security, and a host of political and economic constraints governing artistic labor markets, particularly in the developed world, which may be hostile to the admission of foreign artists, even for relatively short periods (van Graan and Sanan 2015).

The concepts of value and values at an international level discussed previously arise in the global context of cultural diversity, a matter that was brought to international attention through the 1995 report of the World Commission on Culture and Development, *Our Creative Diversity*, and consolidated in UNESCO's 2001 "Universal Declaration on Cultural Diversity." The culmination of these processes was seen in the adoption in 2005 of the UN Convention on the Promotion and Protection of the Diversity of Cultural Expressions (hereafter the Cultural Diversity Convention), which entered into force in 2007.

The convention recognizes the pervasive role of cultural value in motivating the production, distribution, and consumption of art and culture in all their multiple forms. It also acknowledges the differences in cultural values that characterize different national and regional communities, and it promotes the diversity of such values within a context of peace, security, and the observance of human rights. Whether such lofty aims can be achieved through the agency of an international treaty remains a work in progress; nevertheless, a ten-year review of its successes and shortcomings has found that overall the positive outcomes have so far outweighed the negative ones (UNESCO 2015).

An important driving force propelling the initiation and implementation of the Cultural Diversity Convention has been the amalgamated voices of countries of the Global South. These countries have been concerned at the negative impacts they experience from the rise of globalization and the increasing disparities in incomes and wealth between the developed and the developing worlds. Such outcomes reflect the political economy of international trade and cultural relationships in a postcolonial era. The convention has been seen as possibly offering an alternative to the WTO for regulating cultural trade, doing away with the need for the cultural exception arrangements referred to previously. If such a change were to come about, it would represent a small step toward rebalancing power relationships in the international cultural economy, although whether it could be made operational remains in doubt.

The Cultural Diversity Convention situates the process of economic development within the overarching framework of sustainability, a paradigm in which the world is seen as a holistic system integrating economic, social, cultural, and environmental values. Within this context, the convention points to the important role that culture can play in advancing the cause of sustainable development, defined as development that meets the needs of the present generation without compromising the capacity of future generations to meet their own needs (World Commission on Environment and Development 1987, 43). Principles and recommendations relating to sustainable development in different articles of the convention refer both to the role of culture as a facilitator for development and to the potential for the cultural industries to emerge as drivers of the development process.[11]

In 2012, the United Nations set in motion a process to develop a set of Sustainable Development Goals (SDGs) to replace the soon-to-expire Millennium Development Goals (MDGs) that had been adopted in 2000. In drafting the new goals, the United Nations was mindful of the economic, social, and particularly the environmental values implied by the sustainable development model, but it conspicuously ignored cultural values, despite a vigorous campaign by the international cultural community, spearheaded by UNESCO, to have the role of culture in sustainable development recognized and taken on board. Thus, the new SDGs adopted in September 2015 and intended for full achievement by 2030 contain only the most fleeting references to culture, placed in a couple of minor paragraphs dealing with education, heritage, and tourism.

Despite this setback, however, it can be argued that the advancement of a role for culture in sustainable development in the future might never be achievable if this objective were left simply as a component of a set of goals such as the SDGs. Rather, it can be suggested that an international framework oriented toward culture and development such as the Cultural Diversity Convention is likely to be more effective; it has the considerable advantage of being an international treaty imposing specific obligations on signatories, not just a set of aspirations.

To conclude, it is difficult to consider the matter of culture in international relations without referring to the dark side of this picture, the fact that cultural difference underlies many of the conflicts within and between nations in the contemporary world. This phenomenon has, of course, been a feature of relationships between peoples throughout history. Again, there are intersections between economics and culture in this field, such that it is difficult to separate out the relative importance of different imperatives underlying inter- and intranational conflict—the intransigence of some cultural belief systems, for example, compared to the economic drive for command over territory or resources. When cultural factors are implicated in conflict situations, the usual path toward reconciliation that is advocated by concerned voices from all sides is one based on intercultural dialogue. There are many dimensions to these processes—one that should not be overlooked is the role of artists and of the arts generally in promoting peace, communication, and mutual understanding. The significance of these possibilities cannot be overstated.[12]

Conclusion

I have pointed to the many ways in which cultural factors influence processes of long-run transformation in the economy and in society. It is apparent that the role of culture in these processes is so fundamental that theories of economic and social change that fail to take account of cultural factors are likely to provide an incomplete or misleading interpretation of development and its consequences. We have discussed these phenomena in the context of value as understood in economics and in the theory and practice of culture. It could be suggested that economics and culture are uneasy bedfellows, being oriented apparently to the achievement of different objectives and relying on fundamentally divergent interpretations of value. This chapter tries to show that such disparities can provide a springboard for thinking about concepts of value in a wider context than one confined by disciplinary boundaries.

Reconciling differences and recognizing complementarities between value systems can help deepen understanding of how notions of value can be made operational in particular circumstances—for example, in public policy making. In these processes, there may be a tendency for the economic dimensions of value to dominate, pressed not least by those economists who are unable or unwilling to recognize other components of a value system affecting a particular policy. The remarks in the preceding section concerning the virtues of intercultural dialogue can be applied just as readily to the need for a stronger engagement with interdisciplinary dialogue among the humanities and social sciences. The growing discipline of cultural economics, or the economics of art and culture, explores ways of linking economic and cultural interpretations of the world and in so doing represents a positive example of such engagement.

Notes

1. For a comprehensive coverage of art and culture in the history of economic thought, see Goodwin 2006.

2. For a consideration of Ruskin's place in the history of the economics of the arts, see Throsby 2011.

3. For a theory of intercultural competition and the ways in which competition between cultures influences economic performance, see Casson 2006.

4. Similarly, a lot more than values affect people's preferences; see Hausman 2012.

5. Collections of important contributions to the field are in Towse 1997, 2007; Ginsburgh and Menger 1996; and Ginsburgh and Throsby 2006, 2013. Appraisals of the development of cultural economics at various stages can be found in Throsby 1994, 2006; and Blaug 2001.

6. This categorization of the sources of nonmarket demand for the arts follows that developed by economists evaluating environmental values; the theory and methodologies for measuring the benefits from natural capital are directly applicable to cultural capital such as cultural heritage—see, for example, Navrud and Ready 2002.

7. This categorization has subsequently been discussed and elaborated by a number of writers; see, for example, Singh 2011, 24–26. For an overview of the concept of cultural value in economics, see Angelini and Castellani 2019.

8. For a discussion of the relationships between preferences and choice in a cultural context, see Chapter 2.

9. For some discussion on these issues, see, for example, Johnson 2002; and Kramer 2007.

10. For contributions to the field that situate cultural trade in the wider context of overall trade negotiations, see Acheson and Maule 2006; Singh 2008, chaps. 3–4; and Iapadre 2013.

11. For further discussion of these issues, see Throsby 2017.

12. It might be noted that music, as a universal language, exerts a particular fascination in this connection; see, for example, Barenboim 2008.

4 Creating a Culture of Environmental Responsibility

Sharon R. Krause

CONTEMPORARY DISCOURSE IN THE DOMAIN OF ENVIRONMENTAL politics and policy is overwhelmingly cast in terms of human interests (Klein 2014; Purdy 2015; McKibben 1989).[1] This focus is well founded in one sense. Earth systems are remarkably resilient; we may alter or even destroy many species and habitats, but the planet and plenty of its life forms will persist. Human beings, however, are quite vulnerable to toxic waste, resource depletion, and climate change—and to the political, economic, and social instabilities they generate. The focus on human interests, then, reflects the reality that anthropogenic environmental damage powerfully affects us. Beyond that, many environmentalists assume that appealing to interests is the most effective way to motivate collective action on environmental issues. Perhaps it would be nice if more people cared about the well-being of endangered polar bears or dying coral reefs, but caring about nature on its own terms seems to require a form of altruism that is too unreliable to depend on.[2] Self-interest is the passion to be reckoned on.

Yet the appeal to interests turns out to be less effective in the environmental context than we might hope, for varied and complex reasons. In some ways this should not be surprising. After all, societies everywhere inculcate particular values for the purpose of guiding human action in salutary directions because they know that self-interest on its own cannot be relied on to produce collectively beneficial outcomes. Internalizing these values can motivate people to do the right thing even when doing so cuts against interests they believe themselves to have. Moreover, how people conceive their interests depends significantly on the prevailing background of collective values that structures their experience and identities. It is true that human interests are not infinitely malleable, but one of the key themes of this book is that preferences and interests are always embedded in the repertoire of shared values that constitutes culture.[3]

Nowhere is the connection between interests and culture more visible than in the environmental domain. Recent research on climate change, for example, finds close connections between one's cultural identity and one's position on the issue, both across societies and within them (Hoffman 2015, 11). The extent to which people believe that carbon mitigation policies are in their interest, it turns out, depends a great deal on the collective values that shape their experience and identities (9–10). Americans are less likely than people in other developed countries to believe the scientific data about anthropogenic climate change. And among Americans, political party affiliation, which is a good proxy for salient differences in group-based values, is "found to be the strongest correlate for individual beliefs about climate change" (10). Climate politics is not simply a matter of competition among opposing interests, then, but is cultural "at its core" (4). Motivating action on this issue, as on many environmental problems, will require "addressing the deeper ideological, cultural, and social filters" that are in play (5). Thus, while it is true that human interests are at stake in anthropogenic environmental damage, simply appealing to the motive of interest is not likely to generate the outcomes we need. If they are to motivate effective action on environmental issues, appeals to human interests must be combined with efforts to reconstruct the repertoire of shared values that shapes how we understand our interests and how we act on them.

This chapter explores possibilities for creating a new culture of environmental responsibility, drawing mainly on recent work in environmental political theory and philosophy. It begins from the assumption that culture—conceived as a repertoire of shared values—is crucial to understanding the interests people feel themselves to have and that cultural values can powerfully influence long-term changes in society. If we want to improve environmental outcomes, we will need a new culture of environmental responsibility. Key to establishing this culture is novel ways of thinking about what responsibility means. Prevailing views of responsibility in liberal societies treat intentionality and control as preconditions of responsibility, yet people often contribute to environmental damage without intending or controlling their effects. Climate change is perhaps the most obvious example, but the environmental domain is replete with cases in which many agents participate in harmful outcomes for which they cannot reasonably be held responsible, given existing notions of responsibility. This disjunction undermines effective environmental action because when no one is responsible, little gets done. The problem is not limited to misconceptions about the meaning of responsibility either. It also derives from political and economic factors that make it difficult to determine and enforce the responsibility of various agents in particular cases. Creating a new culture of environmental responsibility, therefore, requires not only a new conception of responsibility but also new political and economic practices to support it. The first section of this chapter lays out the conventional liberal view of responsibility and shows why it proves inadequate to contemporary environmental problems. The second section elaborates an alternative repertoire of responsibility, one that distinguishes responsibility as liability from responsibility as accountability, and argues that both have a role to play in the environmental domain. The third section sketches several initiatives at the level of politics, society, and the economy that could support a new culture of environmental responsibility in its plural forms.

The Limits of Liability in a "Sea of Agency"

The most familiar views of moral responsibility in philosophy and political theory take legal liability as their point of departure, which requires both intentionality and control (Feinberg 1970; Nagel 1979; Hart 2008; Raz 2011).[4] We do not normally hold people responsible for something if they did not mean to do it or could not control what happened. Indeed, the "control condition," as the second criterion is sometimes called, is often held to be "the very essence of moral responsibility" in liberal societies (Sommers 2009, 48). Even highly nuanced views of responsibility share this emphasis. Christopher Kutz's excellent analysis of complicity, for example, recognizes that "our lives are increasingly complicated by regrettable things brought about by our associations with other people or with social, economic, and political institutions" and that consequently "we find ourselves connected to harms and wrongs that fall outside the paradigm of individual, intentional wrongdoing" (2000, 1). Kutz's primary concern lies with the harmful actions of collective agents such as states and corporations and with establishing principled grounds for holding individual citizens or stakeholders accountable for the actions of the organizations to which they belong. Yet, despite his nuanced understanding of the interpersonal conditions of human action and his effort to develop a relational approach to responsibility, in the end Kutz defends a fairly standard liability view. For him, we are responsible for (as complicit in) only those harms that result from the actions of collective agents to which we belong when we are willing participants in "a shared venture that does harm," and when we can reasonably have been expected to know about the harms (186).[5] In a similar way, Steve Vanderheiden's treatment of responsibility for environmental injustice, although a highly sensitive and sophisticated account, nevertheless retains a fundamental commitment to the control condition and the principle that we may only legitimately be held responsible for things we choose to bring about (2009, 208, 219–220, 227, 230).

Yet many environmental problems today result from dynamics that are far too complex for any single agent to control, whether individual or collective, and they often involve effects that are generated without anyone actually having intended them. Nobody consciously sets out to warm Earth, for example, and no single participant or group of participants can stop it, yet the effect only transpires because of the contributions that all participants make. Moreover, while their aggregated effects are harmful, the effects of each agent taken individually are negligible. To compound the problem, agents often have few if any alternatives given existing structural conditions. Finally, all agents, both individual and collective, operate in the context of pressures exerted by intersubjective but nonagentic forces, such as markets, and these pressures often contribute to environmental harms. Markets lack the unified purpose, intentionality, and control that we associate with agency—and with responsibility—but they exercise powerful effects on the environment. Together, these factors create what Dale Jamieson and Marcello Di Paola call a "shifting and only partially coherent landscape of agency" that is fundamentally at odds with our existing conceptual resources for ascribing responsibility (2016, 262). The result, as Jamieson and Di Paola say, is that "in this sea of agency it is difficult to assign responsibilities both because responsibilities are enmeshed across units and levels of analysis" and because "it is often just not clear who is responsible for doing what." Consequently, "everyone, even the worst actors, can claim 'plausible deniability'" (268–269).

One might think that this deniability would be freeing. Like the ring of Gyges depicted in Plato's *Republic*, which enables those who wear it to act under a cloak of invisibility that liberates them from the consequences of their actions, the sea of agency lets us off the hook for our environmental effects (Plato 1991, 359d). Yet far from feeling like a liberation, the experience is more commonly one of diminished agency, a sense of inefficacy, even entrapment by forces beyond our control. We find ourselves participating whether we like it or not in the "unintended effects of systemic, interlocking forces and structures" that generate environmental damage that we may regret or even abhor (Jamieson and Di Paola 2016, 263). As Jamieson and Di Paolo put it, "The second I flip on a light switch I am forced into a global network of eco-altering financial and economic interests, political arrangements and avenues of cultural reinforcement" that are "largely unknown to me but which I am at no liberty to side-step" (263). To compound matters, I know that even if I were to go off the grid, my individual refusal would have only a negligible effect. The awareness of our negligibility together with the sense of forced complicity alienates us from our own agency, leaving us "disoriented and skeptical about our capacity to manage our ecological entanglements" (262–263). The flip side of our inability to attribute responsibility is therefore not liberation but disempowerment. This disempowerment helps explain why so many of us remain so passive in the face of escalating environmental problems and why appeals to self-interest so often fail to motivate action. The heart of the problem is how the structural conditions that comprise the contemporary sea of agency interact with our culture of responsibility, meaning the particular repertoire of values that shapes our collective experience and practices of responsibility. To effectively address our environmental problems, we need to reconstruct this repertoire.

Reconstructing Responsibility

To remediate the alienation of agency and empower individuals and groups for environmental action, we must begin by rethinking the meaning of responsibility. Liability is, of course, an important form of responsibility, and it should have a place in our laws and public policies as well as culture. The fact that it is incomplete should not lead us to reject it altogether. Some environmental harms result from actions that do meet the liability criteria, after all, and we need to be able to hold agents responsible in this sense when warranted. Yet we can productively broaden our thinking about responsibility by supplementing liability with a notion of responsibility as accountability.

Accountability has a parallel in the legal concept of strict liability, found especially in litigation around commercial products that have inadvertently caused harm to consumers. Strict liability holds producers responsible for remediating harms caused by their defective products even if the producer was not intentional about the harm or negligent in its actions (Legal Information Institute, n.d.). Responsibility as accountability has a similar form but a broader scope. It gives us a measure of responsibility for any harm to which we contribute, however unintentional the contribution may have been, and even when we lacked control over the outcome.[6] With respect to environmental harms, we are accountable for the often indirect and unconscious parts we play in outcomes such as climate change, habitat destruction, and pollution. In contrast to liability, however, holding someone accountable for a harm in this sense does not imply blame or justify punishment. In view of the fact that the harm is neither intended nor controlled, blame and punishment would be out of place. The woman who must commute by car every day to keep the job that puts bread on the table for her young children deserves no blame for her carbon emissions and the role they play in climate change. Instead of blame, accountability in this context involves acknowledging the harm, making a clear-eyed assessment of the causal dynamics in play, taking honest stock of our contributions, and doing what we can to remediate our effects going forward.

Importantly, accountability also includes an obligation to work for changes in the conditions that form the broader context of our harmful effects. For example, in thinking about my accountability in the context of climate change, my obligation includes not simply switching to LED light bulbs to illuminate my home but also joining with my neighbors to advocate for a cleaner power plant in our area and electing public officials who support alternative energy development, among other things. Seen from this angle, even paying one's taxes can be a (partial) way of exercising accountability, provided that the state directs some of its revenue to remediate environmental harms to which all citizens contribute and to fund the development of more sustainable technologies for meeting collective needs in the future. The obligation to change my effects going forward, in other words, requires me to work cooperatively with others to create new conditions of agency for all of us, conditions that will make it possible for us to avoid reproducing environmental harms in the future. Participating in this collective action is part of what accountability makes me responsible for.[7] Two points are worth emphasizing here: First, accountability means that we can sometimes be responsible for helping repair damage that we cannot be blamed for having caused. Second, although accountability attaches to us as individuals, it requires us to act collectively for change and to work for change not just in our individual lives (by recycling, say, or turning down the heat) but in the larger structural forces that determine what forms of action are normally available to us or incentivized for us.

Accountability so conceived is demanding. To embody it perfectly would mean perpetual engagement on a virtually endless set of environmental effects and the complex conditions that give rise to them. No one could be expected to do that. Still, the impossibility of perfectly embodying accountability does not undermine its value. Just as asking people to be generous does not imply that they must give everything they have to others, so holding people accountable for their environmental harms need not require them to spend every waking hour trying to prevent or repair environmental damage. Different individuals will engage in different ways and to different degrees. There are many ways to be generous, after all—some people tithe 10 percent of their income to their churches, some deliver meals to shut-ins, some go out of their way to help a colleague at work or a stranger in trouble. Yet no one practices generosity in every way all the time. While the ideal of generosity suggests that some kind of contribution to others should be a regular part of one's life, it does not demand that generosity take up all one's life—although trying to perfect the ideal certainly could take up all one's life because the world is full of people in need. Likewise, there are many ways to act on the value of environmental accountability, but none of them has to consume us.

It may be useful here to think of accountability in the way that Aristotle described generosity and all the moral virtues, as a mean between extremes. Generosity on his account is a mean between the extremes of being stingy and being a spendthrift (Aristotle 1984, bk. III, sec. 9–13). It means giving the right amount, in the right way, at the right time, for the right reason, to the right recipient (bk. II, sec. 5). In a similar way (and without endorsing the whole teleological architecture of Aristotle's ethical theory), we might say that environmental accountability is a mean between answering only for harms that you as a discrete individual caused by yourself and can fix for yourself, on the one hand, and indiscriminately trying to fix everything that is wrong with the environment, on the other. Accountability well executed involves being attentive to the big picture of our actions and effects as this bears on environmental harms, remediating them as best we can, and making sensible, focused efforts to create the kinds of change that would enable us to generate better effects in the future. So conceived, accountability is a real advance beyond conventional conceptions of responsibility, and one that could have a transformative impact, but it is not an impossible standard to meet. It is also worth noting that as a cultural value environmental responsibility goes beyond the model of individual virtue as Aristotle conceived it both because it attends to the structural, not simply characterological, conditions of individual behavior and because it orients the individual to collective action for social change as opposed to focusing more narrowly on the quality of one's soul.

If responsibility as accountability bears an affinity to Aristotle's conception of virtue as a mean between extremes, it also shares something with David Hume's notion of moral sentiment and with the broader intellectual tradition of which it was a part.[8] For Hume, moral sentiments are forms of reflective feeling that combine cognition, or reasoning, with affect. In our assessments of right and wrong or good and bad, as Hume sees it, the faculty of practical reasoning is thoroughly integrated with desires and aversions. Insofar as they animate our actions, he thinks, such assessments must incorporate affective concerns because reason on its own cannot motivate action (Hume 1968, 414). Affective concerns guide moral judgment and animate moral action by giving us things to care about. Furthermore, the approval and disapproval that we feel on contemplating particular actions and types of character are themselves sentiments with an emotional valence even though they also involve reasoning. For "when you pronounce any action or character to be vicious," Hume says, "you mean nothing, but that from the constitution of your nature you have a feeling or sentiment of blame from the contemplation of it" (469). Likewise, to judge someone virtuous "is nothing but to *feel* a satisfaction of a particular kind from the contemplation of a character." As he puts it, "the very *feeling* constitutes our praise or admiration" (471; emphasis in original). And our praise or admiration forms the judgment. Moral sentiment is a reflective feeling, of course, which combines affect and cognition, meaning that it involves reasoning and so it is not reducible to mere feeling; Hume's theory includes a sophisticated account of how moral sentiment can be impartial and objective even as it is affectively engaged (Krause 2008, chap. 3). The sense of responsibility as accountability has the hybrid quality that Hume describes. It is partly a cognitive exercise that involves rationally evaluating our roles in often complex sets of causal relations. Yet it is also partly an affective response to harm that involves an emotional investment in limiting and remediating our environmental damage. Accountability, like moral sentiment, is both a reasoned and a felt orientation of normative responsiveness to the world that combines cognitive and affective modes of consciousness.

Responsibility as accountability also has a close parallel in Iris Marion Young's "social connection model" of responsibility (2011, 96). The model is applied to problems of what Young calls "structural injustice," where unfairness is perpetuated systemically through large-scale, impersonal forces (economic, political, and social) rather than through intentional acts of domination by discrete individual agents. She uses the global apparel industry as an example, in which products are often made by impoverished people in developing countries working under exploitative conditions, while the products are consumed by relatively privileged people in wealthy societies. The consumers do not mean to be unjust, often know little about the labor conditions that produced the goods they purchase, and do not control the system. Yet their purchases help sustain that system, and in Young's view "all those who contribute by their actions to structural processes with some unjust outcomes share responsibility for the injustice" (105). Our responsibility tracks the power and force of our effects, as Young sees it. Those whose contributing effects weigh more heavily in the relevant outcome will bear more responsibility for it. People who are wealthy enough to buy lots of clothes produced in third-world sweatshops, for instance, have a larger role in unwittingly perpetuating the exploitation of the sweatshop workers who produced the clothes than do those who buy little. They are also better equipped to purchase their attire from fair trade shops where prices may be higher and to use their resources to publicize and reform the practices of the industry at large (2011, 144–145).[9]

Like accountability, the social connection model begins from the assumption that social life involves interdependent processes of cooperation and competition and that our involvement in these processes implicates us in their effects. Where the effects are unjust, we have an obligation to do what we can to modify them and to reform the processes that produced them. This obligation holds even if we did not intend to bring about adverse effects or did not control the outcomes and even if we had no personal interaction with the victims. Another similarity is that both models are less concerned with blaming people for their past actions than with changing their action for the future (Young 2011, 96–97, 109). And while the responsibility in play attaches to individuals, it cannot be discharged by the individual acting alone. Responsibility for justice "is a responsibility I *personally* bear," Young says, "but I do not bear it alone" because it emerges from my involvement in intersubjective processes (109–110; emphasis in original). "For the same reason," Young continues, responsibility for justice "can be discharged only by joining with others in collective action" that intervenes in social structures "to produce other outcomes" (111).

In contrast to the social connection model, however, the scope of which is limited to human assemblages, accountability in the environmental context also covers our impact on nonhuman beings and things.[10] This means that the sea of agency in which we are asked to exercise accountability includes natural systems and forces along with human ones. To exercise environmental accountability in the context of deforestation or carbon emissions or the decision to throw my old batteries into the trash, I need to grasp how my individual actions and the human systems that aggregate their effects interact with Earth systems to generate the environmental harms in which my agency is implicated. Scientific knowledge contributes crucial information here. It should help shape the background of social understanding and the broader field of cultural values that guide the exercise of accountability, including collective decision making about how to reconstruct the human institutions and structures that shape our agency and its effects going forward.[11] Yet accountability does not require us all to be experts about Earth systems. Consider the way that medical knowledge about the effects of smoking has become a part of the cultural background that informs how many people today exercise responsibility for their health.[12] Much as we do not need to be medical researchers to appreciate that smoking can cause cancer, so we need not understand the complex chemistry and physics behind anthropogenic climate change to grasp that our use of fossil fuels is interacting in powerful ways with Earth systems and to acknowledge that our role in these interactions gives us a share in responsibility for the harms being generated. Exercising responsibility as accountability, therefore, means attending to how our agency interacts not only with human structural forces but also with natural forces and how our actions affect not just other people but nonhuman beings and things.[13]

It should be clear by now that when contrasted with conventional liberal models of responsibility, which ground responsibility in intentionality and control, the notion of responsibility as accountability broadens the scope of our responsibilities. We need to be pluralists about environmental responsibility, meaning that we must distinguish among types of responsibility, acknowledging the importance of liability where standard conditions apply but holding ourselves to account for a wider range of outcomes than is possible on the liability view alone. The value of accountability helps us make sense of our environmental responsibilities in a sea of agency that otherwise obscures them, letting us off the hook far too easily and undermining our own sense of efficacy. This pluralized approach to responsibility illuminates both the breadth and the diversity of our involvements and effects. And even as it broadens the scope of responsibility for environmental harms, it allows us to make important distinctions between the different kinds of responsibility that we may have. These distinctions are important. If it is a mistake to identify responsibility too closely with liability, it would also be wrong to collapse all responsibility into accountability.

Still, the line between liability and accountability is somewhat porous. The more I know about the exploitative conditions of the global apparel industry, for example, or about factory-farmed meat or climate change, the less unintentional my participation will be and the more my responsibility will approach liability as opposed to accountability. Likewise, the liability that one bears as an individual for environmental damage that results from ostensibly intentional actions may be mitigated by political and economic conditions that systematically constrain one's options. I may be fully aware that my job in the petrochemical plant contributes directly to environmental degradation because my job involves secretly dumping toxic refuse from the production process into the waterway running alongside the plant.[14] Yet if this job (or one like it) is the only viable source of income for my family and me, and if whistle-blower protections for employees who report illegal dumping have been dismantled by a government influenced by corporate money, and if political pressure for privatization has eroded unemployment benefits and other social services that would otherwise help me to make ends meet if I were to lose my job for reporting the dumping, then my responsibility in this instance may be better understood in terms of accountability than liability.

This last consideration reminds us that in assessing responsibility for environmental harms we must be attentive to power differentials and varying scales of impact. For example, relative to individuals, large multinational corporations have far more power in determining environmental policies and practices, and their direct effects on the environment can be orders of magnitude greater.[15] For both these reasons, some commentators are critical of efforts to cultivate a stronger sense of environmental responsibility among individuals. They worry that this focus will turn attention away from the kinds of political activism needed to contest the power and effects of large-scale agents such as corporations. As Naomi Klein puts it,

> A lot of environmentalist discourse has been about erasing responsibility: "We're all in this together. . . . We're all equally responsible." Well, no—you, me and Exxon (Mobil) are not all in this together. The idea we're all guilty is demobilising because it prevents us directing our anger at the institutions most responsible. (Forrest 2014)[16]

It is indeed crucial for us to hold corporations liable for their environmental harms when the conditions of liability are in play and to hold them accountable for harms to which they contribute even when their actions do not meet the liability standard. At the same time, however, the power of corporations is subject to the choices of consumers and to pressure from citizens, at least in democratic states. Indeed, the power of corporations is itself partly sustained through the participation and acquiescence of large numbers of individuals. To simply blame corporations for all our environmental problems obscures the power that individuals, acting in concert, can have. We would do better to cultivate a more capacious culture of responsibility, one that enables us to differentiate the kinds and degrees of responsibility that can be reasonably attributed to various sorts of agents under distinctive sets of conditions. A pluralist view of responsibility acknowledges the multiplicity of the sites, sources, and forms of responsibility that operate in the environmental domain given the complex sea of agency in which all participants act. In some cases, attributions of responsibility will have legal or regulatory implications; in others, their force may be cultural, ethical, or political, orienting us to different patterns of consumption, to new forms of production and exchange, to the reform of political institutions, and to invigorated civic engagement.

Fostering environmental responsibility will also require direct efforts to reshape attitudes. In the United States, concerted efforts to change collective values on several issues have had remarkable success in recent years, including substantial reductions in smoking rates and a sea change in the country's orientation to gay people. Differences of opinion still exist on both issues, but the transformations are undeniable. They have resulted from a combination of information dissemination, legal action, new legislation, and the deliberate promotion of alternative repertoires of values. Some of these efforts were carried out by the state, including through public education.[17] Others emerged through non-state-based cultural forms (movies, television, music, visual arts), through civic activism, and through informal, personal interactions. In cultivating environmental responsibility, we can make use of a similar range of resources and techniques. Another model we might look to is the Civilian Conservation Corps (CCC) established in the postwar United States as part of Franklin Delano Roosevelt's New Deal. The CCC trained more than three million men in resource conservation between 1933 and 1942. In addition to inculcating values of environmental responsibility and "active care" for the Earth, it provided professional training that could lead to good jobs and a pool of technical expertise in pollution and resource management (Mapes-Martins 2016, 100–101). The focus of a reconstituted CCC would need to be adjusted for contemporary conditions and challenges, but the basic model could prove valuable. More generally, the public promulgation of what one might call sustainability stories, which exemplify the exercise of environmental responsibility, sharing learning and success, could help nourish a new repertoire of responsibility. As Isabelle Stengers puts it, we need to publicize such stories so that "where one group achieves something, what they learn, what they make exist, becomes so many resources and experimental possibilities for others" (2015, 31, 153).[18]

Although the primary sites for the cultivation of environmental responsibility are political communities, a strong sense of environmental responsibility has the potential to inspire action across national borders. Its promise in this regard comes partly from the fact that it can be affirmed from within a variety of worldviews, much in the way of a Rawlsian overlapping consensus (see Naess 1986, 12–13). Although many worldviews are at odds with environmental responsibility as described in these pages, plenty of others are compatible with it. The different types of environmentalism today, which represent a spectrum that includes eco-feminism, conservative Christianity, neo-Marxism, and green capitalism, among others, speak to this convergence. The fact that the value of environmental responsibility can be affirmed and justified from within multiple worldviews enhances the motivational force it can carry. It also gives the value traveling power across societies, which is crucial given the global nature of many environmental problems and the need for cooperation among otherwise diverse peoples.[19] Moreover, while some aspects of globalization are complicit in environmental degradation today, globalization's ability to disseminate cultural values also can be useful in spreading environmental responsibility. Wealthy nations will need to help developing countries practice environmental responsibility by sharing resources and knowledge that can facilitate genuinely sustainable paths to development; but wealthy nations also have much to learn about sustainability from developing countries and from their own indigenous populations. And much as global interdependence and advancing communications technologies have combined to spread human rights as a repertoire of shared values, albeit often imperfectly, so they have the potential to help nurture global cultures of environmental responsibility as well.

Supporting Environmental Responsibility in Politics and the Economy

For a new culture of responsibility to take hold, however, certain structural features that are characteristic of our contemporary sea of agency need to be addressed and ultimately reconstructed. We need to create the conditions in which the repertoire of values that constitutes environmental responsibility can thrive. Although it would be a mistake to simply reduce culture to political and economic factors, such factors do have an important impact on culture. Recent studies of cultural attitudes among American millennials regarding gender roles and the distribution of labor within the family illustrate this point.[20] While young Americans expressed increasing support for gender equity from the 1970s through the mid-1990s, reports show a decline in this support since then. The dearth of family support policies in the United States is thought to be playing a role. During the same period, researchers point out, support for gender equity has continued to rise among all age groups in Europe, "where public investments in affordable, high-quality child care and paid leave for fathers and mothers are the norm" (Coontz 2017). Many millennials in the United States, it seems, have experienced the difficulties of sustaining gender equity within the family in the absence of a supportive political economy, and "the decline in support for 'nontraditional' domestic arrangements" may reflect this experience. As it turns out, "when young Americans are asked about their family aspirations, large majorities choose equally shared breadwinning and child-rearing if the option of family-friendly work policies is mentioned." Without those policies, the studies suggest, "most young parents will not be able to sustain" their egalitarian cultural values (Coontz 2017). In a similar way, creating a new culture of environmental responsibility will require the right political and economic context.

A full elaboration of that context is beyond the scope of this chapter, but we can sketch some possibilities here. In what follows I focus on three changes in the domains of politics and the economy that could help foster environmental responsibility: (1) principled limitations on the scale and capacities of economic power, (2) eco-constitutionalism, and (3) transparency about effects and costs.

A company that is "too big to fail" is also too big to reliably be held responsible for its environmental impact and too big to allow for the kinds of individual and state actions that the exercise of environmental responsibility will sometimes require. The size of multinational corporations must be contained. In addition to the scale of corporate power, their capacity to influence public decision making needs to be limited. We need to constrain the ability of corporations to directly shape political outcomes through paid lobbying and campaign financing. This means reducing the amount that corporations can spend on lobbying efforts, and it means providing public financing for political campaigns while subjecting corporate contributions to strict limits and public disclosure requirements. We should also be cautious about privatizing the provision of public goods, from prisons and schools to hospitals, roads, and bridges. This is not to say that public-private partnerships never have a place. The point is to remind us that when combined with deregulation and relatively unrestricted free trade, the privatization of public goods has the potential to increase both the scale and the capacities of corporate power in ways that are detrimental to environmental responsibility.

Efforts to pluralize the economy through the development of noncapitalist types of production and exchange also could help limit the power of corporations by multiplying the sites and forms of economic activity. Such alternatives could exist alongside conventional capitalist practices in what J. K. Gibson-Graham (the pen name for coauthors Katherine Gibson and Julie Graham) refer to as a more "diverse" economy. Many already exist, if only in nascent form. Examples include

> the exchange of commodities between and within worker cooperatives, where prices are set to enhance the sustainability of the cooperative; the ethical or "fair" trade of products, where producers and consumers agree on price levels that will sustain certain livelihood practices; [and] local trading systems and alternative currencies that foster local interdependency and sustainability. (Gibson-Graham 2006, 62)

Farmers' markets and community-supported agriculture arrangements similarly provide alternative economic frameworks insofar as they reduce the role of large corporations in both the production and the exchange of food.[21] Alternative transactions already in existence also include the goods and services produced in households, often by women (60). In particular, Gibson-Graham highlight "the incredible range of transactions, forms of labor, and kinds of enterprises through which the work of child care is performed around the world" (72), including "community cooperative child-care," state-funded child care, and "community trade networks and baby-sitting clubs" (74). More diversity would contribute to the limitation of corporate power without requiring an excessively heavy-handed role for the state or replacing capitalism with a command-style economy. Small producers and alternative sites of exchange will likely need support to compete successfully with today's corporate behemoths.[22] Yet large corporations themselves regularly benefit from state support in both direct and indirect ways. Redirecting some of this support to foster a more diverse economy is one way to set principled constraints on the scale and capacities of economic power.

Along with limiting economic power, we can support a culture of environmental responsibility by creating new ecologically oriented constraints on political power. One commentator has referred to such constraints in the language of "eco-constitutionalism" (B. Jennings 2016, 179, 185–187).[23] As the term is used here, eco-constitutionalism means establishing principled constraints on how the power of citizens and states may be exercised over nonhuman beings and things and formalizing these constraints in fundamental law. In the United States, many environmental rules are a function of administrative regulations and public policy rather than fundamental law.[24] They can be overridden fairly easily or even eradicated entirely, as the actions of the Trump administration demonstrate. By contrast, some countries have begun to establish basic protections for the environment in constitutional law. The German constitution, for example, includes provisions for animal rights intended to "protect the lives and well-being of animals . . . [as] fellow creatures."[25] Ecuador's 2008 constitution includes broader protections for "the rights of nature" as a whole, including rights "to exist, persist, maintain and regenerate its vital cycles" and "the right to restoration" from environmental damage.[26] These forays into animal and Earth rights are relatively new, and their impact is still unfolding. They are bound to be subject to contestation and to difficulties of enforcement, much as human rights are. Yet like human rights, they are potentially forceful mechanisms for the limitation of political power. Eco-constitutionalism supports responsibility in part by enshrining basic protections for nature in the laws that constitute the political community and in part by incorporating them into the cultural core of citizenship. Think about how the rights of persons signal to all members of the political community the basic terms of cooperation. Over time, they become internalized in the repertoire of shared values and collective practices that orient democratic citizens and guide them in their relations with one another (Stone 2010, 2, 3). In a similar way, eco-constitutionalism could help generate a new culture of environmental responsibility, one that embeds public values of sustainability in the collective experiences, learning, and identities of citizens.[27]

Finally, we need to create more transparency about what is actually happening in the sea of agency today and more transparency about environmental effects. None of us can become more responsible—whether as individuals, groups, governments, or corporations—without access to accurate information about the assemblages to which we contribute. For example, animal agricultural operations must be required to permit public inspections of the living conditions of the animals they raise and to report the environmental impact of runoff from their operations. Likewise, we need good public data about the environmental and human health effects of the toxins used in the petrochemical and other industries at home and abroad. In part, then, transparency means more access to better information and increased public scrutiny of industrial practices and regulating agencies.[28] Beyond that, transparency also requires us to publicize the full costs of what we buy and what we do. The lower grocery store prices for industrially produced food as compared with the prices for organic produce and meat that is humanely and sustainably raised conceal from view costs that consumers pay in other ways for their ostensibly cheaper food (Pollan 2006, 200–201, 243; Stone 2010, 25–26). Likewise, the fossil fuel industry benefits from many unseen subsidies that people mostly pay for without realizing it. Efforts by environmental economists to make the full costs of our lifestyles transparent are important and have great transformative potential, even if economic costs are not the only ones that should count with us (Olmstead 2016). Acknowledging the full costs (economic and otherwise) of what we do is a key part of establishing both liability and accountability for environmental damage. Together with eco-constitutionalism and limits on economic power, transparency can help support a new culture of environmental responsibility.

Conclusion

Creating this new culture is crucial because the direct appeal to interests is not by itself sufficient to motivate environmental action. Yet if cultural values provide powerful support for human agency, helping generate social transformation over the long term, cultivating the right values matters. Our current culture of responsibility is deeply disabling of environmental action because it presupposes intentionality and control, emphasizes blame and punishment, and saddles the individual with changes that no one can accomplish alone. If the conventional view is how most of us think about responsibility most of the time, there will be many environmental harms for which no one can reasonably be held responsible, and remediating these harms will remain difficult if not impossible. Supporting a new culture of environmental responsibility—conceived pluralistically to include accountability as well as liability—will require the same diversity of approaches that has led to other recent cultural changes from reduced smoking rates to more egalitarian gender norms to increased support for gay rights. They include modifications to existing political and economic institutions as well as legal initiatives, educational outreach, political activism, and inspiration from the art world and the entertainment industry. And like all social transformation, creating a culture of eco-responsibility will require committed leadership both by those who hold power in politics and the economy and by average citizens and consumers.

The complexity of the political and economic systems that structure our action and our environmental impact cannot be wished away. Yet we can learn to navigate this complexity in ways that answer more effectively to environmental demands and to our own need for empowered agency. In fact, a new culture of environmental responsibility can help us regain influence over the complex forces that govern our lives even beyond the environmental domain. Just as it gives us tools to motivate environmental action, responsibility properly conceived equips us to contest—and ultimately to reconfigure—the whole range of structural conditions of political economy that so often entrap us in the contemporary sea of agency. The widespread sense that people have lost control of these forces is reverberating across Europe and North America today. This sense of impotence is being exploited by politicians promoting populist cultural agendas that promise to restore the lost agency of people who feel left behind by globalization, by identity politics, and by democratic deficits in their governments. A culture of environmental responsibility cannot solve all these problems, but it has the potential to be widely transformative by enhancing human agency and by reconstructing the configurations of power that have generated so much alienation. If environmental responsibility is not the only remedy for our contemporary ills, then, it is at least a promising resource for creating a more sustainable future—ecologically and otherwise.

Notes

1. Although the anthropocentric approach has come to dominate public discourse, examples of more ecocentric approaches exist (Naess 1986; Eckersley 2004; Harraway 2008; Schlosberg 2007).

2. In what follows, I treat the environmental domain as a form of "socionatural hybridity" in which human beings interact with nonhuman beings, things, and forces (White, Rudy, and Gareau 2016, xix). In an era of anthropogenic climate change, all ecosystems now bear a human imprint, so the notion of untouched nature is obsolete (McKibben 1989; Purdy 2015; Vogel 2016; Cronon 1995).

3. For further discussion of the cultural context of individual interests, see Chapter 2; see also Chapters 3 and 5 for additional reflections on the relationship between interests and culture.

4. For further elaboration of the limits of the liability model in connection with responsibility for racial and gender-based inequities, see Krause 2015, chap. 3, on which this paragraph loosely draws.

5. Kutz acknowledges that cases such as air pollution caused by the uncoordinated actions of individual automobile drivers strain his model. Because "there is no specific project to which individuals contribute" in such cases, they involve only a "quasi-participatory basis of accountability" (2000, 186), which contrasts with the "shared specific intentions" required to establish complicity as a general matter (189). Kutz addresses the strain by insisting that "the background of interdependent activity and shared values" in which the drivers operate is enough to constitute "a shared venture" (186), and so this disparate collection of individuals may fairly be seen as "a community of accountability" (186). Yet this caveat stands in significant tension with the overall thrust of his theory, which (as he acknowledges here) presses hard on the requirement of a "shared specific intention" as a condition of responsibility. This strain in his view illustrates the difficulty that standard conceptions of responsibility have in the environmental context. It suggests the need for a fundamentally new approach.

6. Accountability has applications beyond the environmental context. It covers our participation, however unwitting, in injustices such as implicit bias, institutional racism, informal dynamics of gender inequality, and the like (Krause 2015, chap. 3).

7. Accountability thus directs the individual to participate in "movements as a form of resistance to what [Michel] Foucault called circulatory power" and also to participate in "alternative circulations of power and material nature in new collectivities," hence to "reconstruction in addition to resistance" (Schlosberg and Coles 2016, 13). This could include (among other things) food movements geared to establishing "food systems which are good for farmers, the health of consumers, and the environment" (14–15), and energy movements that aim to change "the way that energy is produced and distributed" (15).

8. For further discussion of Hume's theory of moral sentiment, see (among others) Forbes 1975, esp. 32–58; Mackie 1980, esp. 14–30; Norton 1999; and Haakonssen 1996. For recent work that takes up the intellectual history of moral sentiment theory, with its emphasis on the reformation of manners and the cultivation of new cultural values, see, for example, Frazer 2010; Forman-Barzilai 2010; Rorty 1998; Ignatieff 2011; and Krause 2008.

9. It is true that the degree to which one's actions contribute to the problem is not necessarily proportional to the degree to which one is equipped to contribute to the solution. Someone with a low income and a large family may buy lots of clothes made in sweatshops, thus contributing to the problem, and be too poor to purchase her family's clothes from fair trade shops.

10. I borrow the language of assemblages from Jane Bennett (2010, chap. 2). I do not attribute agency as widely as Bennett does, however. The language of assemblages is useful because it emphasizes the interactive dynamics through which agency arises and has effects and because it attunes us to the complexities of agency and responsibility in contemporary globalized life. Yet we can and must distinguish agents, who can properly bear responsibility for their actions and effects, from nonagentic forces and causes, which cannot rightly be held responsible for things. This distinction is a crucial condition of possibility for social transformation and environmental change.

11. For discussion of institutional mechanisms for incorporating scientific knowledge into public deliberation about environmental matters, see Dryzek 2016. On "hybrid forums" for decision making in contexts of uncertainty, see Callon, Lascoumes, and Barthe 2001, 21, 26, 181–189.

12. For documentation of the vastly reduced rates of smoking among American adults since 1965, see Centers for Disease Control and Prevention 2018.

13. The "ecovillages" that Karen Litfin (2016) has studied in various parts of the world offer an example of this aspect of accountability. Ecovillagers, Litfin shows, "are unusually sensitive to the consequences of their actions, both near and far" (251). These communities "vary according to cultural and ecological context" ranging from wealthy suburban towns in the Global North to traditional rural villages in the Global South (249). Despite the diversity, however, they share a commitment to living "a low-impact way of life," which they pursue through various combinations of "ecological design, permaculture, renewable energy, community-building practices, and alternative economics" (249, 250). Ecovillages offer concrete examples of how environmental

responsibility could be reframed from a discourse that emphasizes liability and blame to one that focuses on accountability, including a shared approach to creating the conditions for a more sustainable way of life.

14. For an account of one Louisiana man's experience along these lines, see Hochschild 2016, 28–30.

15. Damian White, Alan Rudy, and Brian Gareau point out (citing William Freudenburg and collaborators) that in the United States in 1993, just "*two companies*—Dupont and Freeport McMoran—put out 400 million tons of toxic waste. Together these two companies generated 30% of total chemical toxic waste for the US" (2016, 107; emphasis in original).

16. Timothy Luke similarly warns against focusing environmental responsibility on the individualized "sphere of consumption rather than on the vital sites of production" (1997, 120). With this focus, he says, "a core supply-side changelessness is preserved by enveloping it in a demand-side mobilization for marginal change" (132).

17. For discussion of the relationship between culture and education, see Chapters 5, 6, and 9.

18. On the diffusion of values through social networks, see Bomberg 2012, 423–424.

19. For discussion of this point in connection with the ideal of respect for nature, see Krause 2020.

20. Millennials are the generation of people born between 1982 and 2000. See Coontz 2017.

21. The food movements, transition towns, and decentralized energy grids described by David Schlosberg and Romand Coles (2016, 16) offer additional examples of alternative economic relationships.

22. Some of these changes might involve subsidies, but revising regulatory schemes that disadvantage small producers relative to large ones also could be valuable. On the difficulties of small-scale production in the agricultural sector, see Salatin 2007, 3, 24.

23. In contrast to the approach developed here, Bruce Jennings holds that eco-constitutionalism must involve "the creation of several elite governing entities that can check and balance the more representative institutions such as the presidency or legislature. These elite entities would be insulated in various constitutionally sanctioned ways from the pressures of interest groups" (2016, 185–186). They would resemble the American judiciary in being immune (at least in principle) to political pressures. Another example he offers is "the creation of relatively autonomous regulatory agencies and commissions that have the legal authority to determine policy in some areas independently of the executive or legislative branch" (186). Although he insists that "the spirit of eco-constitutionalism is not deference to expertise" and authority, these proposals do raise questions from the standpoint of liberal democracy, with its commitment to democratic control (however indirect) of government. We need additional checks and balances on the use of power in the environmental domain, but like other checks and balances in liberal democracy, they should be answerable ultimately to the people as sovereign.

24. As Richard Andrews points out, in the United States, "the EPA's [Environmental Protection Agency's] decisions rarely remain settled. Its decisions change economic outcomes for businesses that are regulated, and thus create ongoing incentives for companies to challenge them rather than comply. These challenges include not only petitions and lawsuits, but also attempts to reverse its policies by congressional legislation or budget provisions and by electing presidents with different philosophies" (2016, 156). On this point, see also the work of Bruce Jennings, who refers to environmental regulations in the United States as "little more than side constraints, acceptable so long as they [do] not interfere with profits, employment, or the voracious engine of consumer demand" (2016, 172).

25. The text of Germany's Animal Welfare Act is available at https://www.animallaw.info/statute/germany-cruelty-german-animal-welfare-act.

26. The Constitution of the Republic of Ecuador is available at http://pdba.georgetown.edu/Constitutions/Ecuador/english08.html. The 2010 constitution of Bolivia establishes similar protections. The text of the constitution is available at http://www.worldfuturefund.org/Projects/Indicators/motherearthbolivia.html.

27. For discussion of eco-constitutionalism, including rights for nonhuman parts of nature, and its potential impact on the civic culture of democracy, see Krause 2019.

28. On the environmental importance of transparency and right-to-know laws, see Purdy 2015, 241–242, 244. Scrutiny of regulatory agencies is as important as scrutiny of industries. As Daniel Press and Daniel Mazmanian point out, citing a 2004 study, "For ten of the most common hydrocarbons, the EPA's reports underestimated actual emissions by 25 percent to 440 percent" (2016, 248).

5   Cosmopolitans and Parochials

Economy, Culture, and Political Conflict

Miles Kahler

THE CURRENT ERA OF GLOBALIZATION HAS WITNESSED REPEATED political challenges to economic openness and its consequences from both the left and the right of the political spectrum. Those challenges have centered on economic globalization and the distribution of its costs and benefits within societies. The latest political challengers have diverged from previous critics and opponents in three respects: their coalitions and their programs typically cut across the traditional divides of left and right (e.g., opposition to immigration combined with support for social and economic protections), they have been most prominent in the industrialized North, and they have been more successful than their predecessors. The UK referendum ballot in favor of leaving the European Union, the successful presidential campaign of Donald Trump, and the continuing progress of the Front national (FN)[1] in France and similar movements in other European countries have shaken internationalist assumptions that have grounded foreign policies and global institutions since 1945.

Controversy swirls around the labels applied to these movements: populist, nationalist, antielite, even antipolitics. Their stance toward economic openness has varied: some supporters of Brexit, for example, have embraced both liberalized trade (outside the European Union) and restrictions on immigration. Here, given a focus on the external orientation of these movements and their political opponents, I apply the term "parochials," a label that captures the defensive ethnonationalist stance of most of these movements, whether long-standing European far-right political parties, UKIP's "Little England" hostility toward the European Union, or the isolationist leanings of Trump and his followers. "Parochials" also avoids an assumed identification of these attitudes with the nation-state, rather than more local loyalties (Fitzgerald 2018). Far less attention and analysis has been devoted to the opponents of these movements, those attached to economic and cultural openness, international cooperation, and support for the institutions underpinning that cooperation. Cosmopolitanism has attracted considerable attention from philosophers but less attention, outside the European Union, from those aiming to explain cosmopolitan attitudes and their sources.[2]

Recent political conflict surrounding the stance of individuals and political movements toward other peoples, other countries, and the global order provides an opportunity to investigate the sources of parochial and cosmopolitan orientations. Although this cleavage often cuts across more familiar demographic and socioeconomic categories, material economic interests point to one popular explanation: these are the winners and losers from globalization. That explanation proves to be partial and indirect at best, however. Explanations based on individual socioeconomic characteristics, such as class and economic sector, must be qualified by nonmaterial psychological and cultural attitudes regarding political authority and "others." Often overlooked, parochial and cosmopolitan orientations are also related to geography and the local environment.

Globalization affects different locations in radically different ways, creating environments and local cultures that shape new divisions and coalitions. That critical connection encourages a redefined perspective on culture that is not restricted to national identity but also rooted in everyday, local realities. As J. P. Singh argues in Chapter 1, "preferences arise out of a cultural milieu." That cultural milieu may be local rather than national, and it may shape attitudes toward issues, such as trade and immigration, that are usually considered outside the scope of local politics. Culture both influences and is influenced by individual and group perspectives and narratives toward those viewed as outsiders and the global economic forces that drive economic success and stagnation.

After a brief review and redefinition of the concept of culture in political science and international relations, the sources of political movements (and individual orientations that underlie those movements) that reject aspects of globalization (liberalized trade, foreign investment, immigration) are examined. The cases of the United States and the United Kingdom are at the center of this analysis. Explanations for cosmopolitan attitudes and orientations are considered next. Possible extensions to other cases of parochial and cosmopolitan movements in the industrialized world follow. Finally, a research and policy agenda is presented that incorporates both economic context—the polarizing locational effects of globalization—and local culture, producing a more satisfying and complete explanation for the current contest between cosmopolitans and their opponents.

Interests and Culture in Political Science and International Relations

An evaluation offered a decade ago remains apt: "Culture is not a concept with which most political scientists are comfortable" (Ross 2009, 135). Critics have questioned rationalist assumptions, such as the treatment of preferences as exogenous and individualistic. Despite efforts to incorporate culture as more than a residual in rationalist models, those who embrace an expanded explanatory role for culture have found such amendments wanting.[3]

On the one hand, those who have awarded culture a central role have themselves been criticized for their "cultural essentialism," using culture as "a specific group's primordial values or traits" (Wedeen 2002, 715). As Lisa Wedeen argues, from early accounts of political culture to more recent claims of a clash of civilizations, "most political scientists continue to think of culture as connoting fixed group traits" (716). On the other hand, using culture in a way that avoids such reification and stasis, treating it as "meaning-making," a "social process through which people reproduce together the conditions of their intelligibility that enable them to make sense of their worlds," does not produce an easy resolution of its appropriate treatment in theory or empirical research (Wedeen 2002, 717). A more expansive view of the role of culture does not eliminate the need to assess its significance in explanation or its salience in specific contexts. Investigating culture as a dynamic process of meaning-making in the absence of carefully conducted ethnographic research may also introduce flaws, some of which appear in the analysis that follows. Using survey data on individual attitudes, for example, is often an inadequate proxy for culture because it omits the issues of meaning and context—the shared quality of understanding—that culture entails (Ross 2009, 154).

Despite these caveats, the reintroduction of identity and culture into the study of political preferences and behavior has recently received support in mainstream political science. Christopher Achen and Larry Bartels, under the banner of a realist theory of democracy, have argued that "human thought is deeply conditioned by culture, including group subcultures" (2016, 215). Such attachments and identities are not equivalent to ideologies; they "are emotional attachments that transcend thinking" (228). Although Achen and Bartels do not explicitly associate their group theory of politics with location, Katherine Cramer, in her investigation of rural consciousness, emphasizes that "place identity," which is "a part of at least some voters' fundamental sense of self," may be a more significant explanation of political attitudes than party affiliation (2016, 217).

Defining the scope of cultural units remains a complicated issue of nesting and interpenetration: local cultures—important in shaping individual identities and behavior—are influenced in turn by actors and processes at the national and global levels. Such interpenetration has become even more difficult to trace in an era of digital media that both localize and internationalize information flows. Cultural divides that appear significant in one spatial context may have less political significance when the boundaries of political action change (Posner 2004). In introducing culture to explanations of orientations such as parochialism and cosmopolitanism, orientations that are both individual and collective, these cautions become especially pertinent.

The Rise of the Parochials: Economic Interest or Cultural Values?

Even before the global financial crisis and recession of 2008–2009, new or transformed movements labeled "extreme right" or "populist" had emerged in the industrialized countries. Although placed on the right of the political spectrum, they disrupted that spectrum by combining programs of economic and cultural protectionism in their international orientation with a positive view of social protection and the welfare state in domestic programs. Those movements have recently expanded their appeal in electoral politics and have enjoyed success directly or, more often, indirectly, through their influence on the policies and programs of established political parties. In March 2016, following the previous summer's refugee crisis, AfD, a right-wing party founded three years earlier, entered state parliaments in Germany; in the March 2017 federal election, it became the third largest party in the Bundestag. Promoted by UKIP and the Eurosceptic wing of the British Conservative Party, the United Kingdom's departure from the European Union (Brexit), an unthinkable outcome only a decade earlier, was approved in a June 2016 referendum. Trump, the ultimate political outsider, engineered a takeover of the Republican Party and went on to win the US presidency on a program of opposing immigration and liberalized trade, aligning himself with several of the right-wing European movements. Additional gains were made by nationalists and populists in Austria, where the far-right Freedom Party (Freiheitliche Partei Österreichs [FPÖ]) entered a coalition government (since dissolved), and in Italy, where the populist Five Star Movement and the anti-immigrant League formed a governing coalition. The cosmopolitan center in the industrialized world seemed in full-scale political retreat.

The support that these movements drew from working-class voters—support that often explained their recent electoral success—when combined with their skepticism or hostility toward most dimensions of globalization and European integration, pointed to an explanation based on globalization's redistributive and political effects. The famous "elephant graph" of Branko Milanović appeared to confirm that the main beneficiaries of globalization since 1988 had been, on the one hand, the global middle class, concentrated in the countries of East and South Asia, and, on the other, the global top 1 percent, concentrated in the rich countries. The (relative) losers from globalization were the lower middle class of the industrialized economies, those members of the workforce with lower levels of skills and education. Milanović predicted that the likely outcome from this skewing of the gains from globalization in the industrialized world would be plutocracy (rule by the 1 percent) or nativist and populist backlash (2016, 18–24, 192–211). Interpreting Milanović's graph as a demonstration of zero-sum outcomes from globalization overstates its explanatory leverage (Freund 2016). Nevertheless, the effects of Chinese exports on US manufacturing employment have been well documented (a loss of 2.0–2.4 million jobs between 1999 and 2011); local labor market effects, discussed in a later section, were even more severe (Acemoglu et al. 2016). Even if the effects of technological change on employment and job security were greater than trade or outsourcing, the political interpretation of these effects lent support to antiglobalization movements. Those outcomes also matched the predictions of standard trade theory that workers with less skill and education would be disadvantaged by competition from labor-intensive imports originating in the developing economies.

Despite these apparent connections to globalization, Open Economy Politics, a straightforward assignment of individual preferences, group interests, and coalition formation according to the international division of labor and the predictions of trade theory, has been challenged as an explanation for the rise of movements endorsing protectionism, anti-immigration, and anti-EU policies.[4] In examining individual attitudes toward trade and outsourcing—the transfer of manufacturing activity to other countries as part of global value chains—Edward Mansfield and Diana Mutz (2009) compare individual self-interest, as predicted by international economic position, with predictions based on information or other attitudes unrelated to economic position. In the case of trade, they discover that self-interest is sociotropic: individuals define their stance with reference to likely effects on the national economy. In the case of both trade and outsourcing, information also has significant effects; the sources of that information can be either national or local. In both cases, attitudes toward out-groups are also important, even when those out-groups are racial and ethnic minorities in the respondents' own society. Opposition to economic openness is part of a "broader worldview that defines people as 'us' or 'them'" (Mansfield and Mutz 2009, 602; see also 2013). Another investigation of attitudes toward outsourcing across industrialized countries discovers that exposure to offshoring is not a major determinant of support for right-wing, populist parties, which "appeal to the losers of globalization as a more general phenomenon . . . who seem to share a general distrust of anything foreign" (Rommel and Walter 2016, 26).

Simple economic models also fail to explain electoral support for Trump. The China shock in trade (growth in Chinese import penetration after 2000) has been associated with increased Republican vote share between 2000 and 2016. Other researchers, however, argue that the major determinants of recent changes in Republican vote share (from Obama 2012 to Trump 2016) lie in race and education: those counties with the greatest increase in Republican vote share were on average 98 percent white, with less than 8 percent of their voters holding college degrees. Overall, backlash against trade and "the angry manufacturing worker" damaged by globalization do not appear to have had an important effect on the election (Freund and Sidhu 2017, 3; see also 14–15; Autor et al. 2016). At the individual level, Jonathan Rothwell and Pablo Diego-Rosell (2016) discovered that Trump voters in the Republican primary electorate were not below average in income, did not appear to suffer from economic distress, and were not more likely to be unemployed than other voters. As Mark Rozell documents in Chapter 8, a core constituent of the Trump presidential coalition was individuals who identified primarily as religious and social conservatives; only in certain cases did their economic interests align with his anti-immigrant and protectionist program.

A move to sociotropic definitions of interest, information environments, and attitudes toward out-groups as explanations for parochial and populist movements leads to the domain of culture. Disentangling economic interests and culture is difficult, however. One variable that consistently defines the divide between parochials and cosmopolitans as well as supporters and opponents of globalization is education. Lower levels of education, usually defined as absence of a university degree, are associated with support for far-right parties and for protectionism of all kinds. For example, in the vote for Brexit and in the 2017 UK general election, socioeconomic markers of class were less important than age in determining voter choice, and education, controlling for both class and age, was highly significant (Menon and Wager 2018, 7). Why the less educated should hold more parochial attitudes, however, is unclear: education could be a proxy for skill level in an open economy explanation, but it might also represent lower mobility and sorting by location. Combining Europe-wide and Swiss data, Jennifer Fitzgerald finds that the "most locally attached individuals do not have much education and they are relatively advanced in age" (2018, 83). David Goodhart has linked the attitudes of "Somewheres" to mobility: they are "more rooted and usually have 'ascribed' identities . . . based on group belonging and particular places" (2017, 3–4). As he notes, a majority of the British population live within twenty miles of where they lived when they were fourteen. Attachment to particular places and communities defines "parochial" and connects parochial attitudes to sociotropic definitions of interest that are local rather than national.

Immigration: Globalization Meets Cultural Protectionism

Immigration offers an even more direct link to culture and identity, combining economic anxiety provoked by a dimension of globalization with perceptions of group decline. It has been a driver in the rise of far-right parties in Europe, and it played a major role in the Leave campaign against UK membership in the European Union and the campaign of Trump (Evans and Menon 2017, 53–54, 56). Both perceptions of economic competition from immigrants and cultural protectionism figure in support for anti-immigration movements, but the latter seems to dominate. Pippa Norris argues that "attitudes toward cultural protectionism" were better predictors of radical-right voting than attitudes toward economic issues (with only two exceptions, Italy and Israel): "Negative attitudes toward immigration, refugees, multiculturalism, and economic equality all predicted individual radical right-wing votes" (2005, 167, 182).

Among the factors predicting support for Trump among white working-class voters in the US general election, fear of cultural displacement and support for deporting immigrants living illegally in the United States were important, together with economic pessimism. Actual economic hardship was more likely to predict support for Hillary Clinton (Cox, Lienesch, and Jones 2017). As with other parochial attitudes, education predicts orientation toward immigration, with those lacking a postsecondary degree much less likely to endorse retaining or increasing levels of immigration (Goodhart 2017, 25). Parochial attitudes on immigration, advocating limits or bans, are also closely associated with negative attitudes toward other minorities in both the United Kingdom and the United States (Hooghe and Dassonneville 2018; Sobolewska and Ford 2018).

As in the case of trade, attitudes toward immigration across the industrialized world are often linked less to individual economic position or circumstances than to sociotropic evaluations of its cultural effects on the larger community, a community that can be defined as national or local (Hainmueller and Hopkins 2014; Hooghe and Dassonneville 2018). Although immigration policy is set at national (and European) levels, a strong link to local settings appears in parochial orientations toward immigration. In considering sources of cultural protectionism, anti-immigrant attitudes and anxiety regarding cultural displacement are not related to living in ethnically diverse environments. Eric Kaufmann and Gareth Harris (2014, 10–11) find that opposition to immigration and support for far-right political parties in the United Kingdom declines among those who live in such locations. Of course, the association of positive attitudes toward immigrants in cities with large immigrant populations could be explained in part by out-migration by more xenophobic natives who do not wish to live in such settings. Trump's Republican primary supporters seldom lived in high-immigration locales; their communities tended to be isolated from immigrant populations (Rothwell and Diego-Rosell 2016, 8–9). At a more granular level, an analysis of the 2016 shift from Democratic to Republican (Trump) votes in Macomb County, Michigan, home to a white and predominantly working-class population, indicates that the shift was greatest in white enclave communities with relatively low immigrant and African American populations (Austin 2017a).

Two local effects appear to interact with immigration to produce parochial attitudes and support for anti-immigrant parties. In the United Kingdom, the "rate of change in the non-white British population" in locations with little diversity has produced support for anti-immigration politics (Kaufmann and Harris 2014, 10). Individuals who held strongly negative views on immigration were also most likely to vote for Brexit, but it was perceptions of change in levels of immigration and the likelihood that Brexit would counter those changes that were the most important determinants of a pro-Brexit vote (Goodwin and Milazzo 2017; Evans and Menon 2017, 76). A second effect relates to perceptions of the local economy and its trajectory. An analysis of the Brexit vote found a weak or even negative association between a Leave vote and levels of immigration in a region: perceptions of the state of the economy may have driven anti-immigration views, an effect amplified by the concentration of immigrants in areas with more dynamic economies and younger populations (Colantone and Stanig 2018). In locations with more manufacturing workers, a less-educated population, and concentrations of East European immigrants, the Leave vote increased; in areas with higher levels of income, immigrants were associated with a higher Remain vote (Evans and Menon 2017, 77–78). Across industrialized societies, interaction of the perceived economic trajectory of a given location with levels of immigration appears to predict support for movements that advocate limits on immigration, places where "automation, globalization, and economic restructuring . . . have created sizable pockets of native majority families that have experienced loss of status" (Alba and Foner 2017, 3).

Cosmopolitanism: Rise and Decline?

As in the case of parochialism, defining the constituents of cosmopolitanism precisely—and as more than the opposite of its ideological opponent—has been difficult. Cosmopolitan attitudes and orientations have been both taken for granted and assigned a positive value by many in the scholarly community, which leads to an assumption of cosmopolitanism as an unalloyed good and a social norm. Cosmopolitanism incorporates both attitudes and dispositions as well as a set of practices. The first dimension is defined by "a desire for, and appreciation of, cultural diversity" (Vertovec and Cohen 2002, 13) and the second by "a way of living based on an 'openness to all forms of otherness,' associated with an appreciation of, and interaction with, people from other cultural backgrounds" (Hiebert 2002, 212). Norris and Ronald Inglehart define cosmopolitanism as including both values and identities, which in turn will influence individual orientation toward institutions and policies (2009, 181–182). As a measure of cosmopolitanism, they use tolerance of and trust in those living in other countries.[5] In EU research, absence or relatively low levels of Euroscepticism (i.e., belief that EU membership is good for the individual's country) serves as a proxy for identification with an entity beyond the nation-state.

In these definitions, a cosmopolitan orientation risks being defined by the social and cultural characteristics that explain it. In particular, cosmopolitanism is associated with mobility and other characteristics of elite culture. Such definitions ignore those who become cosmopolitan under duress (migrants and refugees), as well as those who practice "ordinary" or everyday cosmopolitanism at the local level (Hiebert 2002; Lamont and Aksartova 2002). Including this variety of cosmopolitanism is particularly important when investigating the sources of cosmopolitan attitudes and practices, as well as the possibilities for cosmopolitanism among those who do not "trade, work, love, marry or do research internationally" but are not "bereft of the cosmopolitan imagination" (Lamont and Aksartova 2002, 2).

Expanding the definition of cosmopolitanism in this way also permits a redefinition of links between globalization and other transnational connections and cosmopolitan attitudes. As Daniel Hiebert describes, transnational lifestyles, which often strengthen in-group attachments to particular communities, may inhibit cosmopolitan attitudes and behavior (2002, 210). Awareness of globalization may penetrate to the local level without producing cosmopolitan attitudes (Skrbiš and Woodward 2007). Mobility, often identified as an underpinning of cosmopolitanism, need not be limited to crossing national boundaries: moving through different parts of the same city may also produce attitudes of cultural openness (Kendall, Woodward, and Skrbiš 2009, 3). Cosmopolitanism can be locally generated; local need not mean parochial.

Both institutions and practices have been identified as sources of cosmopolitan attitudes. The media (print and television) and the information that they provide regarding other societies have been examined as likely contributors toward more tolerant and trustful views of other governments and societies. Norris and Inglehart array societies on a spectrum of cosmopolitanism; their index includes level of globalization, level of national per capita income, and media freedom. Those living in economically open, high-income and media-rich environments (small, open industrialized economies top the list) are more likely to hold cosmopolitan attitudes—that is, be more tolerant and trusting of outsiders. This information environment, when combined with higher individual use of the news media, produces individuals who are "far more tolerant of outsiders than those who are less attentive" (Norris and Inglehart 2009, 185). However, this definition of the media environment does not include later widespread use of social media as a source of information, an innovation that may undermine these optimistic findings; nor does it examine media and information environments at the subnational or local level.

If the information environment and media institutions contribute to a culture of cosmopolitanism, educational experience and institutions are an equally important determinant of such orientations. Parochials (and supporters of nationalist and extreme-right parties) are concentrated among the less educated in most industrialized societies. Across the industrialized world, those with postsecondary educations make up the core of the cosmopolitan constituency: they are more likely to support free trade, outsourcing, and immigration. In the European context, education predicts a lower probability of individual Eurosceptical attitudes, an effect that has grown as European integration has deepened (Hakhverdian et al. 2013). Enrico Moretti's (2012) economically dynamic innovation sectors, situated in urban locations and often linked to universities, attract university graduates; concentrations of those graduates in turn reinforce a positive economic trajectory that is likely to be associated with cosmopolitan attitudes toward economic openness.

As in the case of parochial attitudes, however, the pathways through which education influences cosmopolitanism are difficult to tease apart. More highly educated individuals could favor policies of economic openness for reasons of material self-interest because such individuals are more likely to possess skills valued in the international marketplace. Pro-immigration attitudes could be a function of economic complementarity: affluent, well-educated individuals benefit from the presence of lower skilled (and lower cost) service providers in many urban settings. Education also has informational effects: individuals may absorb support for free trade and immigration as part of their university training in economics. Such individuals, as described earlier, are much less likely in most societies to support (and take cues from) parties of the extreme right. They are also more likely to partake of a rich media environment dominated by organs that are themselves more cosmopolitan. As Goodhart points out, in many societies, such as the United Kingdom, attendance at university also entails mobility: leaving home and often pursuing a career far from one's birthplace is conducive to cosmopolitanism (2017, 38).

Finally, universities and colleges are also purveyors of a particular institutional culture. Since their foundation in the Middle Ages, that culture has typically been cosmopolitan (at least by comparison to the surrounding local and national milieus). That culture is also based on an element of contemporary institutional self-interest: universities aim to attract fee-paying foreign students and to enhance their cosmopolitan self-image. Cosmopolitan culture in higher education infuses surrounding communities: university towns and cities were among the strongest supporters of Remain in the UK referendum on EU membership. These communities not only attract and retain the highly educated in their populations, they typically provide an everyday experience of cultural diversity.

Beyond higher education, transnational experience—literally crossing borders as a result of family background or practices in work or leisure—has also been associated with more cosmopolitan and less Eurosceptical attitudes. In Europe, apart from immigrant and refugee populations, however, such experience is limited to a relatively small, elite stratum of society; programs to encourage such transnational experience often select for those individuals who are predisposed, on the basis of education or other criteria, toward more cosmopolitan orientations (Kuhn 2011, 2012). In the European Union, though not in other national settings, a final institutional source of cosmopolitan culture lies in European institutions themselves. As documented by Kathleen McNamara (2015), the European Union has a conscious strategy of building a European identity rooted in everyday experience and practice but one that does not confront or conflict with national identities.

Location, Location, Location: Globalization and Local Cultures

In explaining parochial and cosmopolitan orientations as well as the political movements that they sustain, an important missing link allows political economy and culture to be connected: the disparate effects of globalization on local culture and politics. In defending the importance of economic interests as a determinant of attitudes toward foreign economic policy, Benjamin Fordham and Katja Kleinberg argue that our understanding of economic self-interest too often "excludes important group processes through which economic interests shape individual attitudes" (2012, 326). Since economic interests are "shared by groups of people who live and work in close proximity to one another," those individuals might also adopt shared attitudes about a wider universe of issues, such as national sovereignty (326). Although Fordham and Kleinberg are not advancing an alternative based on local culture, they have described the manner in which economic interests can be filtered and interpreted through group narratives at the local level. Many voters use "a local lens when voting—even when participating in national elections" (Fitzgerald 2018, 111).

Regional divergence has become apparent across the industrialized and developing worlds for several decades. This "great inversion"—in which dynamic metropolitan areas have surged ahead economically while smaller cities and rural areas have stagnated or declined—has coincided with technological change favoring agglomeration economies, a weakening of spatial spillovers in favor of knowledge concentration, and a decline in labor mobility (Iammarino, Rodríguez-Pose, and Storper 2019, 273). Spatial effects of globalization have tended to reinforce this divergence among regions and localities. Sociologists have examined the increasingly prominent role of global cities in the current era of economic integration (Sassen 2001). In his recent research on the political attitudes and alignments that are driven by the economic geography of globalization, Aditya Ranganath (2018) demonstrates that clustering of the headquarters of globally oriented superstar firms in specific metropolitan locales define global cities, which in turn emerge as the winners from globalization within their countries. The hinterlands of small cities, towns, and rural locales become relative losers, facing economic stagnation and decline in the face of deepening global economic integration.

These gradual processes produced by technological change, economic openness, and policy choice have been amplified by specific globalization shocks. Financialization and financial shocks, such as the global financial crisis of 2007–2009, produced deep recessions in industrialized economies but did not undermine the position of global cities as financial centers. The local effects of China's entry as a major exporter of manufactures, the China trade shock, affected hinterland localities disproportionately in the United States because trade exposure is much more concentrated than exposure to techno-logical change (Autor, Dorn, and Hanson 2013a, 2013b). A similar trade shock from Chinese imports has been identified in the United Kingdom as a major driver of Remain votes in the 2016 referendum (Colantone and Stanig 2018).

Focusing on the local effects of regional divergence awards a different meaning to an assessment of winners and losers from globalization. First, the complex causal process that produces economic divergence rather than convergence must be attributed to globalization rather than technological change or policy choices. If globalization is assigned primary blame, losers may be identified by sector or class, but the culture of loss and perceived de-cline is most apparent in spatial terms, in certain locales. Recent investigation suggests that the Trump coalition in both the Republican primaries and the general election, like the coalition that supported Brexit, was not defined pre-dominantly by class (the white working class); the educational divide was not equivalent to a divide by income (Carnes and Lupu 2017). Those who perceive themselves as the geographical losers from globalization are not members of a single sector or class, although the economic effects of globalization may be distributed according to those familiar cleavages. In similar fashion, those who viewed the effects of globalization, including immigration, more posi-tively were found in local environments that sustained cosmopolitan orienta-tions, at both the elite level and as everyday cosmopolitanism.

Location and Support for the Candidacy of Donald Trump

With all of the necessary caveats regarding ecological and individualist fal-lacies, county- and metropolitan area–level data on the support for Trump's candidacy produce a portrait of localities that share characteristics support-ing a narrative of national decline and cultural displacement. Trump's victory was owed in large measure to an electoral cleavage between the largest metro-politan areas (and the most globalized in terms of economy and population) and rural and smaller metropolitan areas.[6] The divide between "high output" and "low output" America was sharp and unprecedented: "Trumpland con-sists of hundreds and hundreds of tiny low-output locations that comprise the non-metropolitan hinterland of America, along with some suburban and exurban metro counties" (Muro and Liu 2016). In the counties that sup-ported Trump in the US general election, least well-off households are over-represented. Those counties also have a disproportionately low share of the US foreign-born and a large share (two-thirds) of the white population with only a high school education (Frey 2017). Counties that had experienced the most rapid ethnic or racial diversification since 2000, most as the result of Hispanic migration into small towns in the Midwest, were more likely to vote for Trump, mirroring the findings of immigration and its effects on Leave votes in the UK referendum (Adamy and Overberg 2016).

These areas also displayed signs of recent economic distress, in particular a much slower recovery from the Great Recession and lower wages (Shearer 2016). These income disparities were accentuated by wealth effects: in counties voting for Trump, housing prices had been flat for fifteen years (Kusisto 2016). Local economic hardship also had wider social implications. Rothwell and Diego-Rosell (2016) document two important characteristics of locales with high Trump primary support: reduced life expectancy in the middle-aged white population and low intergenerational social mobility. Trump also overperformed the most in counties with the highest drug, alcohol, and suicide mortality rates—"deaths of despair" (Monnat 2016).

It should be emphasized that all counties (and all locations within those counties) that voted for Trump and embraced the parochial political orientation that he voiced did not display these characteristics. More important, the individuals in these counties who voted for Trump may not have experienced economic distress or hardship; as noted, Trump voters did not seem disproportionately disadvantaged by recent economic developments. But their environments—and their local cultures—would be shaped by their observation of neighbors, children (low prospects for upward social mobility), and rapid demographic changes that pointed to a reduced role in the future. In similar fashion, those living in large metropolitan areas—demographically diverse for decades, economically dynamic, and connected globally—would live in an environment that made acceptance of cosmopolitan attitudes more likely, even if those individuals did not benefit directly from economic and cultural openness. As one observer describes, these effects were deepened as individuals sorted themselves into communities that were more compatible with their outlooks:

> This is more than an ideological gap. The physical landscapes both groups inhabit have become so different that it is easy for urbanites and rural Americans to lose touch with how those in other parts of the country feel. Environments almost certainly play a role in shaping voters' political views. (Leatherby 2016)

Even within a region that has often been taken as synonymous with economic decline, the Rust Belt of the Midwest, one discovers divergent economic fortunes during the era of globalization, economic fortunes that produce lo-cal political effects. John Austin (2017b) discovers two Rust Belts: one with "more knowledge-based, technology-driven and urbanized" economies and the other comprising "small- and medium-sized factory towns" that "have lost their anchor employers and are struggling to fill the void." The former often host institutions and populations that foster cosmopolitanism as well as economic dynamism—colleges and universities, growing immigrant popula-tions, and growing shares of college-educated and professional workers. The latter struggle with the loss of their manufacturing monoculture. The former communities remained solidly Democratic in 2016; the latter were those that flipped from Democratic (2012) to Republican (2016) or nearly did so. Caro-line Freund and Dario Sidhu (2017, 14–15) discover a similar pattern in their sample of counties with similar shares of manufacturing employment: those with less diverse (higher proportion of white) populations and lower levels of college-educated workers displayed the biggest increase in Republican vote share in 2016; counties with more diverse populations and higher levels of college-educated workers displayed the largest increase in Democratic vote share.

Location and Support for Leave in the 2016 UK Referendum
Analysis of the UK vote to leave the European Union reveals a relatively di-verse Leave coalition, biased toward less-educated, older, and low-income voters. Like other movements backing parochial external policies, the Leave campaign cobbled together a broad-based social coalition of at least three distinct groups: "affluent Eurosceptics, the older working class and a smaller group of economically disadvantaged, anti-immigration voters" (Swales 2016, 2). The coalition also included nearly one-third of minority voters, dis-played strong regional concentration, and did not match the existing left-right divide in British politics (7, 27).

The characteristics of locations voting Remain or Leave offered a striking contrast between London, the global city, and similar havens of cosmopolitan sentiment, particularly university towns, on the one hand, and their paro-chial counterparts, on the other: "The referendum revealed a longstanding tension between major cities, at ease with immigration and globalization, and deindustrialised towns that have suffered most from the effects of economic decline, and political negligence" (Menon and Wager 2018, 7; Clarke, Good-win, and Whiteley 2017, 152). Even small differences in distance could produce large political effects, particularly in the north of England. In the city of Leeds, for example, a majority voted Remain; in the town of Wakefield, ten minutes away by train, Leave won by a 30 percent margin (Menon and Wager 2018, 7). Brexit voting patterns tracked an existing pattern of geographical polarization in British elections as big cities have swung toward Labour and voters in towns and rural areas have voted Conservative, a pattern that parallels developments in the United States: "cities are becoming younger, more ethnically diverse, more educated and more socially liberal—while towns are aging, are less diverse, more nostalgic and more socially conservative" (Jennings and Stoker 2019, 157).

Supporting the distinction between "Somewheres" and "Anywheres" identified by Goodhart (2017), the differences between cities and their hinterlands track the divide between a cosmopolitan syndrome (young, better educated, more diverse) and a parochial one ("prone to nostalgia and uneasy about immigration") (Jennings, Stoker, and Warren 2018, 43). The divergence in fortunes was reflected in a vote for Leave that was on average twenty points higher "in those places that had experienced the greatest declines in terms of human and economic capital since the 1980s" (43). The China trade shock contributed to the economic decline of smaller manufacturing centers in the United Kingdom, as it had in the United States. It did not affect the Brexit vote directly, however. The reaction of Leave voters was "local-tropic": rather than responding in a "simple pocket-book fashion," they mirrored a local context and culture of perceived decline, one that produced a cluster of parochial attitudes reflected in the Leave vote (Colantone and Stanig 2018, 201). Overall, the effects of the local environment amplified or reduced the effects of demographic characteristics, such as education: the difference in support for Leave between university graduates and those without a degree was much greater in high-skill areas than in low-skill areas. Locations with poorer economic prospects shaped the voting choices of educated and less educated alike (Goodwin and Heath 2016).

The political outcomes that resulted from these distinct cultural settings required national political movements and leaders who could construct a larger narrative out of the collective lives of these communities and link that shared understanding to national programs. Politicians supporting Remain in the Brexit campaign, who relied largely on national predictions and statistics, failed to make that connection: voters in areas experiencing relative economic decline felt that Remain campaigners were "describing a reality from another planet," a planet centered on the prosperous region surrounding London (Evans and Menon 2017, 62). The power of politicians, schooled in a familiar left-right cleavage, was reduced in the face of the new cosmopolitan-parochial divide. As Achen and Bartels describe, politicians can make their own cleavages, but "not just as they please" (2016, 230).

Cosmopolitans and Parochials: A Global Phenomenon?

The election of Trump in the United States and the UK vote to leave the European Union have attracted an disproportionate share of attention because these two countries at the center of the liberal economic order—and two economies that have benefited from and led that order—produced electoral victories for parochials against a long-standing cosmopolitan elite consensus. The political and cultural bases for their cosmopolitan-parochial cleavages—the demographics of age and education or local cultures based on economic divergence between dynamic urban centers, on the one hand, and town and countryside left behind, on the other—find parallels in other industrialized countries. Both the economic and cultural packages vary from case to case, however. Even in the US and UK cases, trade has played a different role: the Trump campaign excoriated recent trade agreements negotiated by the United States; the Leave campaigners in Great Britain argued that the European Union prevented their country from forging more favorable, trade-enhancing agreements with economies outside Europe.

France: The National Front's Expanding Coalition
In France, the FN (now RN) has expanded its parochial coalition beyond a socioeconomic base among the lower middle class (small shopkeepers and businesspeople) and an ideological core founded in resentful, right-wing colons who returned to France from Algeria in the 1960s. The link between these groups and the old National Front was direct: Jean-Marie Le Pen, its founder, was a veteran of the Indochina War; his first electoral campaign was launched under the banner of the extreme-right Poujadist movement, an antitax, antielite rebellion in the 1950s. In this century, under the leadership of Le Pen's daughter Marine, the movement has modernized and expanded its base, maintaining a hold on its small-business constituency and the far right in the south of France and, at the same time, building support among rural

voters and the working class in the north (Ivaldi and Gombin 2015). The tension between antitax appeals directed to its southern supporters and backing for the welfare state, favored by urban and working-class voters in the north, has made domestic insecurity (antiterrorism) and opposition to immigration and globalization the unifying themes in its political program (Mestre 2013). The most striking parallel with the United Kingdom and the United States, however, is the shift in the movement's geographical base: as it has become a party of rural and working-class voters, the Front attracts less support from the cosmopolitan cities and relies on "more remote urban peripheries," France's "in-between places where farmland gives way to retail sprawl and a sense of neglect" (Ivaldi and Gombin 2015, 10; *The Economist* 2017).

Germany: Alternative for Germany's Support from Those Left Behind

The rise of the AfD, with an ethnonationalist platform opposed to immigration and European integration and promoting ethnonationalism, provides a further test of the cultural and spatial sources for parochial political movements. The German case is complicated by the persistent divide since reunification between a more prosperous and economically dynamic West Germany and a lagging former East Germany. In many respects, most of the former East Germany perceives itself as neglected and left behind. Support for the AfD in eastern Germany tracks closely with the demographic and geographic support for other parochial and populist movements in the industrialized world. Areas with limited immigration display more support for the far right; left-wing parties have greater support in urban centers with substantial immigrant populations (Wuhs and McLaughlin 2019). The AfD also gains support in rural areas and those locations with larger numbers of small businesses, high manufacturing employment, and aging populations—the latter a familiar feature in the east as young people have migrated to urban centers in western Germany. In western Germany, areas with lower-than-average income have tended to support the AfD (Franz, Fratzscher, and Kritikos 2018). Overall, the geography of support for the AfD resembles that of other movements hostile to cosmopolitan elites and promoting parochial platforms: rural and small towns, declining manufacturing centers, aging populations, and perceptions that their communities have few prospects and receive little attention from the government—perceptions exacerbated in this instance by the persistent East-West economic and historical divide.

The Netherlands: Parochialism and Partisan Fragmentation

Other industrialized countries display variations on these patterns. Catherine De Vries (2018) finds an emerging cosmopolitan-parochial divide in Dutch politics that is orthogonal to the left-right cleavage based on class and economic policy. Unlike the United States and the United Kingdom, the parochial divide in the Netherlands does not align well with social conservatism, however, in part because social liberals have been attracted to parochial parties for their anti-Islam and anti-immigrant appeals. Support for the far-right, anti-immigrant Party for Freedom (Partij voor de Vrijheid [PVV]) led by Geert Wilders has not been anchored in older voters, as that platform has in many other industrialized countries, but education remains a critical divide: the best results for the PVV have emerged in "rural areas with higher numbers of immigrants and a lower proportion of more educated voters" (Ehrenberg-Shannon and Wisniewska 2017).

The Netherlands also displays variation among cities in a relatively homogeneous, urbanized country and demonstrates that not all large cities with immigrant populations are immune to the appeals of parochials and their xenophobic messages. Amsterdam, epitome of a global city with a knowledge-based economy, has provided little support for the PVV, but Rotterdam, with an economy based on its port and manufacturing industries, has. Political institutions also matter. Anti-immigrant and Eurosceptic parties such as the PVV have found it easier to win parliamentary representation in the Netherlands given its electoral system based on proportional representation. Cosmopolitan parties, particularly the Greens, have also surged, as they have in Germany. The net result in the Netherlands and throughout much of Europe has been a fragmentation of the party system and pressure on center-right parties, which often move to accommodate far-right parochials, and center-left parties, which lose their former working-class constituents and fail to attract younger, cosmopolitan voters.

Cross-Country Analysis of the New Divide

A recent cross-country analysis of the sources of support for antisystem and anti-EU parties confirms the importance of spatial variables in explaining the rise of parochial political movements (Dijkstra, Poelman, and Rodríguez-Pose 2018). Education remains a critical demographic correlate that tracks the cosmopolitan-parochial divide. (Pro- and anti-European integration attitudes and platforms serve as a proxy for that divide in their analysis.) As we have seen, however, education is also associated with economic divergence, as the well-educated cluster in more dynamic global cities, and those without university degrees shape political culture outside those centers. As Steven Livingston argues in Chapter 6, geographic isolation reinforces educational divides. One variable stands out in explaining votes against EU integration: "Places that have experienced long-term, above-average economic growth tend to vote less for parties opposed to European integration than those that have undergone relative economic decline. . . . Places that have seen better times, often based on past industrial power, are turning in very large numbers to parties opposed to European integration" (Dijkstra, Poelman, and Rodríguez-Pose 2018, 15, 18). Economic trajectory, not income level, is key: richer locales on a downward path are more likely to be more opposed to European integration than poorer ones (19).

Globalization and Populism in Developing Countries

Can the cosmopolitan-parochial divide be extended beyond the industrialized world? Asserting national sovereignty has been part of Vladimir Putin's populist appeal to the left-behind rural communities of Russia (Mamonova 2019). Certainly, regional disparities and divergence are apparent in many developing countries during the decades of globalization. The economic gap between coastal and interior China is only one example (Zhang and Zhang 2003). Populist movements based in disadvantaged regions, whether the northeast of Thailand or the northeast of Brazil, have also been a feature of politics in developing political economies. The antielite platforms of those movements, however, are less explicitly antiglobalization and parochial than those in the industrialized North. Populist movements in the developing world are more likely to frame their appeals as a demand for a fair share of the benefits of globalization, which have accrued disproportionately to urban elites, not as opposition to globalization itself. This fits with the broad support for economic globalization found in public opinion surveys of these countries.

The Future of Cosmopolitanism and Parochialism: Economy and Culture

One cannot argue that the economic insecurity and anxiety induced in certain populations by globalization—whether trade shocks, immigration, or apparent threats to national sovereignty—had no effect on the success of political movements challenging the domestic cosmopolitan consensus. That link was far from direct, however: these movements were not simply movements of globalization's losers, whether defined by class or sector, pitted against better-educated winners who had benefited from the same developments in national and global economies. The link from economy to political behavior and outcomes ran through the divergent locational effects of globalization and the local cultures produced by those different settings.

Although the movements that capitalized on these perceptions of relative decline often deployed nationalist rhetoric and assertions of sovereignty, the operative culture was specific to particular locations and the everyday cosmopolitanism and parochialism that those settings produced. McNamara (2017) has described geographically circumscribed "class bubbles" that have emerged in postindustrial economies, but local cultures of decline and optimism—and the parochialism and cosmopolitanism that they generate—cut across conventional definitions of class and have been readily penetrated by national political campaigns and discourse. "Left" and "right" still carry weight in distinguishing among populists on issues of high salience, such as immigration, but "left" and "right" are increasingly defined in terms of cosmopolitan values originating in globally connected and successful cities and a parochialism based in towns and rural areas experiencing relative decline. As analysis of the 2017 UK parliamentary election results suggest, these divides are likely to persist, creating new identities that will define political behavior into the future.[7]

Renewed attention to political cleavages based on spatial differentiation and divergence has left many questions unanswered. The availability of national-level data has long biased both economic and political research, leading to assumptions that immigration or trade, for example, should have relatively little effect when compared to other variables, such as technological change. The discovery of the localized and severe China shock in trade was a wake-up call for greater attention to disaggregated data that would permit granular analysis of the political economy of globalization. In this respect, political economy followed the path of those investigating internal conflict, where subnational data have transformed the research agenda.

The next requirement is more focused: ethnographic research on the ways in which the positive and negative economic trajectories of particular locations are transformed into political attitudes and mobilization along the cosmopolitan-parochial divide. Two recent studies by Katherine Cramer and Justin Gest offer examples of mapping, respectively, "rural consciousness" (Cramer 2016, 23, 105, 109) and the "countervailing narratives" that take root in "post-traumatic cities" (Gest 2016, 7). Unfortunately, neither Cramer nor Gest is primarily interested in the production of parochial or cosmopolitan orientations through local cultures and identities.[8] As Cramer observes, "This complex set of ideas [rural consciousness] is the product of many years of political debate at the national level as well as generations of community members teaching these ideas to each other" (2016, 213). Jennifer Fitzgerald (2018) argues for the independent effect of local attachment, both psychological and sociological, in explaining support for and resistance to radical right-wing political parties that are anti-immigrant, anti-EU, and antiglobalization.

What is needed is more rigorous mapping of missing links in the relationship between macro-level change (such as the effects of globalization or technological innovation) and the interpretation of those changes in local cultures, cultures that create and sustain parochialism and cosmopolitanism through local institutions and networks. These informal and formal institutions have been linked to economic divergence and its persistence; they also shape local responses to that divergence, defining and mobilizing interpretation and mobilization of their interests (Storper 2018). The nesting of local cultures within national-level institutions, such as the competing political universes produced by social media, is yet another dimension that requires investigation. Variation in the drivers of local cultures occurs across space and over time. On the one hand, the cities and regions left behind have witnessed an erosion of institutions that supported cosmopolitan attitudes, such as labor unions and mainstream religious denominations. Global cities, on the other hand, have developed a rich ecosystem of civil society organizations, among them service sector unions and religious organizations that promote the interests of immigrants, multiculturalism, and a cosmopolitan outlook (Storper 2018, 264).

This spatial reorientation of international political economy provides a missing theoretical and empirical link between two data-rich levels of analysis—national and individual—that have proven inadequate for explaining the contemporary political turmoil that surrounds trade, immigration, and international institutions. If the scholarly task is complex, constructing political and policy prescriptions based on a diagnosis that is both cultural and local is even more difficult. It is, however, essential, since the prosperity of thriving regions and possibly the stability of the global economy is now threatened by a revolt of "the places that don't matter" (Rodríguez-Pose 2018). The past menu of place-based policies directed toward regional and local revitalization—whether in the south of Italy, America's Appalachia, or east Germany—have not been successful and are regarded as "at best inefficient, and, at worst, distortionary and slow[ing] the need for structural reform" (192). The preferred policy, especially in the United States, has been the "bus ticket to Houston": moving individuals to more dynamic, rising regional and local economies and accepting unbalanced growth. The new policy prescription is for place-sensitive programs that accept the need to differentiate among economically lagging and left-behind locales.[9]

Whether such policies are feasible given the political mobilization of resentment and parochialism underway is more questionable. Economic programs directed toward reviving small-town and rural Europe and North America can be imagined, but the very political circumstances produced by these movements make it unlikely that such programs would be implemented. Backward-looking initiatives, such as those aiming to recreate manufacturing and extractive industries that are no longer internationally competitive, are guaranteed to be costly failures. A necessary complement to any policies of renewal, however, will be a new narrative—one that offers a future less threatening and less hostile toward outsiders, whether domestic or foreign. That work of political imagination and communication is not yet at hand.

Notes

Acknowledgments: I thank J. P. Singh, Erik Jones, two anonymous reviewers for Stanford University Press, and the participants at the "Cultural Interests and Values" conference at the Institute for International Cultural Relations, University of Edinburgh, for their valuable comments on an earlier draft of this chapter. I also thank Frieder Dengler, Lucas Dolan, and Bryan Hickel for their excellent research assistance.

1. The FN was renamed Rassemblement national (RN; National Rally) in June 2018.

2. Among philosophical treatments are Benhabib 2006 and Appiah 2006.

3. For a description of efforts to incorporate culture into rationalist models of international relations, see Kahler 1998, 933–941.

4. For a critical review of Open Economy Politics, see Lake 2009b.

5. Norris and Inglehart use "nationalist" to label those who identify strongly with their country (or region) of origin, who express strong pride in their country, and

"who are both less trusting of other nationalities and more intolerant of foreigners than average" (2009, 182).

6. Trump performed less well than Mitt Romney's 2012 result in all locales within large metropolitan areas (Shearer 2016).

7. On the persistence of Brexit identities into the 2017 UK election, see the studies in UK and a Changing Europe 2018.

8. Gest's East London districts were among the few constituencies in Greater London to vote for Leave in the 2016 referendum (Barking and Dagenham, 62.4 percent; Havering, 69.7 percent). Although Gest's second case—Youngstown, Ohio—did not vote for Trump in 2016, the Democratic vote was sharply reduced from 2012 (63.5 percent in 2012 to 49.8 percent in 2016). Gest does examine support for the virulently anti-immigrant British National Party in East London.

9. For details, see Iammarino, Rodríguez-Pose, and Storper 2019.

II CULTURAL INTERACTIONS AND PRAXIS

6 Crossing Borders

Culture, Identity, and Access to Higher Education

Steven Livingston

THIS BOOK SEEKS TO OPERATIONALIZE CULTURE IN A WAY THAT HELPS explain global political economic outcomes. As David Throsby points out in Chapter 3, the challenge but also the opportunity here is that most economists regard culture, if at all, as "exogenous, and largely irrelevant to the behavioral models that are useful in understanding economic decision making." In this chapter, I hope to contribute to an integration of culture with economics with a consideration of culture and class boundary spaces. I propose that the boundaries of economic class are policed by cultural norms. Class is cultural, and culture is policed. The inclination to treat material and ideational calculations as separate and distinct is itself a cultural artifact.

Most international relations perspectives analyze global outcomes with reference to units that identify groups (actors) and their interests. Voters, for example, reward or punish a political party according to self-interested calculations of how well it brings home the bacon—for material interests rather than in the party's appeals to cultural identity (Kinder and Kiewiet 1981). In this respect, many observers conclude that the outcome of the 2016 US presidential election is best understood as working-class retribution for years of neglect from mainstream Democrats. In this view, economic dislocation and shrinking generational economic expectations explains political behavior.

Others emphasize cultural factors, including urban-rural divides and white voter backlash against programs that favor people of color and the emerging minority-majority population in the United States (Sides and

Tesler 2016; Cherlin 2016; Porter 2016). White identity politics ran roughshod over self-interested materialist rationality. As Pankaj Mishra puts it, large proportions of the white working class seem to have misplaced self-interest for a deeply irrational tribal rage (Mishra 2017). Political scientist Diana C. Mutz (2018) finds that the "dwindling proportion of traditionally high-status Americans (i.e., whites, Christians, and men)" were motivated to support Donald Trump because of their sense of relative decline in status. All of this leads us to the central question of this book: If culture trumps material self-interest, what is culture?

Elsewhere in this book, culture is defined as collective experiences, practices, and identities and as something that allows people to make sense of their lives. Culture is also described as dynamic but enduring, as well as flexible but limiting, perhaps in ways similar to Daniel Hausman's point in Chapter 2 about how people's beliefs about constraints limit what they attempt to do. Though intriguing, supple definitions of culture such as these often frustrate scholarship as much as they guide it. Perhaps it is for this reason that the language of cultural studies leaves some social scientists confused and even sometimes a bit tetchy. What are we to make of culture and its relationship to interests?

Following Clifford Geertz, I embrace a semiotic approach to culture and assume that it is found in the constructed meaning assigned by participants to social patterns and behaviors found in society, including their own (Geertz 1973; Keesing et al. 1987). Paraphrasing Max Weber, Geertz reminds us that man is an animal "suspended in webs of significance he himself has spun" (Geertz 1973, 5). Culture is, he says, "those webs, and the analysis of it to be therefore not an experimental science in search of law but *an interpretive one in search of meaning*" (6; emphasis added). Following Gilbert Ryle (1971), Geertz calls this approach "thick description" (1973, 27), the effort to understand the multiplicity of complex, superimposed conceptual structures that play out before the observer.

He illustrates the approach with a retelling of a story offered originally by Ryle. Consider two boys rapidly contracting the eyelids of their respective right eyes. What is going on here? Geertz's famous passage is worth quoting at length:

> In one, this is an involuntary twitch; in the other, a conspiratorial signal to
> a friend. The two movements are, as movements, identical; from an I-am-a-

camera, "phenomenalistic" observation of them alone, one could not tell which was twitch and which was wink, or indeed whether both or either was twitch or wink. Yet the difference, however unphotographable, between a twitch and a wink is vast; as anyone unfortunate enough to have had the first taken for the second knows. The winker is communicating, and indeed communicating in a quite precise and special way: (1) deliberately, (2) to someone in particular, (3) to impart a particular message, (4) according to a socially established code, and (5) without cognizance of the rest of the company. As Ryle points out, the winker has done two things, contracted his eyelids and winked, while the twitcher has done only one, contracted his eyelids. Contracting your eyelids on purpose when there exists a public code in which so doing counts as a conspiratorial signal *is* winking. That's all there is to it: a speck of behavior, a fleck of culture, and *voilà!*—a gesture. (1973, 6)

To the positivist it is all the same. He or she would be found looking for a proper regression model to fit correlations among contracting eyelids and other variables: diet to explain twitching, symptoms of a neurological disorder, age, gender, or what have you. In the meantime, the distinction between a communicative wink and a contracting eyelid would go unrecognized, even before Geertz mischievously adds to the complexity. Suppose there is a third lad, who,

> "to give malicious amusement to his cronies," parodies the first boy's wink, as amateurish, clumsy, obvious, and so on. He, of course, does this in the same way the second boy winked and the first twitched: by contracting his right eyelids. Only this boy is neither winking nor twitching, he is parodying someone else's, as he takes it, laughable, attempt at winking. Here, too, a socially established code exists (he will "wink" laboriously, over-obviously, perhaps adding a grimace—the usual artifices of the clown); and so also does a message. Only now it is not conspiracy but ridicule that is in the air. (1973, 6–7)

Or rather than parody, the insecure mimic might instead be practicing a wink at home before a mirror, "in which case he is not twitching, winking, or parodying, but rehearsing; though so far as what a camera, a radical behaviorist, or a believer in protocol sentences would record he is just rapidly contracting his right eyelids like all the others" (7).

The point of the story is that to understand culture one must strive to untangle the "multiplicity of complex conceptual structures, many of them superimposed upon or knotted into one another" (Geertz 1973, 10). How practically is this done? Much of the central point of this chapter is to address this question: Where does one observe culture at its most conspicuous and decipherable? If we are to take a cultural turn in political economic analysis, how are we to untangle the multiplicity of complex, superimposed conceptual structures that are woven into political life? My answer is that they show up most clearly at points of cultural transgression.

Culture and Boundary Spaces

I assert that the direct experience of what I call boundary spaces offers a laboratory of sorts for revealing the contours of culture and cultural differences, of variation on meaning, that is most germane to politics, especially class politics. Boundary spaces are those places in between conceptual structures: meaning, identity, norms and values, and commonsensically embraced ideas. They are like other complex cultural phenomena: they are hard to define, but you know them when you see them. They are characterized by the subjective experience of stress, curiosity, novelty, disgust, delight, contempt, awe, revulsion, arrogance, fear, anxiety, anticipation, and attraction. These are not necessarily mutually exclusive responses; indeed, the reactions just listed often occur simultaneously and are experienced as arousal. They are most certainly sought after and embraced, though just as often avoided. Edith Turner (2012) speaks of communitas, the joyful human transgressive experiences found around festivals and carnival and other liminal cultural moments in which one is invited to violate cultural boundary spaces and play with identities and roles. The only response not experienced in boundary spaces is indifference.[1]

The boundary space experiences to which I refer here are in some measure similar to Miles Kahler's reference to cosmopolitanism "under duress" in Chapter 5. This is the experience of migrants and refugees, "as well as those who practice 'ordinary' or everyday cosmopolitanism at the local level." As he notes, engagement with boundary spaces does not require a passport: "moving through different parts of the same city may also produce attitudes of cultural openness," which is to say, cosmopolitanism. Irene Wu's discussion in Chapter 9 of study abroad experiences also highlights the sort of liminal experience I draw attention to here. What she calls "soft power relationships" seems to reflect what Kahler means when he speaks to cosmopolitans.

Boundary spaces are where collective meaning and shared experience often fail to be communicated or understood. It is the experience of stepping out of a comfort zone and into alien space, a place where one does not necessarily know what goes with what. Boundary spaces are often contested and experienced with apprehension and fear, or at least confusion. Think, for example, of a simple London sidewalk. It is a cultural boundary space not in the sense that it separates a street from what is found on the other side of the sidewalk. Rather, it is a space where cultural norms and expectations confront one another, where expectations of what goes with what are unclear and therefore unintentionally violated. What do I mean?

Out of custom, in the United Kingdom one walks and drives to the left. The custom developed from the preferences of right-handed swordsmen in the Middle Ages who recognized a self-interested preference for keeping to the left when passing another swordsman. Doing so allowed one's right arm to be positioned in a way that would allow one to swiftly withdraw a sword from the scabbard on the left (*World Standards* 2019). In this way, the scabbard is also kept distant from a potential opponent while the sword could, if needed, be withdrawn with a sweeping arc from left to right and across the body to deliver an incapacitating blow. After a time, the self-interested practice of walking to the left became merely a routine courtesy and cultural practice. Similarly, the display of an empty outstretched hand in greeting and the breaking of bread (never cutting, for that would require a knife, which in the Middle Ages was regarded as bad manners because of the implicit threat it carried), have similar origins.

Conventions are not adopted universally. About 35 percent of the world's population follows the practice of passing to the left, though now usually without swords and scabbards. Many of the other 65 percent who pass to the right are counted among London's 38 million annual tourists. The result is a royally contested boundary space free-for-all where the customs of the native inhabitants and interloping visitors collide, sometimes quite literally.

It is in transgressive moments such as this that we are most acutely aware of our own culture and the culture of others. Passing on the left (or right) in the absence of contestation and tension would appear too natural and unremarkable to be given thought. Navigating and probing boundary spaces, though, allows us to experience our own suppositions, vulnerabilities, and expectations, while sometimes opening up a deeper awareness of the suppositions of others. My approach, therefore, is deliberately transgressive and interpretive. I look for culturally rich moments as they occur in boundary spaces. It is here that we are most likely to sort out the distinctions between winks and twitches, mimicry and rehearsals. If culture is an osmotically derived sense of what goes with what, awareness of it comes most lucidly in the apprehensive experience of liminality.

Yet the flux of liminality and negotiated meaning is too exhausting to be sustained. Pedestrians in London are reminded of walking conventions by signposts telling them where to be. Institutions intervene. Boundaries are policed. In Germany, walking or running on a *Fahrradweg*, a path designated for bicycles, will result in a steady stream of invectives and stern advice to *Wanderer woanders* (walk somewhere else). Peter L. Berger and Thomas Luckmann (1966) observe that people and groups interacting in a social system create stable concepts of others' actions and that these concepts are habituated into reciprocal, institutionalized roles. Habituated roles create the contours of borders and boundaries that come with attendant expectations and customs associated with nation, class, race, gender, and age, among other identities. Borders and boundaries are attended to by guardians (who are themselves fulfilling role expectations), especially parents, schools, workplaces, police officers, religious communities, friends, and school admissions officers. When one approaches boundaries, guardians are there to remind the potential transgressor of the proper expectations associated with his or her role. Guardians in this sense are acutely aware of norms that define where a boundary exists. Those who are the most revealing of transgressions are boundary keepers: those people and institutions responsible for maintaining current practices and standards.

I am especially interested in illustrating my argument with a discussion of the negotiation of class roles defined by access to higher education. Of borders and boundaries, those defining class (drawn by language and accents, manners and personal bearing, clothing, surnames, place of residence) and education are the most closely guarded. They are also the fulcrum of materially based interests confronting class-based culture. And the boundaries between higher education and the working class have perhaps never been as infringeable as they are now. Bright, intellectually gifted young people from postindustrial cities such as Youngstown, Ohio, and Flint, Michigan, face almost insurmountable hurdles in charting a path to a four-year university or college. Historically, a college education and state support for universities and students made transitions between class and higher education feasible, though still burdened by the sort of self-doubt that is too often fueled by family and friends who are eager to keep one from overreaching, or being too big for one's britches. State support for universities and students has shrunk, leaving working-class students outside the gates or saddled with the accumulated debt of $60,000 a-year tuition. How are these new boundaries negotiated by the working class in postindustrial America?

The Cartography of Class and Culture

Leonard Reissman in *Class in American Life*, published in 1959, reports that when first asked, interview subjects often claim that "we don't have classes in our town" only to then take the conversation to a review of class distinctions marbling the town's geography (Fussell 1992, 17). The distinguished historian and literary critic Paul Fussell (1992, 15) once remarked that a frank conversation about social class offers the most dependable way to reveal personal insecurities. Fussell believes that while working-class people tend to be resigned to their position in society and the well-to-do are furtively delighted by the attention given to their good fortune, it is the friable middle class who is most likely to be left tetchy by the topic (Fussell 1992, 16). For Fussell, this reticence is explained by the incendiary nature of class in America. To question a person's position in society is to implicitly question character, assuming that the better sort deserves his or her position in society, as does the ne'er-do-well. Academics in America are just as reticent, it seems, to talk about class, though that has perhaps changed as a result of the 2016 elections. Literary theorist Walter Benn Michaels asserts, "Although no remark is more common in American public life than the observation that we don't like to talk about race, no remark . . . is more false" (Kahlenberg 2017). Michaels continues, "In fact, we love to talk about race. And, in the university, not only do we talk about it; we write books and articles about it, we teach and take classes about it, and we arrange our admissions policies in order to take it into account." Richard Kahlenberg adds, "In part, Michaels suggests, we talk about race to *avoid* talking about class" (2017; emphasis in original). Class differences, therefore, like London sidewalks, constitute a kind of revealing cultural boundary space. And access to education is one of the bright lines that separates classes.

Class tensions have fueled an endless stream of cultural products, from earnest Dickensian engagements with poverty and class to erudite reviews of its growing distinctions to lighthearted but probing comedies. If class apprehensions cannot be ignored, they can at least be plumbed for comic relief (Day 2011).

In the 1960s, class tensions in the United States were exploited for their comedic content by television programs such as *The Beverly Hillbillies, Gomer Pyle, U.S.M.C.*, and *Green Acres*. While intended to be humorous, these shows were also revealing of cultural tropes and expectations of what goes with what. Dull-witted Jethro Bodine and his uncle, Jed Clampett, of *The Beverly Hillbillies* and Jim Nabors's character in *Gomer Pyle* were gentle but socially misplaced rubes among sophisticates (or in Gomer's case, the strict discipline of military life). In the former show, the complexity of class relations was brought into relief by Jed Clampett's Beverly Hills banker, Milburn Drysdale, whose professional interests orient him to Jed's wealth but whose cultural bearing inclines him to treat Jed as the country bumpkin that he is. Jed's cultural bearing and backcountry apparel do not align with his formidable financial authority, making his class boundary lines as confusing as a London sidewalk but also humorous.

The conceit of Eddie Albert's character in *Green Acres* is the opposite of Jed's. Erudite New York City attorney Oliver Wendell Douglas decides his true calling is in the country. As the show's theme song says, "Farm livin' is the life for me / Land spreadin' out so far and wide / Keep Manhattan, just give me that countryside."[2] Just as Jed continues to wear shabby backwoods clothes to signify his class origins, Oliver continues to wear the pressed white shirts and suits of his law-firm life, even while pitching hay and riding a tractor. Meanwhile, his glamorous socialite wife, played by the elegant, European-born Eva Gabor, struggles to get by without her servants. Her misplacement is signified by her struggles in the kitchen—where 1960s women belonged—as she prepares such culinary delights as boiled water soup in her pearls. Again, the risible tug is found in the social tensions arising from a confused juxtaposition in class boundary space.

In more class-conscious Great Britain, the much-admired 1990s-era BBC comedy *Keeping Up Appearances* follows the travails of Hyacinth Bucket (which she insists is pronounced "Bouquet") as she struggles to cement her social superiority with anyone willing (or not) to listen. She is forever planning—and those around her forever ducking—one of her "executive-style" candlelit suppers featuring her Royal Doulton china with "the hand-painted periwinkles." Most often, Hyacinth's lovable but unmistakably lower-class family upends her efforts. Just as she is about to take that desperately desired step up the social ladder, her "bone-idle" brother-in-law, Onslow, appears in his sputtering 1978 Ford Cortina Mark IV with the entire shambolic family in tow. As Hyacinth once said to Richard, her long-suffering husband, "You know I love my family, but that's no reason why I should have to acknowledge them in broad daylight!" (*Wikipedia* 2020). Hyacinth's striving actually underscores an important point about class and cultural boundary space: in all but the most ossified societies, class is, in fact, culturally negotiated space. There is a potential for movement, in part because the boundary space between classes is, at least in some ways, equivocal. It is not out of the question to think that perhaps one fine day Hyacinth will find herself in the white-gloved embrace of her erstwhile social superiors. That is what makes her efforts funny, especially for those who can identify with her position in life. If navigation of class barriers was in fact hopeless, her striving would be only pathetic. The tragic take on Hyacinth's ambition is found in Arthur Miller's *The Death of a Salesman* and F. Scott Fitzgerald's *The Great Gatsby*. In Hyacinth's case, hope mixes with frustration to produce familiar, identifiable, shareable, and humorous tensions. But boundary space confrontations also underscore the point that class and culture are revealed most distinctly at the edges where the rube rubs elbows with the well-to-do. Yet Hyacinth's hope of class deliverance has taken a darker turn in more recent popular entertainment. Bong Joon-ho's 2019 Academy Award-winning film *Parasite* depicts the lower-class Kim family as they struggle to get by in a dingy basement apartment. Their fortunes take a turn for the better after each member of the family infiltrates the luxurious lives of the upper-class Park family. The comic tension takes a darker turn in a way that is perhaps reflective of the twenty-first century's darker struggle with extreme inequality. Upon seeing Mr. Park's disgusted reaction to one lower-class character's body odor, Kim Ki-taek, the patriarch of the struggling family, fatally stabs Mr. Park. Though *Parasite* begins with risible class tensions not unlike those in *The Beverly Hillbillies* or *Green Acres*, they eventually deteriorate into bloody class warfare.

The lines and contours of boundary spaces are demarcated by attributes of culture: accents and grammar, habits of dress, postal codes, vacation destinations, leisure activity, social networks, dental health, automobiles, entertainment preferences, shopping destinations, tableware, and especially education. Material wealth, of course, cuts across all of these attributes, though in sometimes surprising and contradictory ways. A blue-jean-clad billionaire runs against type (at least in clothing) while a large percentage of the American middle class struggles financially to keep up the appearance of affluence (Gabler 2016). At least in some American circles, a middle-class staff worker with an Ivy League education or a poorly paid assistant professor might be held in higher esteem than a tradesperson pulling in a healthy six-figure salary, sans college degree. As distinguishing a wink from an eyelid contraction, navigating cultural boundary spaces between classes is anything but obvious. Access to a higher education might offer a boundary space condition that reveals it more clearly. That is what I undertake next.

Ivy Towers and Tall Walls

As I write this chapter I am attached ever so tenuously to one of the world's great universities, the University of Cambridge in the United Kingdom. One cannot help but feel a sense of awe as one walks the same brick and cobblestone footpaths that were once traversed by Isaac Newton, Alfred, Lord Tennyson, Stephen Hawking, Francis Bacon, and so many other intellectual giants. One enters a room at Kings College (founded in 1441) with the realization that Alan Turing, John Maynard Keynes, Frederick Sanger, E. M. Forster, George Santayana, Anthony Giddens, and Robert Walpole stood in the same room. One has the sense of having *arrived*.

Yet as a visitor, my privileges at Cambridge are limited; indeed, they are quite literally blocked by centuries-old wooden doors that bar interlopers from entering the grounds of almost all of its thirty-one constituent colleges. One is allowed an occasional glimpse through an open door to what lies beyond the wall. The guardians of boundary spaces here are unyielding and ancient.

Other barriers to elite educations are less obvious but no less strict. Stone and wood are replaced by subtler forms of exclusion. Chief among them is social class. In *Good Will Hunting*, actor Matt Damon's stereotypical working-class Boston "Southie" accent and janitorial clothing set him apart from the students and faculty at the unnamed (though obviously MIT) elite university. As a janitor, Damon's character is given conditional access to the university and assigned a tightly proscribed role: pick up after the elite and nothing more. He is a parochial, in Kahler's terms in Chapter 5, barred from the university education that would open him up to cosmopolitan attitudes. He is allowed to transgress space—to be in it but not a part of it. Yet there is a hidden underlying tension. Will's accent and sartorial appearance are at odds with his intellectual gifts (as Jed's appearance and financial standing are at odds), which suggest that he should in fact be both in and a part of the university. His place in class and intellectual boundary space is unclear, confused, and filled with revealing tensions.

One evening, while pushing his broom up and down a hall in the mathematics department, Will does something deeply transgressive. He puts down his janitor's broom and picks up a grease pen to solve a complex mathematical equation that was left as a challenge to students by a charismatic professor named Gerald Lambeau.[3] In this small act of cheeky brilliance, Will transgresses social boundary space and steps from the world of working-class expectations (push a broom) to intellectual engagement and creativity. He steps from one life into another. Lambeau eventually discovers, to his amazement, that the equation was solved by a janitor. It is perhaps revealing that Lambeau's first reaction to this realization is anger and agitation. Yet Lambeau eventually befriends Will Hunting and brings him into the fold of the university elites. The rest of the movie involves Will's personal conflicts in reconciling his profoundly damaged sense of self with the unexpected promise of a life of the mind. He is invited to step through the door but struggles, not for a lack of talent, but because of his own sense of himself. That is the most formidable wall of all.

Let us now step away from Hollywood to enter the world of actual class barriers to higher education. We should begin by noting that of the thirty-eight most prestigious colleges in the United States, more students come from the top 1 percent of income scales than do students from the bottom 60 percent. Furthermore, while about a quarter of the wealthiest college-aged men and women in the United States attend an elite college or university, less than one-half of 1 percent of children from the bottom fifth of American families do. At elite colleges, at a time when the poor have gotten poorer and the very rich have gotten much richer, "the share of students from the bottom 40 percent has remained mostly flat for a decade" (Aisch et al. 2017). If one is wealthy, or at least upper-middle class, one has a far greater chance of attending a prestigious university, irrespective of intellectual capabilities.

What explains this trend? Why is there so much boundary space between the working class and a college education? A part of the answer is that lower-income students no longer have the same structural opportunities that were once available to them to go to college (Leonhardt 2017a). Embracing

neoliberal orthodoxies about shrinking the role of government, state legis-
lators have made deep funding cuts to their universities. According to one
estimate, individual state spending per student in inflation-adjusted dollars
has fallen 18 percent nationwide (Mitchell, Leachman, and Masterson 2016).
Arizona leads in both percentage reductions in spending per student and in
percentage increase in tuition costs, a staggering 50 percent in the former and
almost 80 percent in the latter. Even the world-class public university system
in California experienced an almost 30 percent reduction in spending while
students faced a whopping 72 percent increase in fees. With these financial
trends, education is out of reach of many working-class students. But other
structural impediments exist.

One way working- and middle-class students have funded college in the
past has been with Pell Grants. Even this opportunity is closing. At the public
colleges in the 2017 New York Times Index, the average share of last year's
freshman class receiving Pell Grants—which means they typically come from
the bottom half of the income distribution—fell to 21.8 percent, from 24.3 percent in 2011–2012 (Leonhardt 2017b). As state investment in education shrinks
and costs go up, Pell Grant support has diminished. If Pell Grants are drying
up, what about other educational pathways across class boundary space?

As a working-class American growing up in the 1960s and early 1970s, my
own college education began much differently. After my father failed to secure
the same sort of assembly-line factory job for me as he had for my three older
brothers, I decided that being a farm laborer was not the life for me. I knew
that working on a farm in exchange for rent, as I had been doing since just before turning age sixteen, was not sustainable, even though I had managed to
make my way through high school under the arrangement. After walking off
the farm, the first door I walked through in Flint, Michigan, led to a US Army
recruiter, who promptly signed me up for a six-year enlistment in an artillery
unit in exchange for educational benefits that I was promised following my
honorable discharge. These were the early steps on my path through boundary spaces between classes.

The Servicemen's Readjustment Act of 1944, commonly known as the GI
Bill, transformed American higher education, indeed, American culture. By
1956, almost nine million veterans had made use of the GI Bill education benefits in some way, with over two million attending a college or university. The
Vietnam War produced a small but still significant surge, one that I caught
the end of in 1978 when I started college in earnest following my military ser-

vice. I had also managed to take community college courses during my enlistment, holding a textbook in one hand and an M16 rifle in the other. In the end, I count myself as one of the 2 percent of the American professoriate to come from a working-class background.

Today, in an era of high-tech warfare, the days of large ground-force armies are over. Even volunteering for military service is out of reach for many working-class youths, in part because of their educational background (Feeney 2014). The institutions that facilitated working-class and middle-class upward mobility—affordable land grant colleges, the GI Bill, and Pell Grants—are less effective, leaving bright and capable young people behind. This is without question a great and widening barrier to working-class students trying to navigate social boundary space. Looking at individuals born between 1981 and 1991, one study finds that as many Harvard students came from the top 1 percent as from the bottom 60 percent in wages and wealth (Kahlenberg 2017). In Great Britain, similar patterns are evident. Only 11.5 percent of Oxford's students are from working-class families, and 12.6 percent of Cambridge's students come from the working class (Davis 2010). High-achieving, low-income students are less likely to apply to prestigious universities in the United States than are their high-achieving, high-income counterparts.

Adding to the mystery is the fact that very selective institutions offer high-achieving, low-income students enough financial aid to make it possible for them to "pay *less* to attend a selective institution than the far less selective or non-selective post-secondary institutions that most of them do attend" (Hoxby and Avery 2012, 1). High-achieving, low-income students self-select to attend less prestigious colleges, if they attend college at all. Why do so many low-income, high-achieving students appear to base their selection of universities on their achievement while others base it on their income?

Caroline Hoxby and Christopher Avery find that relative to high-achieving, high-income students, high-achieving, low-income students are more isolated from other high achievers, both in terms of geography and in terms of the high schools they attend. Put simply, they tend to live in places where one does not see a lot of people going to Harvard, Yale, or Princeton: "In fact, their lack of [geographical] concentration is such that many traditional strategies for informing high-achieving students about college—for instance, college admission staff visiting high schools or after-school programs that provide mentoring—are probably prohibitively expensive" (2012, 1–2). Furthermore, high-achieving, low-income students have much lower chances of meeting a mentor—a guide through class boundary space—who has attended a selective college. Isolation from those who might guide and inspire leads many talented, capable working-class students behind, unable to do what Will Hunting did and transgress class and educational boundary lines. "The economic segregation of selective universities is the highly predictable result of a number of admissions policies that generally exclude working-class students, particularly those who are white" (Kahlenberg 2017). In a 2005 study, William Bowen, Martin Kurzweil, and Eugene Tobin have found that among the thirteen selective colleges in the United States, the following recruitment profiles had measurable effects on chances of admission, all other factors being the same:

- Being a recruited athlete boosted one's admissions chances by 30.2 percent.
- Being an underrepresented minority increased one's chances by 27.7 percent.
- Being a legacy applicant increased one's odds by 19.7 percent.
- Being a first-generation college student improved one's odds by 4.1 percentage points.
- Being from the bottom income quartile offered no improvement in odds. (Bowen, Kurzweil, and Tobin 2005)

In another study of elite private colleges, Thomas Espenshade and Alexandria Radford (2013) found that, holding academic ability constant, upper-middle-class whites were three times more likely than low-income whites to be admitted to selective private colleges. Nevertheless, some of these low-income students are very high achievers. According to Hoxby and Avery, at the time of high school graduation, these students have grades and college aptitude test scores that put them in the top 4 percent of all US secondary school students in the United States. "The problem is," they say, "that most high-achieving, low-income students do not apply to any selective college so they are invisible to admissions staff" (2012, 6).

At the same time, Hoxby and Avery find that high-income students are strongly disinclined to apply to nonselective institutions: "High-income students dislike higher net costs but (all else equal) like higher sticker prices" (2012, 19). Stephen Joel Trachtenberg, the former president of George Washington University, at one point the most expensive university in the United States, understood this dynamic. Trachtenberg convinced affluent applicants that GW was "worth a lot more money by charging a lot more money" (Carey

2015). He likened college to vodka, a flavorless beverage: "But people will spend $30 for a bottle of Absolut because of the brand. A Timex watch costs $20, a Rolex $10,000. They both tell the same time." The number of applicants at GW surged from some six thousand to twenty thousand, the average SAT score of students rose by nearly two hundred points, and the endowment jumped from $200 million to now well over $1 billion (Carey 2015).

It's a Long Way from Here to There

Hoxby and Avery's explanation for the disinclination of skilled, working-class students to apply to highly selective universities focuses on the effects of geographical and social isolation. Students who are less likely to meet graduates of highly selective universities and less likely to be visited by a recruiter from such an elite university are unlikely to apply to one. This certainly makes sense. Coming from a family of six, I was only the second sibling to graduate from high school. My father and mother had a seventh- and sixth-grade education, respectively. In my family, achievement was measured in years worked in a General Motors factory: forty-two years for my father, forty-seven years for a brother, thirty years for another brother, and nine years for a third, who left Flint for a career as a plumber in Florida. And none of the sons and daughters of the GM factory workers who went to high school with me went to Harvard or Yale, or indeed to college at all, except one, who attended Central Michigan University on a football scholarship. Indeed, many of my high school graduating class of 1974 went on to serve prison terms, join the army, or die young (and sometimes all three).[4]

It was in the army that I met my first intellectual, a young lieutenant-colonel named John Shalikashvili. In army logic, after I graduated with honors from both basic training and artillery school, I was assigned as the battalion commander's personal assistant and driver. LTC Shalikashvili went on to become Chairman of the Joint Chiefs of Staff during Bill Clinton's presidency. He spoke five languages and possessed a keen intellect. Although I worked for him for only about two years, we remained in touch after my transfer to a nuclear missile unit in Cold War Europe and, eventually, the end of my enlistment. His mentorship provided the needed guidance, if only in offering an example of what a brilliant person looks like and how one comports oneself in professional settings.

But what about those bright working-class students who are not so fortunate as to fall into the hands of a brilliant mentor? What signals are they given as to what life might hold in store? How deep is their isolation? Earlier, I said that the boundary space between social class is filled with tensions that are sometimes plumbed for insightful humor. Class differences, however, are not always managed so benignly in popular imagination or cultural expression. British writer Owen Jones underscores the social tensions expressed by the disparaging terms applied to the white working class in Great Britain. He illustrates it with a comment found in the *Daily Mail*:

> Look around the supermarket, the bus and increasingly now on the road, you will encounter ever-growing numbers of tattooed, loud, foul-mouthed proles [members of the working class], with scummy brats trailing in their wake, who are incapable of acknowledging or even recognizing a common courtesy, and who in their own minds can never, ever, be in the wrong about anything. (O. Jones 2016, Kindle location 716)

These are the chavs, the British term for what might be called "white trash" in the United States (Isenberg 2016). During the primaries, the *National Review*'s Kevin Williamson (2017) spoke of "the white working class's descent into dysfunction." Trump supporters are "in thrall to a vicious, selfish culture whose main products are misery and used heroin needles" (Williamson 2017). They blame their condition on "outside forces" rather than their own life's choices, a sentiment echoed by popular blogger Erick Erickson when he tweeted that "a lot of Trump voters have failed at life and blame others for their own poor decisions" (Rich 2017). In his own cutting critique of the white working class, Williamson (2017) concludes, "Donald Trump's speeches make them feel good. So does OxyContin." In *Coming Apart: The State of White America, 1960–2010*, sociologist Charles Murray (2012) argues that white working-class Americans are in the condition they are because they have abandoned the family values and civic virtues that once defined their lives. In *Hillbilly Elegy*, J. D. Vance's 2016 memoir, the white working class is vilified as system cheats and scammers. He describes a hardscrabble life, though unlike my own family in Flint; Vance's hillbilly family from eastern Kentucky usually had the benefit of indoor plumbing. His mother was a junkie who married almost as often as she moved from one house to the next. Whether chavs or white trash, the white working class is roundly chastised as drug-addled losers without redemption. And, of course, Hillary Clinton summed up the sentiment with her pithy "deplorables" description for the white working class (Chozick 2016).

Trump's election uncorked a flood of ink dedicated to understanding the white working class and its irrational support of a vulgar New York billionaire real estate developer. The analysis of liberal pundits, as Barbara Ehrenreich notes, has boiled down to, "Are they stupid or just deplorably racist?" (Ehrenreich 2017). On the left, the *Daily Kos* (2016) published an article titled, "Be Happy for Coal Miners Losing Their Health Insurance: They're Getting Exactly What They Voted For." Another example of this is offered by the left-leaning *Guardian*, a British newspaper with a sizable operation and following in the United States. The theme is often the same: these slow-witted people still support him and say the darndest things. "'If they'd leave him [Trump] alone and quit contriving stuff against him, he'd do a hell of a job,' said . . . a retired elevator technician. 'If they get rid of this contrived stuff, he'd be a hell of a president'" (McCarthy 2017).

In the *Guardian* piece, and many others like it, the accompanying photographs underscore the cultural clichés. One photograph shows an older man, shirtless and with a face fixed by a vacant stare. One can see in the photograph a copy of the Bible propped up for display in the window behind him. The overall impression is of an older man who is deeply religious, vacuous, disheveled, and blindly supportive of a deeply flawed president.

A common visual trope of the white working class involves a display of shirtless, overweight, aging men with sagging bodies. In *Keeping Up Appearances*, Hyacinth's brother-in-law, Onslow, is overweight, "bone-idle," and always slovenly dressed in a poorly fitting undershirt that exposes too much underarm flesh. He signifies the strange relationship between religious conservatives and a thrice-married, genitalia-grabbing reprobate, as Mark Rozell discusses in Chapter 8. As with many clichés, the problem is that it is not entirely true. *New York Post*'s Salena Zito (2017) notes that much of Trump's support comes from people living in the second ring of suburbs, the so-called exurbs: "For the most part, the people who live in those regions are pretty much happy with him." The same conclusion is reached by urban geographer Joel Kotkin (2016):

> Much of the New York and Washington press corps has concluded that Donald Trump's surprising journey to the Oval Office was powered by country bumpkins expressing their inner racist misogyny. However, the real foundations for his victory lie not in the countryside and small towns, but in key suburban counties.

It's that friable middle class and its sensitivity to class status that Fussell speaks of that explains Trump as much as the voting habits of any group. If the *Guardian* wanted to depict the typical Trump supporter, it would have done well to use a photograph of a socially and economically insecure middle-class man driving a Range Rover while turned out in a Tommy Bahama shirt and Titleist cap. As Zito (2017) notes, "The people who live in those outer rings of cities aren't just separated by geography; they're separated by culture, traditions and aspirations that differ from those of their city cousins." They are like Hyacinth Bucket, though not nearly as endearing, anxiously clawing their way into the fold of people like Trump who have made it. Yet it is the white working class that gets the blame for the disaster that is Trump:

> Because "class" had for so long been a forbidden word within the political establishment, the only inequalities discussed by politicians and the media were racial ones. The white working class had become another marginalized ethnic minority, and this meant that all their concerns were understood solely through the prism of race. They became presented as a lost tribe on the wrong side of history, disorientated by multiculturalism and obsessed with defending their identity from the cultural ravages of mass immigration. The rise of the idea of a "white working class" fueled a new liberal bigotry. It was OK to hate the white working class, because they were themselves a bunch of racist bigots. (O. Jones 2016, Kindle locations 753–761)

This form of class hatred has become an integral, respectable part of modern British culture, one found in newspapers, television comedy shows (Onslow here), films, blogs, social networking sites, and everyday conversations (719–723). And in America, reporters, anthropologists, and sociologists write about the white working class as if it were an exotic culture (Frank 2004; Bageant 2007; Zernike 2012; Skocpol and Williamson 2012; Hamper 1991; Lamont 2002).

This for me points to the more important form of isolation experienced by bright working-class students. They remain socially isolated and too often scorned and dismissed. Their isolation is phenomenological and not merely a matter of geographic isolation, though the two often accompany one another. The barriers standing before working-class students to a four-year college, prestigious or otherwise, do not typically come in the form of ancient wooden doors set in Medieval masonry walls. They are psychological and reinforced by years of conditioning that tells even the brightest and most ambitious working-class student, "You do not belong here." This is the social space that exists for working-class Americans today. Boundary spaces are often contested and experienced with apprehension and fear, or at least confusion. The public narrative about the white working class has of late put up additional obstacles to the successful navigation of the boundary spaces of class in America. As Berger and Luckmann (1966) observe, people and groups interacting in a social system create stable concepts of one others' actions, and these concepts are habituated into reciprocal roles. Habituated roles create the contours of borders and boundaries that come with attendant expectations and customs associated with nation, race, gender, age, and class. Borders and boundaries are attended to by guardians, including admissions officers at universities. These guardians remind the one attempting to cross the boundary of what will be expected when he or she takes on a new role. I propose this as an interpretation of the experience of university education for white working-class Americans today.

Conclusion

This chapter begins with an epistemological and methodological proposition. I claim that the semiotic turn in anthropology offers the best chance of differentiating the winks from the eyelid contractions in the Ryle-Geertz analogy. I suggest that culture is found in the constructed meaning assigned by participants to social patterns and behaviors found in society, including their own, and that particular moments or relations—the heightened awareness experienced in boundary spaces—are best suited to discovering important distinctions. In such places, untangling the multiplicity of complex, superimposed conceptual structures—thick description—is most likely to come before the observer.

We see so little of that sort of analysis today by intellectuals and political pundits. The vitriolic reaction to white working-class Trump voters raises an important question: Why do so many intellectuals, often privileged by both race and class (the latter sometimes vouchsafed by academic tenure), seem to look at events with so much more race guilt than class guilt and animus? Why is there so little empathy for the white working class? Is it because too many of us do not know anyone in the working class, including the janitor who pushes the broom around in the evening after most of us have gone home for the day?

Joe Bageant's (2007) *Deer Hunting with Jesus: Dispatches from America's Class War* offers a model for the sort of sensitive interpretive analysis that Geertz calls for. Returning after thirty years to "dirt-poor" Winchester, Virginia, Bageant examines the lives of the working poor, including members of his own family. As with Vance's *Hillbilly Elegy*, Bageant draws on his own life experiences to chronicle the boundary spaces between the people of Winchester and those of the middle and upper classes that inhabit the growing number of exurb communities reaching toward the Blue Ridge Mountains along the I-66 corridor from Washington, DC. Unlike Vance, Bageant is not judgmental and demeaning of those he describes. He paints a picture of a permanent underclass that is taken advantage of by the Republican Party and Fox News but disdained by Democrats and liberal intellectuals. In so doing, he plumbs the full expanse of the boundary spaces separating his friends and family from their presumed better sorts. I believe this is the sort of respectful, thoughtful, lived ethnography that separates good from thin—and perhaps even damaging—use of culture as an analytic device for scholarship.

Notes

1. For an extended and erudite discussion of the experience of the "other," see Said 1994.

2. The lyrics to "Green Acres," by Vic Mizzy, are available at https://www.lyricsondemand.com/tvthemes/greenacreslyrics.html.

3. Lambeau is played by Swedish actor Stellan John Skarsgård. His accent and confident bearing underscores the role of language in the navigation of social space, a point that is signaled for a third time in the movie by British actor Minnie Driver. Driver's posh British accent and her enrollment at Harvard University demarcate her place in social space relative to Damon's Southie brogue and broom.

4. In 2013, Flint was declared the most dangerous city in the United States, with 2,729.5 violent crimes per 100,000 residents. With a population of 101,632 people that year, it had 63 murders and 1,930 aggravated assaults (MarketWatch 2013).

7 Ideology, Economic Interests, and American Exceptionalism

The Case of Export Credit

Kristen Hopewell

EXPORT CREDIT, AN IMPORTANT BUT UNDERSTUDIED AREA OF trade policy, has recently emerged as a major subject of political contestation within the United States and competition among states internationally. As one of the primary tools used by states to enhance the competitiveness of their exports, export credit—the use of loans and other forms of financing by states to boost exports—has taken on renewed strategic importance in the wake of the 2008 global financial crisis, with states focused on expanding exports to bolster economic growth and employment. States around the world have been aggressively expanding their provision of export credit, led most strikingly by an explosion in the use of export credit by the BRICs (Brazil, Russia, India, and China).

Amid this trend, the United States is a significant outlier, moving in the opposite direction of eliminating or severely circumscribing its use of state-backed export credit. Once an obscure bureaucratic agency, virtually unknown to the general public, the Export-Import Bank of the United States (EXIM) burst onto the public stage, becoming a highly contentious focus of national political debate. The Tea Party made the bank a prime target of its campaign to dramatically reduce the size of government and its role in the economy. As a result, EXIM was forced to cease all operations for five months in 2015, and the vast majority of its lending activity (approximately 85 percent) was blocked for nearly four years.

This chapter analyzes the sources and implications of American excep-tionalism in the area of export credit. As I show, the US case is puzzling be-cause not only is the United States unique in unilaterally constraining its use of export credit, but in doing so, it is relinquishing an important industrial policy tool: the restriction of export credit undermines the ability of US firms and industries to compete in critical sectors and encourages the offshoring of advanced, high-value-added manufacturing and related activities. Why then has the United States moved in the opposite direction of other states and taken steps that many consider an act of economic self-sabotage? I ar-gue that American exceptionalism on export credit cannot be understood without reference to culture, specifically the spread of an ultra-free-market ideology predicated on the denial and erasure of the role of an active state and industrial policy in driving the United States' economic success. Market fundamentalist ideology has shaped the construction of American economic interests and preferences in the area of export credit, leading to policy outputs that depart radically from other states.[1]

While often overlooked in conventional analyses of international trade politics, the case of export credit highlights the role of culture in shaping the formation of economic interests and preferences in trade policy. Following from the sociological and anthropological approach to culture laid out in Chapter 1, culture can be understood in the broadest sense as public mean-ings that enable groups of people to make sense of the world and that in turn orient their actions. Ideology, as a form of human meaning-making, is thus an important part of culture. By focusing on the role of culture in explaining American exceptionalism on export credit, this is not to deny the importance of other factors: as the following analysis shows, the institutional and material resources of the Tea Party have undoubtedly played a major role in enabling it to exert such immense influence over US policy, but its campaign against EXIM is driven by ideology. Although a state's trade policy is commonly as-sumed to be a reflection of its underlying economic interests, the case of ex-port credit underscores the fact that such interests are not predefined (see also J. P. Singh's discussion of North-South trade relations in Chapter 1). Eco-nomic interests and policy preferences are not simply the product of material forces but socially constructed, with the result that cultural forces such as ideology play a significant role in shaping how a state's economic interests are defined and interpreted.

Ideology, Industrial Policy, and American Hegemony

There has been a resurgence of interest in industrial policy—policies designed to promote the competitiveness of a country's firms and industries (Rodrik 2008; Stiglitz, Esteban, and Lin 2013). Among advanced industrialized states, this interest has been fueled by concerns about their declining share of global manufacturing amid growing competition from emerging economies, such as China (Figure 7.1) (Warwick 2013; OECD 2013). Many states are increasingly seeking to use the policy tools at their disposal to actively intervene in markets to promote the competitiveness of their firms and industries and thereby boost exports, employment, and growth (Lazonick 2008; Robinson 2011).

Yet amid what has been described as a "renaissance of interest in industrial policy" (Warwick 2013, 47), the United States is unique in constraining the use of an important industrial policy tool—export credit. By restricting its own use of export credit, the United States has hampered the ability of its firms and industries to compete in key sectors. In the name of free markets, the United States has tied its own hands—restraining the scope for the state

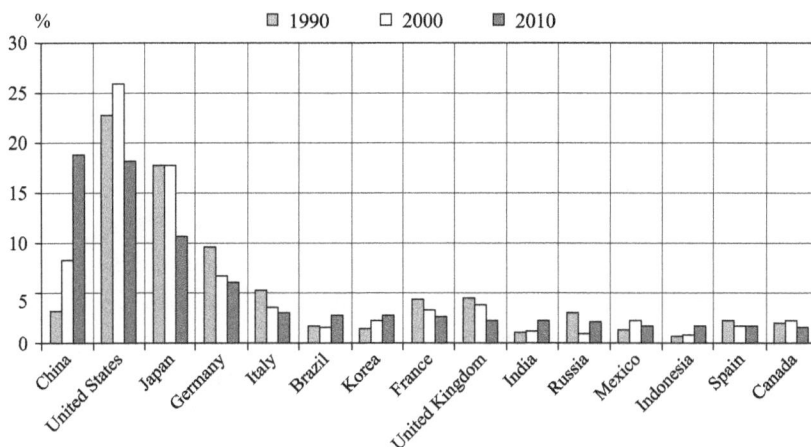

FIGURE 7.1 Percent share of global manufacturing, selected years.
SOURCE: Data from Organization for Economic Co-operation and Development *OECD.Stat* database, at https://stats.oecd.org; United Nations *National Accounts Main Aggregates Database*, at http://unstats.un.org/unsd/snaama/Introduction.asp.
NOTE: Manufacturing in this figure refers to industries belonging to International Standard Industrial Classification (ISIC) divisions 15–37.

to intervene in markets to promote US economic interests—not because it was compelled to by external forces but because of constraints imposed by a powerful internal domestic political movement, the Tea Party, in the thrall of market fundamentalist ideology. I argue that two intersecting ideological currents—related to the role of the state in the US economy and the sources and extent of American power in the international system—have helped give rise to and fueled the campaign against EXIM.

First, the Tea Party's campaign against EXIM is rooted in a failure to recognize and appreciate the role of an active state and industrial policy in building US economic supremacy—and, by extension, its political dominance. Despite trumpeting the virtues of unfettered markets, the United States has always made use of industrial policy, and, indeed, this has been critical to its economic success (Lazonick 2008; Schrank and Whitford 2009; Weiss 2014). Thus, as Fred Block and Matthew Keller argue, "prevailing accounts of the US as a liberal market economy are deeply misleading" (2014, 20). The United States—like all other successful developers—has exemplified the vital role of the state in supporting industrial development (Chang 2002; OECD 2013; Warwick 2013). Yet this reality is systematically erased by the prevailing ideology that obscures the true underpinnings of US economic power. Within American popular discourse, there is a collective "amnesia" about the contribution of government to America's economic success as a result of a deliberate campaign to delegitimize the role of an active state (Hacker and Pierson 2016, 89). In the words of Block, proponents of market fundamentalism created "a fictive American past in which the substantial economic role played by government—from the founding—was made to disappear" (2011, 4). Unlike many states that are more open and explicit about their developmental agendas, the US developmental state has been largely hidden and invisible to mainstream public debate (Block 2011).

Second, the Tea Party's anti-EXIM campaign is also tied to a fictitious idea of how America obtained its global economic and political dominance, shaped by what Jeff Faux calls the United States' "national delusion of exceptionalism"—faith in America's natural, inherent superiority and the belief that, in a fair game with a level playing field, the United States will inevitably prevail (2012, 47). This view is widely found throughout American political discourse. President Barack Obama in his 2012 State of the Union Address, for example, asserted, "Our workers are the most productive on Earth, and if the playing field is level, I promise you: America will always win"

(Faux 2012, 47). This stance cuts across the political spectrum, with Obama's statement echoing those of earlier presidents, such as George W. Bush, who similarly proclaimed in his 2006 State of the Union, "With open markets and a level playing field, no one can outproduce or outcompete the American worker" (Faux 2012, 47). The assumption that the United States will always triumph in a world of free markets belies the fact that the United States gained its economic supremacy not through free markets and open competition but through an interventionist state actively engaged in fostering its economic development, and the United States consolidated its dominant position not through a level playing field but by using its hegemonic position to tilt the rules of the multilateral trading system in its favor (Wilkinson 2011).

The Tea Party's effort to eliminate US export credit—a product of its broader antipathy toward the state—rests on a lack of recognition that without an active state, the US position in the global economy will be weakened. The Tea Party attack on EXIM is also shaped by an overestimation of the United States' current power in international affairs, manifest in the assumption that either other countries will follow its example by restricting their own use of export credit or that the United States will be able to force them to do so. This can be seen as a form of hegemonic hubris—an excessive confidence in the United States' ability to dominate the global economy and its governance and a failure to recognize the extent to which it is being diminished by contemporary power shifts.

The Battle over EXIM

Export credit represents an instance of US industrial policy being made the subject of intense public debate. In this section, following a brief discussion of the changing global political economy of export credit, I turn to examine the origins and impact of the Tea Party's campaign against EXIM. I make the case that the Tea Party's opposition to EXIM is rooted in an ideologically driven faith in free markets and the continued inevitability of US power. As I show, the Tea Party's effort to dismantle the bank—and ultimately other elements of US industrial policy—threatens to undermine US manufacturing competitiveness in the face of rising challengers. Regardless of the specific fate of the Tea Party as a political movement, or of EXIM, these ideological and political forces have deep roots and widespread popular support and are therefore likely to remain prominent and continue to shape American public policy for some

time (concerning the impact of another conservative ideological movement—
the religious right—on contemporary American politics, see Chapter 8).

The Global Political Economy of Export Credit

Every major economy has an export credit agency (ECA) that provides various forms of financing to facilitate and expand exports, including direct loans
to foreign buyers, insurance and loan guarantees, working capital financing,
and finance for large-scale infrastructure and industrial projects. Official
export credit occupies a crucial niche, filling gaps in, or helping bolster the
availability of, private financing. ECAs are heavily involved, for example, in
long-term export financing, including financing for complex, multibillion-
dollar sales such as aircraft and infrastructure projects. In such sectors, ECA
support can help make transactions more commercially attractive by mitigat-
ing risks of financing or by providing another source of funding to diversify
risks. As Andrew Moravcsik states, export credit is "the financial lubricant
that keeps the international trade system going" (1989, 176). Approximately
sixty ECAs are in operation globally, providing $300 billion in trade-related
finance annually (Akhtar 2015).

For many countries, state provision of export credit is a core part of their
industrial policy and national export strategies. The importance of export
credit has only been amplified since the global financial crisis. During the
crisis, when the availability of commercial credit contracted dramatically,
government-backed export credit played a critical role in filling the gap in
trade finance and keeping international trade moving, preventing the financial crisis from spiraling into a worldwide depression (Auboin 2015). The en-
suing implementation of new Basel III financial regulations diminished the
availability of private lending for certain forms of trade, increasing the need
for state-backed export credit (Akhtar 2015). Even the World Bank (1993) and
the WTO—long-standing champions of free market economics—recognize
state-backed export credit as an important industrial policy and development
tool, as well as a means to address market failure and a vital source of coun-
tercyclical lending. As one WTO official summarized, "It simply makes sense
for ECAs to play a role in financing trade."[2]

EXIM was created as part of the New Deal in 1934. In FY2014, EXIM authorized more than 3,700 transactions totaling $20.5 billion, which supported
$27.5 billion worth of exports and 164,000 jobs (EXIM 2014). It is a small gov-
ernment agency with less than four hundred staff that regularly generates

revenue; in 2014, for example, EXIM contributed $675 million to the US Treasury. To illustrate of how it operates, EXIM supports the American aerospace sector by supplying financing to facilitate the sale of Boeing jets to foreign buyers. Given the size of these transactions, the purchasing airlines usually require loans to make the purchase possible. EXIM can step in to provide direct loans when commercial financing is unavailable or to guarantee (and thereby reduce the cost of) commercial loans. Aerospace is just one industry supported by EXIM and its counterparts around the world.

The global landscape of export credit has changed profoundly with the rise of the BRICs. Since 2000, export credit provision by the BRICs has surged from less than 3 percent to 40 percent of the world total (EXIM 2015). The vast majority has come from China, which constitutes 90 percent of the export credit activity of the BRIC countries and is now the world's largest export credit provider. In 2014, China supplied $58 billion in medium- and long-term export credit support—far more than the $12 billion provided by the United States and, indeed, more than all the wealthy G7 countries combined—and an additional $43 billion in overseas investment financing to promote its exports (EXIM 2015) (Figure 7.2).

China is aggressively using export credit to foster industrial upgrading and the global expansion of its firms. Export credit has been the driving

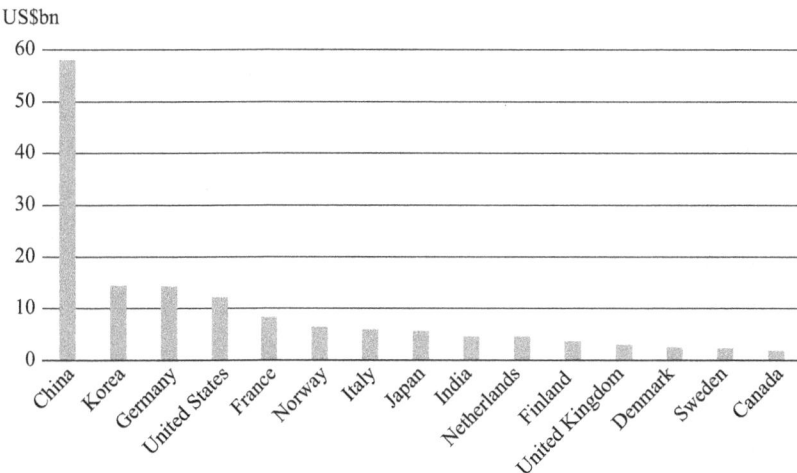

FIGURE 7.2 Official export credit volumes, 2014 (in billions of US dollars).
SOURCE: EXIM 2015.

force, for example, behind the much-reported expansion of China's activities in Africa, Latin America, and elsewhere; while often mistakenly described as aid, most of China's foreign lending is, in fact, export credit—loans tied to the export of Chinese goods (Bräutigam 2009). Export credit is a central part of China's strategy to escape the middle-income trap by transitioning from exporting consumer to capital goods. Although smaller in scale, the other emerging economies use export financing strategically in key sectors to significant effect (such as Brazil in construction, Russia in nuclear energy, and India in transportation and energy). The dramatic expansion in the use of official export credit by China and the other BRICs poses a serious competitive challenge to the United States and other traditional powers. Beyond the BRICs, most other major economies are significantly expanding their export credit offerings to enable their firms and industries to better compete in global markets (Hopewell 2019).

The Rise of the Tea Party

The Tea Party has emerged as a potent force in US politics, transforming the American political landscape. It is made up of a combination of forces—grassroots activists, advocacy organizations backed by ideologically motivated wealthy donors, and influential right-wing media outlets. The Tea Party burst onto the scene in early 2009, prompted by the election of Obama and Democratic majorities in the House and Senate (Ashbee 2011; Maxwell and Parent 2012). The movement was propelled by fears on the right that Obama and the Democrats would reshape US policies by tightening regulations, raising taxes, and expanding social programs, as well as by anger at the bank bailouts and stimulus package triggered by the financial crisis (Skocpol and Williamson 2012; Van Dyke and Meyer 2016). The emergence of the Tea Party was thus, in part, a response to the more assertive and visible use of industrial policy by the United States (Schrank and Whitford 2009). It is estimated that close to a quarter of the US population supports the movement or evaluates it positively (Barreto et al. 2011).

Among the leading funders of the Tea Party are billionaires David and Charles Koch—tied as the fifth wealthiest individuals in the United States—who have been highly active in financing ultra-free-market political campaigns (Mayer 2016). The Koch brothers organized a network of wealthy conservative donors, channeling hundreds of millions of dollars to an integrated set of libertarian, antigovernment political organizations. As Theda

Skocpol and Alexander Hertel-Fernandez document (Skocpol 2016; Skocpol and Hertel-Fernandez 2016), the Koch network has worked to penetrate and capture the Republican Party and pull its agenda to the right on political-economic issues. Americans for Prosperity, the hub of the Koch network, is now thoroughly intertwined with the Republican Party. For candidates seeking support from the Koch network—whose vast financial and staff resources now exceed those of the Republican Party itself—the price is accepting its ultra-free-market policy agenda. The Koch network monitors the activities of Republicans in Congress to ensure that their legislative agendas and votes match its preferred positions. Those who are not sufficiently aligned with its agenda risk being unseated in primary campaigns, as the Koch network backs challengers espousing more extreme free market views. The Koch network has thus played a major role in the extraordinary rise and political influence of the Tea Party and driving Republican candidates and officeholders toward increasingly extreme economic positions.

The Kochs obtained their fortunes from Koch Industries, a large industrial conglomerate with substantial oil and gas operations, and most of the other network participants similarly derived their wealth from businesses. There are some complementarities between the business interests of network participants and the agenda that the network seeks to advance, such as reducing taxes, loosening government regulations, undermining labor unions, and opposing environmental regulations. Yet, drawing on an extensive study of the Koch network, Hertel-Fernandez and Skocpol (2016) argue against a reductionist interpretation that equates its political objectives solely with the interests of Koch Industries or the company ties of other wealthy donors in the network. Propelled by a deep antipathy toward the state, its political advocacy goes beyond "mere corporate self-interest," pursuing many causes far beyond the narrow scope of its business interests—and even some that contradict those business interests, such as opposing tax cuts and subsidies for the private sector. While the interests of mainstream business and the Koch network align on certain issues, "the Koch network promotes a much more sweeping, ideologically inspired free-market agenda" (Hertel-Fernandez and Skocpol 2016).

The Tea Party Campaign Against EXIM

The Tea Party campaign against EXIM began in 2010, when Republicans won control of Congress. Organizations advocating a free market agenda—

including Americans for Prosperity, Club for Growth, Heritage Action, Cato Foundation, Mercatus Center, and American Enterprise Institute, many of which were created and/or backed by the Koch network—began mobilizing opposition to EXIM and made abolishing the bank one of their key political goals. This was a top-down initiative, orchestrated by Koch-funded groups, rather than arising from the grass roots; indeed, most Tea Party members had never even heard of EXIM before. As one organization representative described, "We launched a major grassroots education campaign. When we first started, people didn't even know what EXIM was. They had no idea what we were talking about. Folks would say, 'Huh? What's wrong with FM radio?'"[3] Through this grassroots mobilization led by influential promarket groups, "EXIM became the cause célèbre" of the Tea Party as the movement gained prominence in Washington.[4]

Although the bank has periodically been subject to criticism from free market conservatives, in the past any such opposition had been overcome by the bank's powerful supporters in industry and Congress and never substantially disrupted its functioning (Becker and McClenahan 2003). This changed with the rise of the Tea Party. EXIM is authorized by sunset legislation that requires regular congressional reauthorization; unless legislation to renew its charter is approved by Congress, the institution expires. For nearly eighty years, Congress had routinely reauthorized the bank's charter, usually with little or no controversy. However, the Tea Party began mobilizing opposition toward EXIM in advance of its 2012 reauthorization. Although the bank was reauthorized by Congress, the Tea Party succeeded in limiting its authorization to two years, rather than the normal five—ensuring that the fight over the bank's existence continued without pause while the Tea Party campaign against it gained momentum and grew in strength. Subsequently, when the bank's authorization expired on June 30, 2015, the Tea Party used its sway in Congress to block reauthorization.

The Tea Party objects to EXIM as a deviation from free markets, arguing that it represents "crony capitalism" and "corporate welfare."[5] The bank's opponents contend that government support for business and exports is "unnecessary" and "inefficient" (Mercatus Center 2014), and as Senator Marco Rubio puts it, "the government shouldn't be picking winners and losers" (Raju and Everett 2015). According to Representative Jeb Hensarling (TX), then chair of the House Financial Services Committee, which has jurisdiction over the bank, and one of its most powerful opponents in Congress:

The best way to level the playing field for American exporters and manufacturers is not with taxpayer subsidies, guarantees and politically driven lending, but instead with more opportunity. . . . A pro-growth agenda—including fundamental tax reform, American energy independence, cutting burdensome red tape and reducing abusive lawsuits—will do more to help our exporters, manufacturers and small businesses than the Export-Import Bank ever could. (Weisman 2015)

Critics complain that the bank interferes with the market and forces US taxpayers to assume the risks of foreign loans that should be the responsibility of the private sector. They further protest that EXIM uses American taxpayers' money, in the words of Hensarling, "to help foreign corporations, including businesses that are owned by the governments of China, Russia, Saudi Arabia and the United Arab Emirates" (Weisman 2015). The Tea Party contends that American economic success is rooted in free markets: as one representative stated, "I don't think we've ever benefited in any market by taking a protectionist stance. We protect our markets by building better products."[6] And, in the absence of EXIM, the Tea Party maintains that "the free market will step in."[7] Those seeking to eliminate the bank express confidence in the competitiveness of US industry: to quote Republican Study Committee chair Bill Flores (TX), "We know American businesses are capable of competing in a free and open market, without government interfering" (Cirilli 2015).

The campaign against EXIM is not just about the bank itself but about legitimating the Tea Party's broader campaign to restrict the role of government. In the words of Senator Ted Cruz (TX),

If we're to have credibility on reforming government across the board, if we are to have credibility on reforming welfare, to get off of dependency and get back on our own feet, we need to demonstrate as a first step that we can wean giant corporations of that same dependency of the federal government. (Raju and Everett 2015)

EXIM was chosen strategically to show that the Tea Party is going after all forms of welfare, not just those targeting the poor and middle class. As a representative of Heritage Action stated, "If you're going to be successful in reforming entitlements, you don't have moral credibility if you don't take on corporate welfare—and you can't do better than Exim" (Mascaro 2015). The campaign against EXIM is explicitly intended to build a new "free market populism" on the right (Carney 2011).

The Tea Party's credibility as a popular grassroots movement had been tarnished by its financing by the billionaire Koch brothers. Targeting EXIM, however, enabled the Tea Party to deflect such criticism by presenting itself as leading the charge against big business. Similarly, for Republicans, according to Hensarling, "this is an important fight for our party to have" because "we have been tagged as the party to some extent of big business" (Bair 2015). Going after public subsidies to big business resonated strongly in the aftermath of the financial crisis, with the Tea Party's campaign against EXIM feeding off public outrage at the bailouts of Wall Street banks and the auto industry. The EXIM campaign generated flattering headlines for the Tea Party and its supporters in Congress (such as "Smackdown: Conservatives vs. Big Business" in *Newsweek* [Cadei 2015] and "Jeb Hensarling Takes a Swing at Corporate Welfare" in *Fortune* [Blair 2015]) while enabling the Tea Party to turn the tables and paint its opponents (whether Democrats or moderate Republicans) as the handmaidens of big business.

The Tea Party mobilized its considerable political machinery in opposition to EXIM, including organizing educational and political action campaigns directed at its grassroots supporters (which in the case of Americans for Prosperity alone consists of 2.8 million members); holding town hall meetings across the country; using its considerable financial resources for large-scale advertising campaigns, such as hostile TV ads against Republicans who had not come out in opposition to the bank; disseminating report cards evaluating Republican candidates on where they stood on EXIM; lobbying members of Congress and their staff in their districts; and directing lobbying on Capitol Hill.[8] As a representative of Americans for Prosperity described, "This little never-heard-of bank, it became kind of a litmus test for people who wanted to prove their potential free-market bona fides" (Mascaro 2015). The reach and influence of the Tea Party put immense pressure on Republican members of Congress and presidential candidates to oppose EXIM reauthorization.

Billionaires Versus Big Business

EXIM has extensive support from the business community. In response to the Tea Party, business actors united in a massive campaign to defend the bank. As one representative bluntly stated, "We've had to wage a full-scale frontal assault."[9] Given that the Tea Party campaign against EXIM has been primarily bankrolled by the Koch brothers and other wealthy donors, one representative of US industry captured the unusual nature of the resulting face-off as "billionaires versus big business."[10] The bank's supporters argue that it plays a vital role in facilitating US exports and supporting US jobs. They point out that the risk to taxpayers is minimal—the bank has a default rate of well below 1 percent, lower than most commercial banks, and a high recovery rate. Since EXIM charges interest and fees, it generates revenue for the American government, sending $6.9 billion in profits to the Treasury over the last two decades. Its supporters argue that eliminating EXIM will put US firms and industries at a competitive disadvantage and cause US corporations to lose global market share. In short, to quote the United States' former lead trade negotiator, Ron Kirk, "You have all of those interests saying, 'Wait a minute, this is critically important to us'" (Mascaro 2015).

In fact, for many years business actors have been seeking to expand the resources and scope of the bank to enable the United States to better keep pace with its competitors. According to a representative of US industry, "We'd like the bank to be put on steroids."[11] Relative to the magnitude of US exports, EXIM's funding authority has sharply declined over the past forty years, and the United States has fallen behind other states in the provision of export credit (Hufbauer, Fickling, and Wong 2011). South Korea, for example, now provides more than twice as much support to its exporters, even though the US economy is ten times larger and exports three times more (EXIM 2015). In addition, the export credit provided by other states is generally more flexible, less restrictive, and less cumbersome and difficult to access, making US financing less competitive. Consequently, prior to the explosion of controversy surrounding reauthorization, many actors—including the Obama administration and some members of Congress—had called for increasing the bank's lending ceiling, making its lending policies less restrictive, and expanding coverage to encompass a broader range of exports such as services (Bergsten 2014; Hufbauer, Fickling, and Wong 2011). Ultimately, however, the objective of reforming US export credit to "fight fire with fire" (Bergsten 2014) was eclipsed by the struggle to simply keep the bank alive in the face of the Tea Party challenge.

For many American policy makers, officials, and business actors, the controversy surrounding EXIM came as a shock. According to Kirk, "It caught a lot of people off guard. . . . I don't think anyone believed it would grow to this extreme" (Mascaro 2015). America's corporate leaders express bewilderment

at the storm of opposition to EXIM's reauthorization and the extreme difficulties they have faced attempting to secure the continued functioning of the
bank. As one business representative explained:

> The Tea Party has got a whole army working on this. They put out so much
> misinformation—they pump out this stuff like it's coming out of a firehose.
> We can't keep up with this—the whole coalition [of business actors support-
> ing EXIM] can't keep up with this. People say, "Corporations rule America,"
> but look at this. This has been a massive effort: every Fortune 100 company is
> around the table at NAM [National Association of Manufacturers] or the US
> Chamber [of Commerce]; we've had daily conference calls for a year on this, all
> kinds of consulting firms on hire, working full time on this; we've had fly-ins
> bringing hundreds of people in to lobby on Capitol Hill. This whole situation
> is "through the looking-glass"! You have all of corporate America and all of
> the Democrats and a sizable number of Republicans and the White House—
> and we *still* can't get it done. Who would dream we couldn't get it with all this
> backing?[12]

Another echoed this sentiment: "We're just left saying to ourselves, 'What the
hell is going on here?' We've been crying our heads off, but we've been almost
completely hamstrung politically."[13] Remarkably, business found its economic
interests being overridden by the ultra-free-market ideology of the Tea Party.
This was all the more surprising because, as one industry lobbyist stated,
"We're usually the darlings of conservatives and most Republicans—we get
fierce championing and support from Republicans."[14] But even Republicans
who have traditionally been allies of business and privately support EXIM are
hesitant to champion it publicly, fearing the political heat from the Tea Party.
In the current political climate, a business representative explained, "no one
on Capitol Hill wants to hear from large companies anymore—to represent
large companies on Capitol Hill is to put a target on your back."[15]

The Disruption of US Export Credit

The EXIM fight created a deep split among Republicans. Although the majority of Republicans in Congress continued to support the bank, the Tea Party
campaign against EXIM gained the support of most congressional Republican leaders, as well as the majority of Republicans on the pivotal House Financial Services Committee, which has responsibility for reauthorization of

the bank in the lower chamber. EXIM also became a focal issue in the 2016 presidential primaries. As a result of pressure from the Tea Party, virtually every Republican presidential candidate campaigned against the bank—with candidates devoting entire speeches to this once obscure agency. With its significant political clout, the Tea Party succeeded in preventing congressional reauthorization of the bank's statutory charter, forcing it to shut down and cease issuing new loans as of July 2015. Approximately two hundred transactions worth more than $9 billion were stopped in the pipeline. Only in December of that year, through a rare procedural maneuver, were its advocates able to pass a four-year reauthorization for the bank.

Even though EXIM was reopened, its operations still remained sharply constrained. For nearly four years, Tea Party–aligned members of the Senate blocked appointments to EXIM's board of directors, leaving the bank without the quorum necessary to approve any transaction over $10 million. EXIM could only approve small export deals, not large orders for goods like aircraft, satellites, and major manufacturing equipment. This had a significant impact on the workings of the bank because large deals constitute 80 to 90 percent of its loans, and it left major exporters like Boeing, General Electric, and Caterpillar without access to official export credit in the United States. The bank's full lending power was not reinstated until May 2019, when the Senate finally confirmed three new board members and restored its quorum. However, after just four months of being restored to full operations, the bank's new charter expired in September 2019, and it once more became the subject of a renewed fight over reauthorization and faced being shut down again unless reauthorized by Congress. The bank was ultimately reauthorized for seven years in December 2019.

The Tea Party has been highly satisfied with the results of its campaign against the bank: as one representative stated, "This is the most successful campaign we've ever had."[16] The Tea Party has vowed to continue fighting the bank, using its influence in Congress to tie up EXIM in continual battles for its reauthorization while limiting its scope and operations such that it is too encumbered to function effectively. As one industry representative summed up, "They will continue to do everything they can to gut the bank."[17] For nearly a decade, the battle over the future of EXIM has consumed an enormous amount of time, energy, and resources—of the bank's staff, American policy makers and political leaders, and the country's major business actors—and the conflict shows no signs of abating.

Implications for American Manufacturing

The Tea Party's continuing offensive against EXIM has potentially significant implications for the United States' advanced manufacturing industries. US spending on export credit is already dwarfed by China, and eliminating EXIM would make the United States the only major economy in the world without an ECA. Eliminating EXIM or constraining its room to maneuver threatens to seriously impede the ability of US firms to compete in key sectors. While the bank only supports a relatively small percentage of US exports (about 2 percent), its financing is concentrated in capital equipment and services (so-called big-ticket exports): aircraft, satellites, transportation equipment, large agricultural equipment, product-manufacturing machinery, oil and gas, mining, power plants, and major infrastructure projects. In these sectors, exports represent a significant proportion of output, and EXIM supports a far greater proportion of exports. These capital goods sectors—technology-intensive and high-value-added—are a cornerstone of the advanced manufacturing activity that remains in the United States, along with associated engineering, research and development, and other high-value services. These are also precisely the sectors that China is moving into as it seeks to develop more advanced industries and foster the global expansion of its firms (Hopewell 2018). More than half of EXIM's financing, for example, goes to infrastructure projects, primarily in emerging economies, an area where China is an increasingly prominent global player. China's goal is to become a major competitor to the United States and other rich countries in advanced manufacturing within the next decade, and its strategy of using export credit to foster industrial development is proving remarkably successful: as one official stated, "In almost every capital goods sector, China is going from a bit player to being one of the biggest."[18]

The Tea Party contends that companies should seek private financing rather than rely on a government agency; however, private financing is more costly than the lower rates offered by ECAs, and in emerging markets bidders are often required to supply ECA financing. Consequently, eliminating EXIM financing increases the incentive for many of the largest US firms to shift their sourcing and production to foreign countries where they can secure ECA support, with consequent losses to the US manufacturing base and employment. State-backed export credit is particularly important in facilitating sales to emerging markets, where less-developed banking and capital markets limit the availability of private financing. Emerging markets now account for the majority of global economic growth, and China, in particular, is making aggressive use of export credit in these markets as a platform to expand its global presence and market share (Bräutigam 2009). A director of Acrow Corporation, an engineering company that makes prefabricated bridges exported to emerging economies, where customers cannot readily access private financing for large infrastructure projects without ECA backing, described eliminating EXIM as follows: "For us to pull another arrow out of our quiver, it's irrational, it's terrifying and it's inappropriate when one considers the reality of the global marketplace" (Weisman 2015).

In certain sectors, it is impossible to export without the backing of an ECA. This is the case, for example, in the market for building and operating nuclear power plants. As an industry representative explained:

> We simply cannot make a bid without ECA backing. It is often a tender requirement [i.e., a requirement to bid for a contract]. That doesn't mean you are automatically kicked out of a tender competition for noncompliance, but they could. And, if it's a nuclear reactor, you will be kicked out because you will never find a commercial bank that will finance building a nuclear plant for eighteen years.[19]

Because of their capital reserve requirements, commercial banks simply will not extend multibillion-dollar loans for such long periods: "EXIM will do eighteen years. Commercial banks can't even come close." The result, he continued, is that "for our industry, there's no question about it: if we lose EXIM, we're out of it. EXIM keeps us in the game. We can compete based on our other advantages, but not without this." For such companies, in the absence of EXIM financing, their only option is to relocate production abroad to gain access to foreign ECA support. According to one industry representative,

> A multinational like Westinghouse or GE will look out for itself and continue to compete. If it can't get ECA support here, it will source the content from somewhere else. So we'll see a shifting of content out of the US. Westinghouse might continue to win tender but without US content and US jobs.[20]

With rapidly growing demand for energy in emerging economies, the market for nuclear equipment and services will potentially reach $750 billion over the next decade (CSIS 2013). Without export credit support, the United States has been locking itself out of the global market and ceding the field to its competitors.

EXIM plays a similarly important role in supporting the US aerospace sector. Boeing is the United States' largest exporter and the largest recipient of EXIM financing, with the bank typically supporting about 10–15 percent of Boeing's aircraft sales. As of 2014, EXIM was supplying $32 billion in financing to support the export of Boeing's jets to buyers in thirty-four countries (US Government Accountability Office 2014). Not only does Boeing face intense competition from its European rival Airbus, which receives substantial ECA support, but China is also aggressively seeking to penetrate this sector. Aerospace is a priority area of China's industrial upgrading plans. Its aviation companies enjoy substantial state credit support from China's ECAs, and similar support was an essential factor in the emergence of Airbus as Boeing's main rival. By eliminating its use of export credit, the United States has thus been relinquishing an important tool for maintaining its competitive position in the aircraft sector.

The disruption of export credit has caused the United States to lose exports and employment, with foreign buyers turning to other suppliers that can offer ECA financing (Hopewell 2017). For example, prior to its shutdown, EXIM was supporting about 60 percent of sales by US satellite companies. Given the high cost of satellites, export credit financing is a key factor in choosing between US and other suppliers and often even a pass-or-fail criteria for satellite deals. Without access to EXIM financing, US firms have lost three preexisting satellite orders to competitors in Canada and France, which were able to provide ECA financing, causing the loss of hundreds of US jobs, and they have been locked out of competitions for new contracts where ECA support is an explicit bidding requirement (Calmes 2015).

American multinationals have been relocating production to countries where they can secure ECA support. General Electric, for example, one of the largest users of EXIM financing, was bidding on over $11 billion worth of projects requiring ECA support when the bank was shut down. Bids for these projects, primarily in emerging markets, will not be considered without the backing of an ECA. GE has therefore been striking agreements with foreign ECAs willing to finance its exports and shifting manufacturing from the United States to those countries. This has included moving production of underwater oil and gas equipment to Great Britain, along with a thousand jobs; production of gas-powered engines and three hundred fifty jobs to Canada; aircraft engine production to Canada; turboprop aircraft engine manufacturing and a thousand jobs to the Czech Republic; and five hundred jobs producing generators and aeroderivative turbines to France, Hungary, and

China (Calmes 2016). GE's motives are simple: "We're doing this because if we don't, we can't submit a valid tender" (Lawder 2015). For their part, countries on the receiving end of this investment freely acknowledge that they are benefiting from the disruption of the US Export-Import Bank: as one official stated, "Frankly, it's been great for us."[21] Constraints on export credit are thus contributing to diminishing the industrial base in the United States while strengthening that of its rivals.

While large multinationals are able to change their production strategies and relocate manufacturing production overseas to access ECA support, smaller US firms—and, of course, US workers—simply do not have that option. By limiting export credit, the United States has been directly undermining its own exports and jobs at a time when they are already under threat from emerging competitors (Chin and Gallagher 2015). As one US industry representative stated, "Eliminating EXIM will do in the last part of the US manufacturing sector, increasingly hollowing out the US export base. The consequences may take many years to appear, but that's what's coming."[22]

Confronted with the suggestion that eliminating EXIM would damage US competitiveness, given that its rivals are providing substantial amounts of export credit to their firms, Tea Party opponents are quick to dismiss such concerns. The following response, provided by the Club for Growth, is typical: "So what? If other nations engage in corporate welfare, that is no reason for the United States to follow suit in the name of a level playing field. We don't need to import other nations' bad policies" (Roth 2015). The Tea Party maintains that China only hurts its own economy by providing state-backed financing for its exports—based on the assumption that any state intervention inevitably creates inefficiencies that impede economic growth.[23] The Tea Party further claims that if the United States stopped its use of export credit, its resulting success would have a "demonstration effect," encouraging others to do the same.[24]

The Tea Party contends that eliminating EXIM would enable the United States to "lead by example" in efforts to eliminate government-backed ECA programs internationally and that the United States can use the existing system of global trade rules and disciplines to force other countries to cede their own use of export credit.[25] In reality, however, the United States has been trying for years to bring China and other emerging economies under international disciplines, but such efforts have been unsuccessful (Hopewell 2019). Given the centrality of export credit to their development strategies, the emerging economies have little incentive to relinquish their use of this tool.

A representative of the US Chamber of Commerce expressed it thus: "Their economies depend on their ECAs. I don't see a world where they're suddenly going to say, 'Okay, we don't need our ECAs.' That's just not realistic."[26] The same is true of the United States' other competitors—in the words of one US industry representative, "The notion that if we unilaterally disarm, we'd be better off is ridiculous. We're shooting ourselves in the foot right now. None of our trade competitors are going to pull back. They're doubling down on support while we're sitting here debating whether EXIM should exist."[27] The Tea Party's assertion that the United States can simply convince or compel other states to restrain their use of export credit thus reflects an unduly optimistic view of America's current power in the global political economy and its ability to shape the behavior of other states.

Conclusion

As this analysis shows, at a time when many states are increasing their use of export credit amid a widespread embrace of industrial policy, the United States is a conspicuous outlier. As a result of the Tea Party's ideologically driven campaign against EXIM, the United States' ability to use export credit to support its firms and exporters has been severely disrupted. By circumscribing the activities of its export credit agency, the United States has been undermining the competitiveness of important industrial sectors and contributing to the movement of advanced, high-value manufacturing abroad. The case of export credit thus illustrates how a powerful ideologically driven domestic political movement has shaped the construction or interpretation of US interests and policy preferences, leading to policy outputs that depart radically from other states and hamper the United States' ability to maintain its economic primacy in the face of new emerging challengers. Culture—specifically the antistate ideology of the Tea Party—plays a critical role in explaining American exceptionalism on export credit. This case thus demonstrates the importance of cultural forces, such as ideology, in the formation of economic interests and policy preferences in the area of trade.

Notes

Acknowledgment: This research was supported by an Economic and Social Research Council (ESRC) Future Research Leaders grant (ES/N017390/1).

1. The following analysis draws on Hopewell 2017. It is based on field research conducted between 2015 and 2016, primarily in Washington, DC, but also in Paris and Geneva, involving more than thirty-five interviews with representatives of the leading actors in the pro- and anti-EXIM campaigns (including Tea Party organizations, business associations, and nongovernmental organizations); US government officials and negotiators; and OECD, WTO, and foreign officials.

2. WTO official, interview by the author, Washington, DC, July 2016.

3. Tea Party representative, interview by the author, Washington, DC, July 2015.

4. Government official, interview by the author, Washington, DC, July 2015.

5. Tea Party representatives, interviews by the author, Washington, DC, July 2015.

6. Tea Party representative, interview by the author, Washington, DC, July 2015.

7. Tea Party representative, interview by the author, Washington, DC, July 2015.

8. Tea Party representatives, interviews by the author, Washington, DC, July 2015.

9. Business representative, interview by the author, Washington, DC, July 2015.

10. Industry representative, interview by the author, Washington, DC, July 2015.

11. Industry representative, interview by the author, Washington, DC, July 2015.

12. Business representative, interview by the author, Washington, DC, July 2015.

13. Business representative, interview by the author, Washington, DC, July 2015.

14. Industry lobbyist, interview by the author, Washington, DC, July 2015.

15. Business representative, interview by the author, Washington, DC, July 2015.

16. Tea Party representative, interview by the author, Washington, DC, July 2015.

17. Industry representative, interview by the author, Washington, DC, July 2015.

18. Trade official, interview by the author, Geneva, July 2016.

19. Industry representative, interview by the author, Washington, DC, July 2015.

20. Industry representative, interview by the author, Washington, DC, July 2015.

21. Foreign official, interview by the author, November 2016.

22. Industry representative, interview by the author, Washington, DC, July 2015.

23. Tea Party representative, interview by the author, Washington, July 2015.

24. Tea Party representative, interview by the author, Washington, DC, July 2015.

25. Tea Party representatives, interviews by the author, Washington, DC, July 2015.

26. US Chamber of Commerce representative, interview by the author, Washington, DC, July 2015.

27. Industry representative, interview by the author, Washington, DC, July 2015.

8 Strangest of Bedfellows

*Why the Religious Right Embraced Trump
and What That Means for the Movement*

Mark J. Rozell

THE 2016 PRESIDENTIAL CANDIDACY OF DONALD J. TRUMP POSED
a special challenge for many religiously motivated voters, especially those associated with the religious right movement that has long anchored the Republican Party. As a candidate for the Republican nomination, Trump advocated
strong socially conservative views, declared himself pro-life, and reveled in
the endorsements of such leading religious right figures as Phyllis Schlafly and
Jerry Falwell, Jr. (Weigel and Del Real 2016; Costa and Johnson 2016).

Yet for many religious conservatives, Trump—who is thrice married, had
carried out public extramarital affairs, is often crude and even vulgar in his
language, as well as formerly pro-choice and a contributor to Democratic candidates' political campaigns—lacked the personal character and political al-
legiance to the Republican Party to carry forward their cause. During the Republican presidential nomination process, several candidates had much more
credible credentials than Trump to seek the votes of religious conservatives.
More than the others, Senator Ted Cruz (TX) posed the most serious threat
to Trump's nomination and attracted the support of many religious conservatives, but ultimately Cruz's campaign also faded.

Even after he achieved the party nomination, many questioned whether
Trump could retain the kind of strong social conservative support that his
Republican presidential nominee predecessors had achieved. Some notable
religious right figures, such as Russell Moore and Michael Farris, spoke forcefully against Trump's candidacy throughout the election campaign (L. Turner

2016). That was understandable. When Trump ran for president, he admitted that he was not a regular attendee of religious services; he stated that he has never sought God's forgiveness; when asked to cite his favorite Bible verse or testament, he declined to answer; when he spoke at Liberty University, the nation's largest Christian university, he twice cursed (a violation of the university's student code), and he then referred to Second Corinthians as "Two Corinthians"—a gaffe that elicited laughter from many student attendees of the speech and was widely reported as evidence of his complete unfamiliarity with the common discourse of evangelical Christians (Taylor 2016).

Trump also struggled to articulate his views on some critical social issues, and sometimes his positions were out of sync with religious conservatives. Most prominently, at one point during the campaign, he suggested that women seeking abortions outside legal restrictions would have to be prosecuted—a position he later somewhat pulled back from (Flegenheimer and Haberman 2016). During the campaign he said that he was "fine" with gay marriage and called his own views "irrelevant" to the issue, given the decision of the Supreme Court to legalize same-sex unions (Stokols 2016). And then some religious conservatives declared that Trump simply was opportunistic in seeking their support and not sincere about any promise to promote a social conservative agenda. *National Review* writer Maggie Gallagher (2016) at one point predicted that "Trump is going to throw social issues under the bus" if elected.[1]

Nonetheless, religious conservatives voted overwhelmingly for Trump and were key to his victory in the general election. Despite his personal character, concerns about the authenticity of his social issues positions and about whether he would do as promised if elected, and his lack of comfort with evangelical discourse,[2] Trump won the white evangelical vote—the core of the religious right—with 81 percent, according to the major media exit poll (Huang et al. 2016).[3] He actually outperformed the unquestionably socially conservative past GOP presidential nominees Mitt Romney and George W. Bush. Impressive as well, he won the Catholic vote, which, unlike in several of the more recent presidential elections, broke more strongly in favor of the GOP nominee than the overall popular vote. Trump's 60–37 percent margin among white Catholics over Hillary Clinton anchored his 52–45 percent margin among all Catholics (Martínez and Smith 2016).

Culture and values were key to Trump's triumph of the religious right. He may not be the kind of politician whose personal conduct religious conservatives want to embrace, but on the key social and cultural issues of the day he has staked out positions consistent with the views of the religious right. Not to be underestimated is that in a binary choice election, his 2016 opponent, former secretary of state Hillary Clinton, personified for the religious right the progressive social values that they deplore.

Furthermore, in this campaign context, culture and values for many religious conservatives were about more than social issues. White evangelical and born-again Christians, the core of the religious right, have long been suspicious of globalization and multiculturalism. Trump's lambasting of various US trade agreements with international partners and his attacks on international organizations and agreements played very well with social conservatives who perceived the United States as a loser in the movement toward globalization. Similarly, evangelicals united behind Trump in their support for his anti-immigration platform and the promise to build a wall along the Mexican border. For them, international commerce, migration, and the perceived loss of US international dominance threatened Western culture and values. Evangelical support helped Trump cement his protectionist arguments with moral coatings such as America First or Make America Great Again.

The Religious Right and Trump: The Context

Most people outside of the religious right find the movement's embracing of Trump to be highly perplexing, even outright hypocritical. Indeed, in the late 1990s, religious conservative leaders and activists strongly advocated the impeachment of President Bill Clinton due, they claimed, to his deep character failings and misuses of power. Yet two decades later, the movement supported for president a man whose personal character flaws and misuses of power vastly exceed those of the former president. The easy conclusion is that the religious right is guilty of situational morality—standards apply differently, depending on who happens to hold power. No doubt that is accurate, but more of the context is needed to explain the shifting moral standards of the religious right.[4]

The social movement in the United States widely known as the religious right comprises a collection of socially conservative and politically active born-again and evangelical Christians, as well as some ultraconservative Catholics (Wilcox and Larson 2006, 6–9). Importantly, this movement comes out of a unique subculture in the United States that is intensely suspicious of mainstream political and social institutions and that rejects many of the conventional norms of a democratic society. At once, this subculture claims moral superiority in what it considers a corrupted society while pursuing access to levers of power in that society in order to conform the mainstream culture more to its own idealized image of the United States.

Not to be overlooked is the linkage of social and cultural issues to the broader economic factors that played a substantial role in religious conservative support for Trump. A strong basis of Trump's evangelical support in particular was his attacks on globalism, multiculturalism, and immigration as the causes of the decline of certain sectors of the US economy. His "make America great again" theme evoked for conservative evangelicals an idealized past American greatness, when the county was predominantly white, Christian, and not challenged economically by other rising nations. Also, white Catholic support substantially helped anchor Trump's triumph in some key Midwest and upper Midwestern states where his economic populist message resonated strongly in communities devastated by the decline of the manufacturing sectors (Kmiec 2018).

Thus, whereas social and cultural values largely drove religious conservative support for Trump in 2016, material factors also played an important role. Socially conservative Catholics no doubt favored Trump's pro-life positions, but many of these voters from working-class backgrounds had long supported Democrats over Republicans because of economic interests. Convincing working-class Catholic voters to put social issues ahead of economic self-interests is not easy, but Trump's aligning of the social and perceived economic interests of those voters was a powerful combination.

The following analysis thus examines the connection between the social-cultural values that drove religious conservative support for Trump, as well as the material factors that played a key role. Indeed, economic factors are filtered through a cultural lens for socially conservative, religious right voters. Antipathy to globalization, immigration, and multiculturalism among the religious right—and in Trump's representation of that anxiety—has both material and cultural roots, but admittedly it is very difficult to disentangle them. The linkage between culture and materiality is what most analysts miss when they hold economic factors and cultural factors as separate in examining the demography and political preferences of the religious right.

Conservative Catholics for Trump

Although Trump fared better among evangelicals than among Catholics, his margin among the former was only slightly better than those of past GOP presidential nominees, but his margin among the latter was substantially stronger.[5] Given the large concentrations of Catholic voters in upper Midwest states that were key to Trump's Electoral College victory, it is reasonable to argue that the Catholic vote played the most substantial role in the 2016 presidential campaign outcome. But, of course, in an election so close and with the support of a coalition of many groups, it would be easy to argue that any one of them was the key to his victory. What is unarguable, though, is that a coalition of conservative evangelical and Catholic voters anchored Trump's victory. It is remarkable, perhaps, that for four decades religious conservative leaders have wished for a strong evangelical-Catholic voters alliance that would transform US politics (D. Hudson 2008) and that the best success of this effort at the presidential election level happened through the candidacy of Trump.

In 2016, Democratic Party nominee Hillary Clinton won the popular vote handily, but Trump won the Catholic vote, and that was important in the Electoral College given the heavy concentration of Catholics in the key battleground states. Some of the US Catholic bishops were vocal in the election on the immigration issue and especially in opposition to Trump's promise to build a wall along the US-Mexico border, as well as on issues of social and economic justice (Pitts 2016). Yet Catholic voters demonstrated their independence from the political signaling of church leadership, as they have done in many elections. Scholar Mark M. Gray (2018) notes that a key to Trump's victory was not so much the overall national majority but the GOP nominee's performance among Catholics at the state level in the states that mattered most.

The Catholic vote was once distinctive, a reliable component of the New Deal Democratic Party coalition (Prendergast 1999; Gayte, Chelini-Pont, and Rozell 2018; Heyer, Rozell, and Genovese 2008). As social issues came to the fore in the 1970s and as Catholics began to move from the immigrant underclass to the middle class and above, many Catholics became either politically independent or Republicans. In most of the more recent presidential election cycles, the self-identified Catholic vote has closely mirrored the national vote. In that regard, the Catholic vote generally is no longer distinctive, although, as we saw in 2016, a minority of religiously devout and politically active Catholics is persuadable on religious grounds and numerous enough to make a difference in close elections.

Polling data late in summer 2016 showed Trump handily losing the Catholic vote. What happened? In postelection analyses, most observers proclaimed that the polls had failed to project the likely outcome of the presidential contest. The short and convenient answer given by most was that the polls were wrong. In fact, most of the national polls had the numbers extremely close to the actual outcome of the popular vote. The national polls generally were more accurate in 2016 than in 2012, but no one complained in 2012 because the polls, the popular vote, and the Electoral College outcome all aligned. The polling data in 2016 were flawed in some key battleground states in which state-level polls repeatedly projected numbers in Clinton's favor and did not capture a possible late surge for Trump. Poor polling in the states where it mattered most to the Electoral College outcome magnified the story of polling error in 2016 (Cohn 2017). Ultimately, the Catholic share of the electorate declined, and whereas the popular vote went comfortably Democratic, the Catholic vote went Republican.

Importantly, after polling data projecting a big slide in Catholic support for Trump, the GOP nominee softened much of his usually strident rhetoric on such issues as immigration and deportations, as well as some of his policy positions. It is highly likely that given the power of the Catholic vote in several of the very critical states in the Electoral College, Trump tamped down some of his strident appeals and also made a specific outreach to Catholic voters that did not capture much media attention but delivered the message for its intended audience.

Ralph Reed, founder of the Faith and Freedom Coalition, notes that the Trump campaign microtargeted Catholic voters "deliberately and extensively," particularly in the key upper Midwest states with large Catholic populations, and that there were a "number of outside efforts" ongoing to support these Trump campaign efforts.[6] Among those efforts outside the campaign apparatus was the Faith and Freedom Coalition, a successor to the Christian Coalition, which targeted about fifteen million faith-based voters in battleground states. Reed estimates that about one-third of those contacted were Roman Catholic.[7]

Additionally, according to Trump campaign speechwriter F. H. Buckley, a key effort was led by the Catholic Advisory Committee, organized by Deal

Hudson, that pushed the importance of Catholic outreach and arranged for the candidate to appear on EWTN (the global Catholic television network) and to put out a video on the occasion of the canonization of Mother Teresa, among other efforts (Buckley 2016).[8] The Clinton campaign had no comparable effort of targeted outreach to Catholic voters. There was no Catholics for Clinton VIP group or other such entity to rival the dedicated efforts on the GOP side. Possibly Clinton perceived her selection of a Catholic running mate, Senator Tim Kaine (VA), as her campaign's Catholic outreach, although historical evidence suggests that the vice presidential nominee is not a significant factor in voting choices (Jelen 2018).

Furthermore, for the religiously devout Catholic, it mattered that Trump was unwavering on his pro-life stand on abortion. Among those Catholics (and evangelicals, of course) for whom the life issue is predominant, was it more important that Trump had been married three times and had extramarital affairs or that he would appoint pro-life judges to the Supreme Court if elected? The question obviously answers itself. Most voters do not put personal character considerations over the potential impact on millions of lives from the policies likely to be promoted by the successful candidate for office. The continued vacancy on the Supreme Court elevated the importance of that factor to the voting preferences of Catholic conservatives in 2016. Trump made it clear that he would appoint a pro-life judge to the court if elected, and during the campaign he released a list of conservative jurists he would consider for the position (*NBC News* 2016). The importance of the court appointment to Catholic conservatives cannot be underestimated.

Consider as well the strongly felt sentiment among many Catholics that core elements of the Obamacare health plan intruded on religious liberties. Obamacare regulations compelled Catholic charities to pay for contraceptive coverage, in violation of the consciences of many devout Catholics. The understanding that Hillary Clinton as president would continue such regulations weighed heavily on many socially conservative Catholics. The stance of Obamacare offers another instance of this chapter's argument regarding the overlap of material and cultural values.

Another key factor in the election was that the widely hyped Latino surge in voting did not materialize. Political observers repeatedly stated that Trump's rhetoric on immigration, while mobilizing some voters, would cause a substantial countermobilization among Latinos who had not voted in large numbers in past elections. Surprisingly to these analysts, Latino voting dropped from 2012 to 2016, and although Clinton won a commanding majority of their votes, she achieved a substantially lower percentage of Latino votes than did Barack Obama in 2012 and 2008 (Krogstad and Lopez 2016). The drop-off in Latino voting was a big factor in the Catholic component of the electorate dropping by 3 percent from 2012 to 2016. In brief, Trump did better than Clinton at mobilizing his Catholic base, and he held down his losses among normally Democratic-voting Latinos (Richomme 2018).

Finally, Trump did especially well among Catholic voters even after he criticized Pope Francis as "very political" and naïve about the immigration issue (Rappeport 2016) and after the pope had criticized the GOP candidate for advocating that the United States build a wall along its southern border with Mexico. Specifically, on February 18, 2016, in response to a question about Trump's proposed border wall with Mexico, the pope responded: "A person who thinks only about building walls, wherever they may be, and not building bridges, is not Christian. This is not the gospel" (*National Catholic Register* 2016). Given the enormous worldwide popularity of the pope, it was reasonable that many political analysts believed at the time that his signaling of disapproval of the Republican presidential candidate would potentially discourage some Catholics from voting for Trump. Nonetheless, the frequently touted "Francis effect" on US politics simply did not materialize in the 2016 presidential campaign. Indeed, Trump struck back, calling the pope's criticism "disgraceful" and continued, "No leader, especially a religious leader, should have the right to question another man's religion or faith" (Rappeport 2016). Trump's response perhaps even helped him with some of the conservative Catholics whose support he sought, as many of them are not enamored of Pope Francis, and they tend to agree with the characterization of the pope as "very political," heading in a more liberal direction than they would like on social and economic issues as well.

Finally, material considerations surely played a role in Catholic voting, as did cultural-moral values. As noted, Trump's economic populism and attacks on globalization likely influenced many working-class Catholic voters who also liked his social issue positions. Adding to the complexity of disentangling the cultural and the material is the fact that Catholic voting in the United States over time has moved from solidly one-party (Democratic) to two-party competitive, a process that occurred with the increased material well-being of Catholics. For many years, Catholics were immigrant outsiders to the mainstream US culture, and they lived in the inner cities, joined labor unions, and reliably voted Democratic. As their children and grandchildren achieved higher education and economic status, Catholic voting began to splinter. As the Democratic Party in the 1970s especially began to openly embrace abortion rights, gay rights, and a liberal cultural order, some Catholics began to move their loyalties away from the Democratic Party on account of social, not material concerns (Prendergast 1999).

For Trump, the key in 2016 was that the Catholic habit of voting Democratic had long disappeared, and he was able to draw support from some of the more affluent who had developed a Republican voting habit, some social conservatives turned off by the Democratic Party stands on cultural issues, as well as working-class Catholics attracted to his unique economic message that year.

Conservative Evangelicals for Trump

Trump's candidacy did not easily attract support from conservative evangelicals, but he won them over time with his commitments on policy and a promise to appoint only pro-life judges to federal courts. The evangelical component certainly was as much a key to Trump winning as the Catholic vote, and by one measure perhaps even more so (Rozell, 2018). Trump won Pennsylvania, Michigan, and Wisconsin—states with significant Catholic populations—by about 107,000 votes combined. There are substantial numbers of evangelicals as well in those states. If Trump merely did as well as Romney and John McCain among evangelicals in those states, he likely would have lost two or three of them and the presidency and the Catholic vote would have been irrelevant to the outcome.

Nonetheless, after all of the hype about Trump's success with evangelical voters, let us not forget that the election was a binary choice with a very unpopular Democratic Party presidential nominee. Indeed, during the election, a Pew Research Center poll found that for evangelicals, voting against Hillary Clinton was a stronger motivator than voting for Trump (Pew Research Center 2016; Land 2017).

An October 2016 *Washington Post/ABC News* poll found that 70 percent of evangelicals had a negative view of Hillary Clinton, whereas her national negative rating was 55 percent. Undoubtedly, the unfavorable view of Clinton made it much easier for skeptical evangelicals to support Trump (Bailey 2016).

Despite being a United Methodist who frequently attended religious services, taught Sunday school, and attended weekly prayer breakfasts when she was a US senator, most evangelicals perceived Clinton not as a faith-based politician but as a liberal feminist activist, and her pro-choice stand was for them a strong disqualifier.

Yet Trump did make very significant commitments to conservative evangelicals in the campaign, and these certainly mattered. In June 2016, Trump addressed the Faith and Freedom Coalition conference, where he held up a list of judges he would consider for appointment to the Supreme Court and exclaimed, "And by the way, these judges are all pro-life!" (CNN 2016). In September 2016, Trump (2016) issued a letter to pro-life leaders stating his commitment to defund Planned Parenthood if the organization continued to provide abortion-related services. He also stated he would act to make the Hyde Amendment "permanent law to protect taxpayers from having to pay for abortions." Trump's choice of Mike Pence, a strong social conservative, as running mate also gave the GOP nominee substantial credibility with the religious right.

The day after the election, president of the Family Research Council Tony Perkins assessed the importance of Trump's multifaceted strategy to reach religious conservatives: "First, he chose a pro-life conservative running mate, he did not try to weaken the party's platform, and he laid out a list of potential justices that he said are pro-life. . . . We've never had a Republican nominee do this. And I think he basically closed the deal in the last debate when he went into late-term abortion in first 15 minutes" (Stewart 2016).

Also notable, though, is that evangelical voters themselves have changed in their assessments of the moral character of candidates for public office. In the 1990s, conservative evangelicals were a strong united voice of opposition to President Clinton based in large part on their perception of his poor moral conduct. As Robert P. Jones (2016) notes, even as late as 2011, only 30 percent of white evangelical Protestants considered it possible for a person who had committed an immoral private act to be fit to hold public office. By the time Trump was the GOP nominee in 2016, fully 72 percent of that group deemed immoral personal acts irrelevant to one's ability to hold public office. Jones's analysis is on target: "The Trump era has effectively turned white-evangelical political ethics on its head. Rather than standing on principle and letting the chips fall where they may, white evangelicals have now fully embraced a consequentialist ethics that works backward from predetermined political ends, refashioning or even discarding principles as needed to achieve a desired outcome" (R. Jones 2016).

For the case of religious conservative evangelicals, it is especially complicated to draw out the economic bases of their voting decisions because their support for Trump was so incredibly one-sided. Much of the teaching of evangelicals embraces economic upward mobility and even rationalizes material success as based in hard work and merit—values that align with Trump's view of himself. The confluence of values on cultural and material issues, along with intense disdain for the alternative in the presidential election, made the voting choice so much easier for conservative evangelicals despite Trump's personal flaws.

A number of scholars in the past have written admiringly of the religious right's successful transition from extremism to political pragmatism (Moen 1992; Rozell 1997; Rozell and Wilcox 1998). Movement leaders for the past three decades have strongly urged activists to support candidates who could win elections and move policy goals forward rather than give votes to candidates who were more authentically religious conservatives. In this context, it is not surprising that past religious right presidential candidates such as Pat Robertson, Gary Bauer, and Mike Huckabee have not been able to secure a GOP presidential nomination, or even come close. Yet prior to Trump's campaign, there did not appear to be any serious risks to the credibility of the religious right movement by making pragmatic compromises to support mainstream Republican candidates for the presidency. The movement's support for Trump challenges that credibility, although at the halfway mark his presidency showed some real policy gains for religious conservatives.

The Trump Presidency So Far

Now in the third year of Trump's presidency, there is much to suggest that he is fulfilling his commitments to religious conservatives who supported him. And give credit to those who placed their bets with candidate Trump: on the singular most important decision of lasting import of his young presidency, he has delivered two solid conservative jurists to the US Supreme Court. That is a big victory for the religious right, and its supporters have every reason to consider their backing of candidate Trump to have been a very good decision.

And given the advanced ages of some current court members, it is likely that Trump will be able to further swing the court to the right. The possibility of *Roe v. Wade* being overturned is more real now than ever. Less noticed but very important is that Trump is making numerous lower federal court appointments, further influencing the development of constitutional law on social issues for many years after he eventually leaves office.

There are other important successes so far for religious conservatives. In his first days in office, Trump, by executive action, reinstated the so-called Mexico City Policy, derisively known as the gag rule—the ban on federal dollars for international family planning agencies that provide abortion-related counseling or services. That issue has long been a political football, put in place by Ronald Reagan and either overturned by every Democratic president or reinstated by every Republican one since. Commitment to this ban has, since the 1980s, been a core issue for religious conservatives (Rozell and Das Gupta 2009). To any who considered that perfunctory, the president then appointed a leading anti-abortion activist to be the director of the federal program that provides funding for family planning services for poor citizens and those without health insurance.

Although most secular Americans associate the religious right nearly exclusively with the abortion issue, almost nothing riles up social conservatives as much as issues of schooling—a public good but where cultural values influence provision. Social conservatives have a strong antipathy toward what they perceive as an antireligion and even anti-Christian ideology pervading public education. Trump has scored with social conservatives in his appointment of their fellow traveler Betsy DeVos as secretary of education and in his strong support for so-called school choice. The president has committed to supporting policies that promote education vouchers—a highly controversial idea but one that resonates with religious conservatives who believe that funds used for public education should be available for parents instead to send their children to private religious-based schools. Such a policy would begin to defund public schools while transferring tax revenues to religious academies—a longstanding goal of the religious right.

Numerous other actions of this presidency resonate with the religious right. Pence—his very selection itself an affirmation of Trump's pro-life credibility—prominently participated in the annual March for Life procession. No other presidential administration has had that high-level direct participation in the march. There are appointments of other social conservatives such as DeVos and Department of Housing and Urban Development (HUD) secretary Ben Carson.

The president issued an executive order travel ban on citizens from seven Muslim-majority nations. Although the controversial ban remains bottled up in court challenges, it featured a special dispensation for persecuted Christians. The president's travel ban action is highly unpopular, yet white evangelical Christians have expressed very strong support for it (G. Smith 2017).

During the presidential campaign and at the February 2, 2017, National Prayer Breakfast, Trump promised to eliminate the Johnson Amendment (White House 2017), the legislative enactment that since 1954 has prohibited all 501(c)(3) nonprofit organizations from endorsing or opposing political candidates. Many religious conservatives have opposed the amendment because of its legal restriction on religious congregations making political endorsements and participating in political campaigns, under threat of loss of their tax-exempt status. On May 4, 2017, the president issued an executive order that substantially weakened IRS enforcement of the amendment. Although religious conservatives would have preferred that this executive order completely repeal the Johnson Amendment, as Trump had promised, doing so would require an act of Congress. What made the president's executive order meaningful was that it removed a long-standing threat of legal action that worked as a deterrent to religious congregations directly participating in political campaigns. In his Rose Garden ceremony touting the new executive order, the president stated: "This financial threat against the faith community is over. . . . You're now in a position to say what you want to say. . . . No one should be censoring sermons or targeting pastors" (Wagner and Bailey 2017).

Moving the US embassy in Israel to Jerusalem was another big victory for evangelical conservatives who had long advocated that action. Both Democratic and Republican presidents for years had said they favored this move but ultimately decided against it. Trump's action again suggested to social conservatives that he keeps the promises he made to them, no matter how politically difficult.

In short, religious conservatives feel validated in backing Trump for president and believe that he will continue to pay back their loyalty. And with historically poor public approval ratings, the religious right is the singular, unwaveringly loyal constituency of Trump. According to public opinion polls, Trump's support among white evangelicals is substantially higher than his approval rating from the public generally. Looking at the first one hundred days of the administration, Trump's early major religious right sponsor Jerry Falwell, Jr., gushed with praise for the new president: "I think evangelicals have found their dream president. I think reuniting Israel with America after eight years of treating them badly, appointing Neil Gorsuch to the Supreme Court, appointing people of faith to his Cabinet in almost every area . . . I think he is attacking ISIS so that Christians being murdered in the Middle East will stop. All those things that evangelicals love" (Bailey 2017). Falwell continues to sing the praises of Trump more than halfway into the president's term, even advocating that other social conservatives emulate Trump's combative and aggressive style of attack politics (Boston 2019).

Falwell and other socially conservative backers of the president are correct that they have gotten a lot for their votes. Yet this odd relationship between faith-based voters and a womanizing, thrice-married worshipper of global capitalism carries big risks for those who are so uncritically supportive of the president. Political leaders come and go, but principles should be enduring. The challenge for the religious right in embracing Trump is how to get around the character issue. It lacks credibility to claim that character matters when one political leader has consensual affairs but then overlook it when another has done the same and even worse by bragging, as Trump has done, about committing sexual assault (Fahrenhold 2016).

In the 1990s, many Americans accepted the harsh judgments of religious conservatives toward Bill Clinton's extramarital conduct as consistent with the religious right's deeply held moral beliefs. Many religious right leaders spoke eloquently about the public consequences of validating morally repugnant conduct by a national leader who is supposed to be a role model for our young citizens. Nonetheless, public opinion was not on the side of religious conservatives. Most of the public had made a pragmatic judgment that the personal conduct of one man was not nearly as important as the consequences of his policies on the nation and the world. Clinton's policies were popular, and the country ultimately concluded that although his personal conduct was far from noble, the balance favored keeping him in office to continue his agenda.

There was no lack of clarity at that time as to where people stood on the issue of personal character in public life. The religious right proudly owned its passionate commitment to traditional morality and did not waver despite ultimately losing the battle over the hearts and minds of Americans regarding

Clinton's fate. In the end, when the Senate failed to vote to remove the impeached president, a large majority of Americans agreed that that was the right action and were relieved to get back to other national business rather than focus on Clinton's character (Andolina and Wilcox 2000).

Given that background, is it any surprise that many Americans see the religious right–Trump alliance as a kind of marriage of convenience—nothing more than both parties using each other for their own gain? It has not gone unnoticed by the public that many of the same religious conservative leaders who condemned Clinton's personal conduct have embraced Trump as an authentic man of God and have conveniently overlooked the forty-fifth president's character.[9]

Here is the dilemma for the religious right: the movement tied itself firmly to the fate of a deeply flawed character and of a presidency that could have easily ended in impeachment, criminal prosecutions, or something far worse, such as a major international incident. Furthermore, almost all of the gains the movement has made so far with Trump—the big exception being the Supreme Court and other federal judicial appointments—are easily reversible. Much of what Trump has done so far is through appointments and direct executive actions; these are fleeting victories. Courts have stepped in to delay and restrict portions of his travel ban. Even with large partisan majorities in Congress, he could not quickly repeal Obamacare, and he is learning just how really complicated it is to get things done through legislating rather than executive orders. Now past the halfway point of his presidency, there are few significant legislative achievements to his credit.

With such a shaky start, poor poll numbers, and a substantial loss of Republican seats (forty-one) in the House of Representatives in the midterm elections, the president's hands are further tied on policy, and he continues to be the target of serious legislative investigations of the executive branch, even after being impeached by the House of Representatives. Many establishment Republicans are distancing themselves from their president, leaving Trump with one foundation of solid support remaining—the religious right. If he is a one-term president, look to the next president to undo most of what he has achieved so far through direct executive actions and possibly through legislative initiatives sent to the president.

However this presidency ends, it is hard to imagine that religious conservatives one day will be celebrating the achievement of Trump's promise to revive the greatness of an imagined American past. More likely, the movement will be in a defensive posture answering for its compromises in order to have been temporarily at the seat of power. The loss in credibility could potentially be enormous.

Notes

1. Like the forecasts of many political experts who declared that Trump had no chance of winning the presidency, Gallagher's prediction turned out to be incredibly wrong.

2. In June 2016, religious conservative columnist Cal Thomas interviewed Trump and gave the GOP candidate a chance to articulate his views on religion and whether he seeks forgiveness. What is striking is how Trump turns the topic instead to how well he was faring with evangelical voters:

THOMAS: Every president has called upon God at some point. Lincoln spoke of not being able to hold the office of the presidency without spending time on his knees. You have confessed that you are a Christian. . . .

TRUMP: And I have also won much evangelical support.

THOMAS: Yes, I know that. You have said you never felt the need to ask for God's forgiveness, and yet repentance for one's sins is a precondition to salvation. I ask you the question Jesus asked of Peter: Who do you say He is?

TRUMP: I will be asking for forgiveness, but hopefully I won't have to be asking for much forgiveness. As you know, I am Presbyterian and Protestant. I've had great relationships and developed even greater relationships with ministers. We have tremendous support from the clergy. I think I will be doing very well during the election with evangelicals and with Christians. (Thomas 2016)

3. Edison Research collected the survey for the National Election Pool, a consortium of ABC News, Associated Press, CBS News, CNN, Fox News, and NBC News. The relevant exit poll question was: "Would you describe yourself as a born-again or evangelical Christian?"

4. Chapter 7 adopts a similar approach in explaining the context of the cultural ideology of the Tea Party that led to the pressures to slowly eliminate export subsidies to firms as immoral and antithetical to capitalism.

5. Portions of this section originally appeared in Rozell 2018.

6. Ralph Reed, email interview by the author, January 4, 2017.

7. Reed, email interview.

8. See also F. H. Buckley, email interview by the author, January 2, 2017. Buckley is a professor of law at the Antonin Scalia School of Law at George Mason University.

9. An especially harsh judgment of the strong conservative, evangelical support for Trump comes from Professor Jeremy Gunn: "One might have hoped that Trump would finally drive the evangelical community back to its moral senses. Instead, he seems to represent the final triumph [of] secularism, wealth, gambling, and

braggadocio, and pornography, carpet bombing of populations, racism, and pre-varication over the community that once professed its belief in the nonviolent and transcendent message of Jesus Christ." Jeremy Gunn, comments on "Debate on Inter-religious Strategies" panel at the "Religion and Presidential Elections in the USA" conference, September 22–23, 2016, Aix-Marseille University, Aix-en-Provence, France.

9 Applying the Soft Power Rubric

How Study Abroad Data Reveal
International Cultural Relations

Irene S. Wu

A YOUNG PERSON'S DECISION TO ENROLL IN A FOREIGN UNIVERSITY is the culmination of the student, family, and community's social, cultural, and economic aspirations. In Chapter 6, Steven Livingston worries that children of America's working class today regard a college education as not only beyond their economic reach but also unrealistic as a cultural aspiration. It is precisely this combination of palpable cultural anxiety and strained economic conditions, which J. P. Singh highlights in Chapter 1, that leads all authors in this book to argue that economics cannot be shorn of cultural considerations.

The Soft Power Rubric is a conceptual approach that links empirical data to address a major question in international politics: How does one measure a country's soft power and cultural influence? A country has soft power when it can persuade, rather than force, other countries to its point of view. The Soft Power Rubric reconceives soft power as when foreigners think of *us* as "we," rather than as "they," and emphasizes the perspective of the countries at the edge, rather than at the center of the international system. A country's ability to attract foreign students to its universities is one common way to understand its soft power in the international community.

This chapter examines the underlying political economies of soft power through data that reveal the preferences of students from countries that send the most students abroad and of Sub-Saharan African students who study abroad. This uncovers unexpected soft power relationships that both South Africa and Malaysia cultivate as international education hubs, which complicates our understandings of North-South or core-periphery postcolonial relations. In addition, the data also reflect the slowing growth of France's educational ties with other countries. The Soft Power Rubric unveils important networks of cultural relations, offers a path forward to bring cultural data into empirical modeling, and points to fruitful areas for future work. The chapter also offers a contrast with other authors in this book who emphasize a reaction against globalization.

Reconceiving Soft Power in the International System

"Soft power" captures the notion of a country's persuasive, cultural influence in the international system. It is a critical counterweight to the idea of hard power—economic leverage and military might (Nye 2004). Guns and money are not the only resources that matter in the international system. Values, ideas, and information are also influential (see Chapter 3 for a similar point). At the end of the Cold War, it may have been burgers and rock and roll that drew people to walk West rather than East when the Berlin Wall fell (Gans 2013).

There are dozens of monographs on the soft power of individual countries. Yet the literature lacks a theory that enables empirical comparison of soft power resources across countries and over time. In this chapter, I draw on insights from the field of political communication and other allied fields to offer key observations that make this measurement possible and compose a data set that opens new vistas for research on soft power in the international system.

The first insight is that when studying media broadcasting, political communications scholars are as, if not more, interested in the reaction of the audience than in the intent of the producer. For example, Ien Ang (1982) has studied the complex reaction of Dutch audiences to the US television series *Dallas* in the 1980s and finds that audiences were attracted by their own desire to escape reality and to the program's family drama, not by the show's presentation of an American worldview, as cultural critics have feared. This suggests that when researching the soft power of the United States, for example, it is far more important to focus on the reaction of others than the declarations of the US government.

To make this insight more abstract, suppose soft power is present when foreigners think of *us* as "we" rather than as "they." That is the ultimate form of foreigners accepting another country's point of view. A country does not so much have soft power *over* another country, but rather countries have soft power relationships *with* each other. Getting to "we" and "with" suggests that these societies are integrated, in whole or in part.

The second insight from political communication is that we can detect social integration in changes in the direction and volume of interaction among people. Karl Deutsch (1966) and Richard Merritt (1966), in their studies of nationalism, use indicators of postal mail correspondence and other observable interactions among people to track integration within a country over time. Similarly, if soft power relationships exist where there is partial integration of two countries, then that would be observable in the interactions among people across borders.

The Soft Power Rubric reveals the volume and intensity of people-to-people interactions that form the basis of many individuals' views of foreign countries. People interact with foreigners in many ways, including by migrating, studying abroad, traveling, and watching foreign movies—the basic elements of the everyday political economies of the Soft Power Rubric. To explore the practical application of this new view of soft power, I have composed a data set on migration, study abroad, and travel for over two hundred countries from 1960 to 2015 and a data set on foreign movie audiences for about fifty countries from 1970 to 2015. Taken together, these four indicators provide a nuanced picture of the personal interaction of people across nations and opens the possibility of comparing soft power of countries across time. This Soft Power Rubric provides empirical markers that can ground qualitative studies of individual countries.

What do these soft power data mean? The measurements of economic and military power provide some insight into how to assess soft power. Gross domestic product (GDP), which reflects the sum total economic production of a country as measured by financial value, is a measure of economic power (Kuznets 1959). The number of military bases, aircraft carriers, or armed forces personnel are measures of military power. In both economic and military cases, the thing measured is power resources. More resources likely means more success, but there is no guarantee. A bigger GDP does not guarantee the upper hand in a trade negotiation. More military bases do not ensure victory in war. However, more resources do make success more likely, and the depletion of resources heightens the risk of failure. The same is true for soft power. More soft power resources is no guarantee of success in persuading another country, but the lack does heighten the likelihood of failure.

These data have an important role in communities shepherding their soft power resources. The data are drawn from UN-related organizations—the UN Population Division, UNESCO, and the WTO. Elinor Ostrom (2003), in her principles of how communities govern scarce resources, points to the importance of access to transparent data and reliable scientific explanations. Chapter 4 also emphasizes the need for communities to have clear information on the state of the environment and the scientific understanding for how to take care of it as a foundation for building a culture of responsibility. Similarly, for a country's soft power to flourish, communities should have both data and an understanding of how soft power accumulates and dissipates.

Finally, taking the perspective of the influenced rather than the influencers, the Soft Power Rubric builds on the idea that a country's soft power resources do not reside in and are not the primary responsibility of the state but rather are resources held by the whole community. This echoes Sharon Krause's argument, in Chapter 4, that social problems like the quality of the environment cannot be properly addressed without fundamental shifts in cultural values. Environmental responsibility is more than individual liability of individual economic actors, she argues, rather it is accountability of the entire community for the whole outcome. Similarly, the depth of a society's soft power resources depends not only on the quantity of individual interactions with foreigners but also on the quality. When a stranger stops at the lunch counter, does she leave with only a sandwich or also with directions to the festival and tips on handling the upcoming snowstorm? It is the visitor's whole experience in the community that determines whether she recommends that her friends travel there in the future. Soft power is one political benefit that accrues to societies that observe the ancient values of hospitality.

Wu Soft Power Rubric

The Soft Power Rubric is a group of time series data that tracks changes in the interactions that people have with foreigners. Three series are direct people-to-people interactions, emigration, study abroad, and travel abroad; the fourth is a mediated interaction, watching foreign movies. Emigration, permanently moving family and home to another country, reflects a person's ultimate integration into a foreign society. Study abroad reflects a person's serious interest and commitment to understanding another society by spending substantial financial resources and formative time in a foreign country. Travel

Short-term attraction	Watch a movie	Visit a country	Study abroad	Emigrate	Long-term attraction

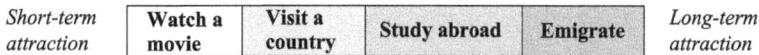

FIGURE 9.1 Wu Soft Power Rubric: Indicators of social integration across borders.

abroad reflects a short-term interest in a foreign society. For each of these three series, international institutions have collected data for many countries for many years already. Watching a foreign movie expresses an interest or curiosity about another country. Data for this are available but are less comprehensive than those of the three other series.

These four indicators, as shown in Figure 9.1, range from short-term attraction, such as buying a ticket to see a movie from another country, to long-term attraction, emigrating to a foreign country. What matters is not how many movies a country produces, but rather how many foreigners choose to watch them.

The quantitative data in the Soft Power Rubric reflect how integrated countries are. In this approach, soft power is not an outside force that causes migration, for example. What drives migration is a combination of dynamics including the person's knowledge and social contacts, his or her professional skills, the broader economic and social conditions, and policy decisions made by both originating and destination countries. A government's decision to grant more or fewer visas, for example, affects the number of immigrants. The change in the number of immigrants, combined with changes in the other indicators within the Soft Power Rubric, is the change in soft power relationship between countries. Many dynamics such as policy shifts, technology change, and environmental conditions contribute to changes in soft power. This conception of soft power makes it possible to discuss the United States' soft power relationship with Canada as distinct from its soft power relationship with China or with countries in Europe.

While the Soft Power Rubric unveils the intensity and volume of integration between countries, it does not reflect the quality of the relationship. For example, the number of immigrants in one country may reflect how attractive that country is, while in another country the same number reflects those fleeing violent conflict in neighboring regions. Once Soft Power Rubric indicators are established, only further inquiry into the history and context of the interaction can provide the full picture. For example, in the 1990s after the end of the Cold War, anti-Americanism and critiques of US hegemony by its Western European allies increased to a level even greater than what had flowed from Eastern European countries during the communist era. However, the Soft Power Rubric indicators show deep integration between the United States and Western Europe, suggesting that such critiques were borne in part out of frustration and disappointment among countries that have close ties, a qualitatively different kind of conflict than among countries with weak ties.

In Chapter 2, Daniel Hausman regrets that economists often exclude culture from their models to fully explain the creation of interests and preferences. The challenge becomes how to include it, especially given the insight from Chapter 3 that financial value inadequately captures cultural value. The Soft Power Rubric, which uses social interactions as a measure, is one response to the call of several authors in this book to look beyond the usual economic indicators for explanations of people's preferences. The Soft Power Rubric captures a picture of how countries are tied together and offers an alternative to financial indicators like trade, investment, and currency flows.

One practical advantage of the Soft Power Rubric is that data for these indicators are collected by international institutions and available to the public for free. Public opinion surveys, while also good measures of soft power influence, are expensive to conduct, generally do not have historical time series, and often are not easily accessible to researchers (see Goldsmith and Horiuchi 2012). Further, such surveys are not able to cover the number of countries available in the Soft Power Rubric. Soft power indexes that rank countries using a single algorithm are useful in their simplicity but lack flexibility (see McClory 2016). For example, France may attract many visitors from one country and many students from a second; an index tends to mask these distinctions rather than drawing them out. Further, if the algorithm is not transparent, then it is challenging to confirm the results of the index.

The quantitative indicators for migration, international education, travel, and movies are each deeply embedded in their own scholarly literature. It is striking that while these four fields remain largely separate how interrelated their concerns are. For example, in the field of international education, scholars use the push-pull model to explain students' decision-making process; it categorizes the dynamics that push students abroad and pull them toward certain destinations (Mazzarol and Soutar 2002). From the field of tourism come the ideas of destination image, what travelers think about a locale, and place identity, how those who live in a locale think of their own community

(Karl, Reintinger, and Schmude 2015). Migration scholars place a high priority on understanding the transnational identity of those whose everyday lives regularly reach across borders (Vertovec 2001; Robins and Aksoy 2001; Golbert 2001). From the research on movies arises the debate over whether the success of cultural productions in world markets is explained best by understanding the international power structure or as subject to regular business cycles (Straubhaar 1991). Each of these concerns is relevant to phenomena in the other three fields. The Soft Power Rubric brings together not only the quantitative data but also the overlapping and reinforcing cognitive frameworks from these four fields.

Education: Interaction Builds Soft Power Resources

An underlying principle of the Soft Power Rubric is that interaction is necessary to understanding and that empathy is an essential precursor to foreigners thinking of *us* as "we" rather than as "they." International education creates opportunities for people-to-people interaction across borders, the fundamental building blocks for trust and potential cooperation.

Three insights from past research on trust, culture, and social integration shed light on how education can build soft power resources.

- On trust, Ostrom's (2003) empirical and experimental work shows that reciprocal interaction can increase people's willingness to cooperate. Trust is not simply an act of faith but a choice based on experience and self-interest.
- On culture, Gary Fine (2012) reminds us that it is not an outside force that is a catchall explanation for the unexplainable. People create and perform culture as they interact with each other. His "tiny publics"—small groups of people, like a book club or a team of video gamers—work together, hold common values, share a past, and look forward to a future and are key to understanding how cultural forces came to be.
- On tracking social integration, Deutsch (1966) looks to the volume and direction of communications as an indicator of how close-knit communities are. For example, Merritt (1966) shows that in the mid-eighteenth century more postal mail was exchanged between the US colonies and Great Britain than among the US colonies themselves.

By the early nineteenth century, the reverse was true, with more mail delivered among the US states.

Carol Atkinson's (2014) work on US military training of elite foreign officers where social interaction is both structured and frequent is one of the strongest examples of how to build soft power resources through international education. Furthermore, Atkinson links US military training of elite foreign officers to long-term democratization around the world. In the Middle East, for example, Tunisia and Egypt send officers to the United States for military training, while Syria and Libya do not. During the Arab Spring protests of 2011, the Tunisian and Egyptian militaries backed the protestors, while in Syria and Libya they did not (Atkinson 2015).

Through qualitative surveys and quantitative analyses, Atkinson (2014) shows that nondemocratic countries that regularly send officers to the United States for military training are more likely to transition to democracy than those that do not. Her quantitative studies of about 170 countries over a forty-year period show autocratic countries that participated in US military exchanges were more likely to acquire democratic political institutions than those without military exchanges. Her work also shows positive impact on democratic transitions and democratic practices, like basic freedoms of speech, religion, political participation, and workers' rights.

Compared to foreigners in civilian universities, foreign military officers are likely harder to influence through socialization, Atkinson (2014) notes. They are typically older, midcareer professionals who have been chosen by their respective governments and are committed to return to service in their home countries, with political systems that range from democracies to dictatorships. However, US military institutions take a structured approach to ensure that foreign officers interact with many parts of society, in contrast with the freer, less-organized approach of civilian universities (Atkinson 2014).

US military elite schools divide students into seminar groups of fewer than twenty that train and study together for a semester at a time, unlike students at civilian universities, who have different classmates in each class. Within a primary seminar group, students are likely to remain friends for life. Foreign military officers are fully integrated into these seminar groups. Special for foreign students, however, are the required field studies that take them into American communities to observe life off campus and outside the military. Foreign military officers come to the United States with their families and are paired with sponsor families to integrate them into community life. The officers experience America not only through their own lives but also through the eyes of their family members (Atkinson 2015). Atkinson's (2014) surveys show that travel and social interactions are among the things the foreign military officers rate mostly highly about their experience in the United States.

Other studies of international education show the consequences of not integrating foreign students with the host community. China's foreign military training program segregates foreigners on a different campus from Chinese military officers, report John Van Oudenaren and Benjamin Fisher (2016). The foreign officers are instructed in English, as many are not able to speak Chinese. When surveyed, foreign alumni regret that there were few opportunities to talk unofficially with instructors or with People's Liberation Army (PLA) officers.

In the civilian world, in France's elite Grandes Écoles, while international students receive the same training as French students, they are flagged as foreign, given different degrees upon graduating, and are excluded from professional opportunities available to their French classmates. These practices undermine the meritocratic model held up by French republican ideals, argue Brigitte Darchy-Koechlin and Hugues Draelants (2010). The Grandes Écoles are prestigious in France, but outside the country French universities like the Sorbonne are more widely recognized. The authors suggest the Grandes Écoles' failure to fully integrate international students undermines the schools' ambitions to be a major influence in creating an international, not just a French, elite.

Case study literature on international education indicates that study abroad can enhance students' opinion of their host country if students have an overall positive experience, frequent interactions with hosts, and feel welcome and integrated into the host community. The next section presents the quantitative data to uncover which countries have relationships built on international education exchange.

The Audience's Perspective, Part 1: Where Do Countries Send Their Students?

A key insight of the Soft Power Rubric is the value of observing interaction from the perspective of the audience, not the projector of power. In political communication, research is just as focused on how people receive and understand a message as how people send a message. One seminal example is Ang's (1982) study of Dutch viewers' reaction to the hugely popular US soap opera *Dallas* in the 1980s, a flagship example of the American cultural imperialism that concerned European governments. Ang's qualitative investigation finds viewers pay little attention to the distinctively American aspects of the show. Instead, some fans are emotionally attached to the characters and drama of the family dynamics. Others value the spectacle of beautiful people and things. The show is at once realistic in the characters' problems and fantastical in its melodrama and material context. Ang's methodological insight is that to understand the impact of a television show it is important to ask the viewers. To apply this insight to international education, rather than focusing on the countries that host the most students, this analysis takes as its point of departure the countries that send the most students abroad to enroll in foreign universities.[1]

Where do students go to study abroad? Figure 9.2 shows the countries who sent the most students abroad for university education in 2015: China, India, Germany, South Korea, and Nigeria.

Unpacking this data further, Figure 9.3 shows where these five countries sent most of their students. The figure shows the top five destination countries for each sending country. Thicker arrows reflect more students traveling to a country.

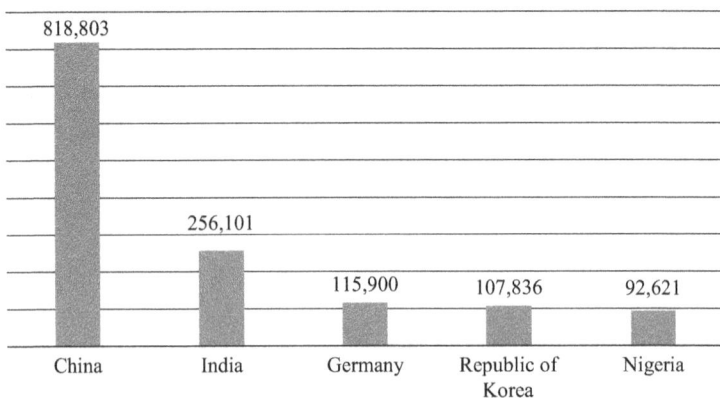

FIGURE 9.2 World's top five countries sending students abroad, 2015.
SOURCE: Data from UNESCO Institute of Statistics *UIS.Stat* database, at http://data .uis.unesco.org.

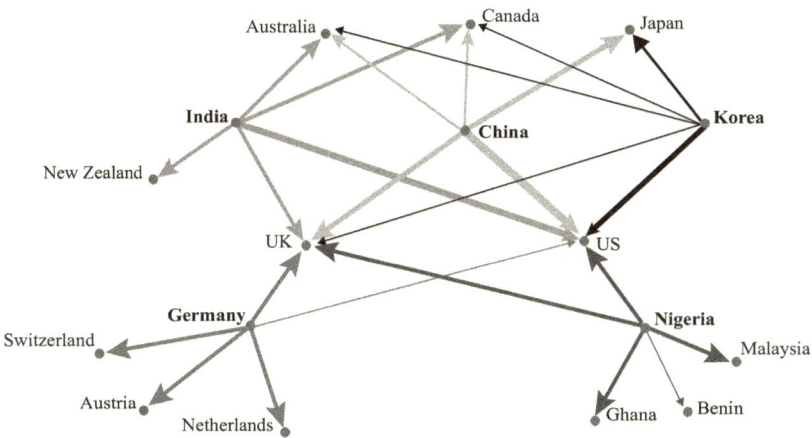

FIGURE 9.3 World's top five destinations for students from the world's top five sending countries, 2015.

SOURCE: Data from UNESCO Institute of Statistics *UIS.Stat* database, at http://data .uis.unesco.org.

For all five sending countries, the United States and the United Kingdom are major destinations. For Indian, Chinese, and Korean students, Canada and Australia are important destinations. Many Chinese and South Korean students go to Japanese universities. Many German students enroll in universities in other European countries. Many Nigerian students study abroad not only in nearby Ghana or Benin but also in Malaysia. The next section considers the emergence of regional hubs like Malaysia.

The Audience's Perspective, Part 2: Where Do Sub-Saharan Countries Send Their Students Abroad?

The Soft Power Rubric makes visible countries that have significant influence but are usually not thought of as leaders, like Malaysia in Figure 9.3. Malaysia appeared when the point of departure was the top five sending countries. If the point of departure changes, then other regional hubs emerge. If, for example, instead of the top five sending countries in the world, the point of departure is all the Sub-Saharan African countries that send students abroad, the analysis uncovers new insights. Figure 9.4 shows the top five foreign destinations of Sub-Saharan African university students in 2015. France, otherwise absent in the global analysis, takes the lead for Sub-Saharan African students.

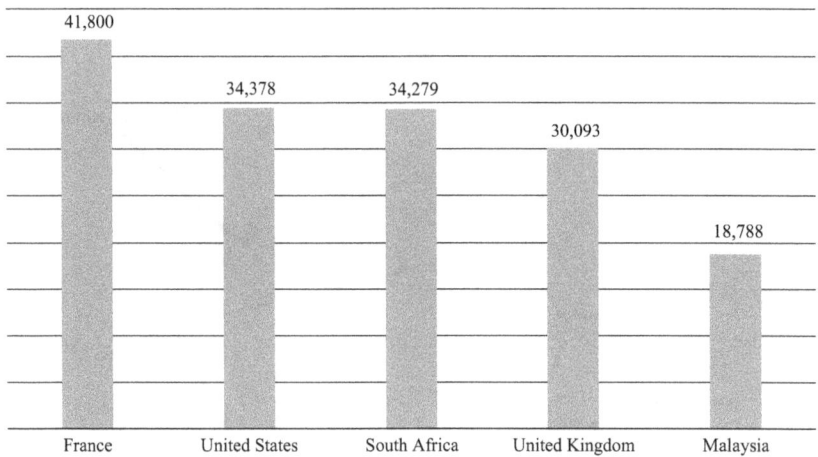

FIGURE 9.4 Sub-Saharan Africa: Top five foreign destinations for students, 2015.
SOURCE: Data from UNESCO Institute of Statistics *UIS.Stat* database, at http://data.uis .unesco.org.

The leading destination on the African continent is South Africa. Malaysia is the leading Asian country. The next sections take each of these three countries in turn.

France

France is a major destination for students from Sub-Saharan Africa. Of the top ten countries that send university students to France, six are former colonies: five countries in Africa and Vietnam. The remaining countries are China and European countries. See Figure 9.5.

France remains a major hub of international education, but the number of foreign students enrolled in its universities has not grown at a rate as rapid as that of the United States, the United Kingdom, and Australia. Figure 9.6 shows the number of foreign students in these four countries from 1970 through 2015. The number of foreign students enrolled in French universities grew continously from 1970 to 2015. However, by 2000, the United Kingdom and, by 2010, Australia had both surpassed France as host for international students.

Many of France's foreign students are from former colonies. Figure 9.7 compares the number of foreign students in France that came from former colonies and other countries from 1970 to 2015. Most foreign students at

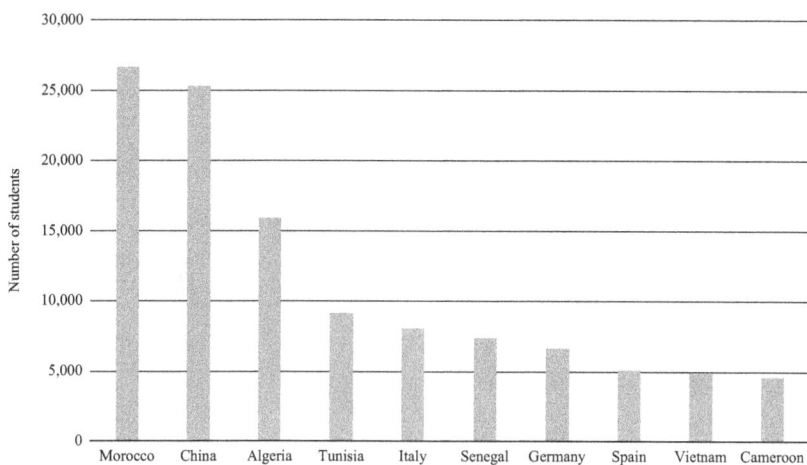

FIGURE 9.5 France: Top ten countries sending students, 2015.
SOURCE: Data from UNESCO Institute of Statistics *UIS.Stat* database, at http://data
.uis.unesco.org.

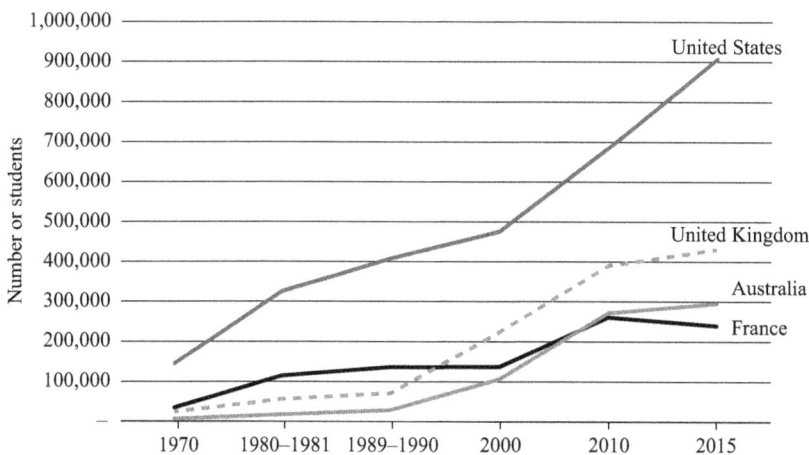

FIGURE 9.6 United States, United Kingdom, France, and Australia:
Total foreign students hosted, 1970–2015.
SOURCE: Data from UNESCO Institute of Statistics *UIS.Stat* database, at http://data
.uis.unesco.org.
NOTE: Because of incomplete data, 1980 figures sometimes reflect 1981 data, and 1990
figures sometimes reflect 1989 data.

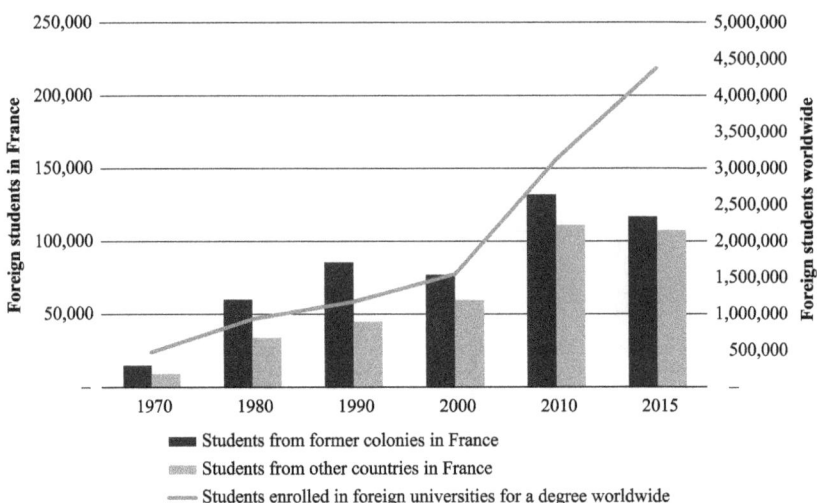

FIGURE 9.7 France: Foreign students from former colonies and other countries, 1970–2015.

SOURCE: Data from UNESCO Institute of Statistics *UIS.Stat* database, at http://data .uis.unesco.org.

French universities during that period were from former colonies. In 1990, about three-quarters were from former colonies; in 2015, about half. The reasons students from former colonies continue to be drawn to France are complex. France and French society are highly regarded around the world. Alice Kaplan (2013) captures the glamor of Paris in *Dreaming in French*, recounting the personally and professionally pivotal year that Jacqueline Bouvier Kennedy, Susan Sontag, and Angela Davis each spent studying in France. Especially striking is the account of Kennedy's year abroad. Her postwar France, mired in economic austerity and undergoing physical reconstruction, still retains its cultural prestige. Also, the French government established school systems in their colonies that taught in French and awarded credentials recognized by the French university system. The government awarded scholarships to colonial elites to study in France; in turn, they send on their children. Education converts hard power into soft power; and the soft power resource can be handed down from generation to generation.

In Chapter 1, J. P. Singh includes an exploration of the persistently unequal trade relationships between industrialized North and developing economies in the South. He argues that the pattern of trade and the lack of concessions granted by the North to the South are because of paternalistic cultural values held by the North. The data on international tertiary education both confirm and complicate Singh's argument. The historical pattern revealed in Figure 9.7 shows the conversion of French colonial military and economic power into cultural influence. At the same time, David Throsby, in Chapter 3, reminds us that economic decisions—like deciding which university to attend—are influenced by cultural values, such as what families believe about a foreign country and its universities. The regard for the former colonial center is a mixture of practical considerations and deeply engrained cultural values. As Hausman suggests in Chapter 2, the effects of economics and culture are not causal and unidirectional, but mutual and interactive. Economic choices influence culture; cultural preferences lead to economic choices.

South Africa

South Africa is the leading soft power country in Africa and a regional hub for higher education. Figure 9.8 shows which countries sent the most students to South African universities in 2015. Zimbabwe has the largest foreign student community in South Africa. Streams of students also come from other parts of southern and eastern Africa and also from the United States.

The rise of South Africa's soft power resources is also reflected in its ability to attract immigrants, foreign students, and foreign visitors (Wu 2018). The next two figures contrast the pattern in visitors to South Africa before

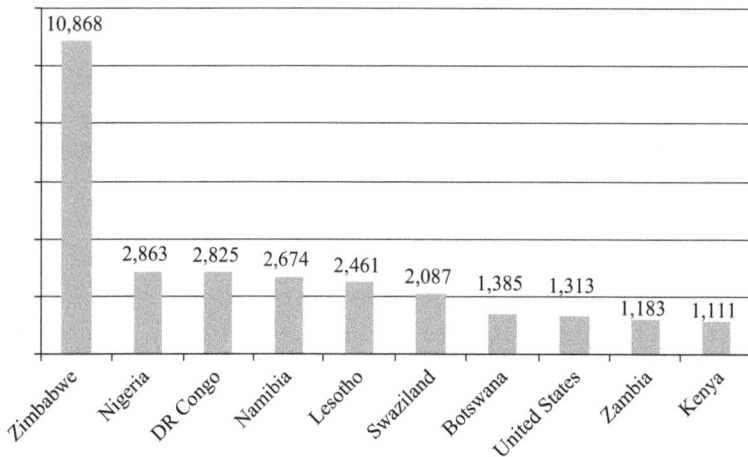

FIGURE 9.8 South Africa: Top ten countries sending students, 2015.
SOURCE: Data from UNESCO Institute of Statistics *UIS.Stat* database, at http://data .uis.unesco.org.

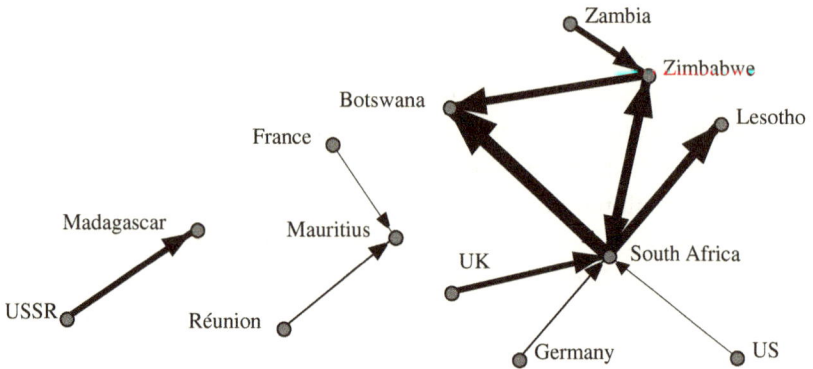

FIGURE 9.9 Foreign visitors to SADC, 1990.
SOURCE: Data provided to the author by UN World Tourism Organization.

and after the end of apartheid. Figure 9.9 shows, for 1990, the largest flows of foreign visitors into some of the member countries of the Southern African Development Community (SADC). The figure shows three main destinations: South Africa, Mauritius, and Madagascar. Thicker arrows reflect more visitors traveling to a country. Figure 9.10 shows the 2015 data for major flows of foreign visitors into SADC. South Africa has become overwhelmingly central to the region. Foreign visitors come to South Africa from more countries, from more regions of the world, and in greater numbers.

When apartheid ended in 1994, South Africa went from pariah to paragon. It installed a democratically elected government and took its place as soft power leader in the region. Figures 9.9 and 9.10 are a visual representation of South Africa's leap from diplomatic isolation to the only country representing the African continent in the G20. In Figure 9.10, dashed lines indicate a smaller flow of visitors than solid lines.

Malaysia
Malaysia promotes itself as a value-for-money education hotspot (Arachi 2005). Malaysia's education ministry aims to improve the ranking of Malaysian universities in global lists and to make Malaysia an educational hub. To meet surging domestic demand for university education, the government's 1996 reforms established alongside the public universities a private higher education sector that could also attract foreign students (Kassim 2014).

As Figure 9.11 illustrates, the number of foreign students in Malaysian universities nearly tripled between 2005 and 2015.

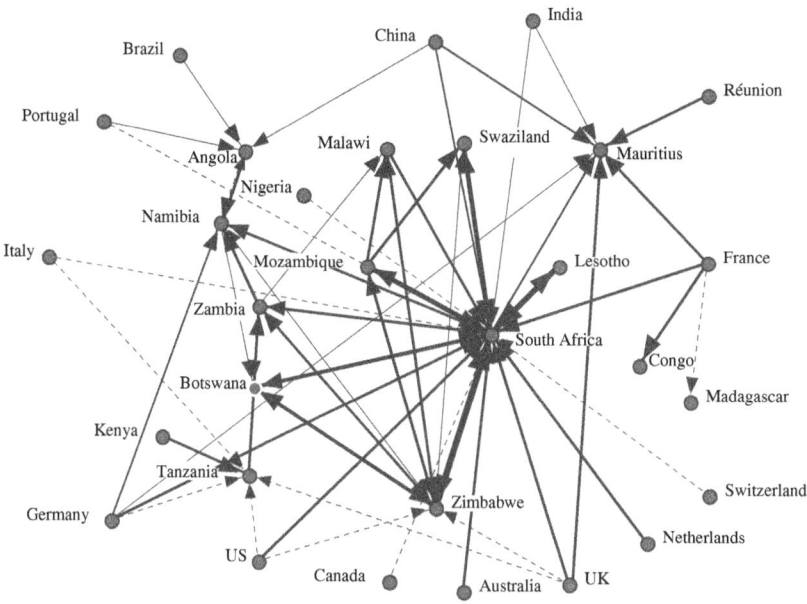

FIGURE 9.10 Foreign visitors to SADC, 2015.
SOURCE: Data provided to the author by UN World Tourism Organization.

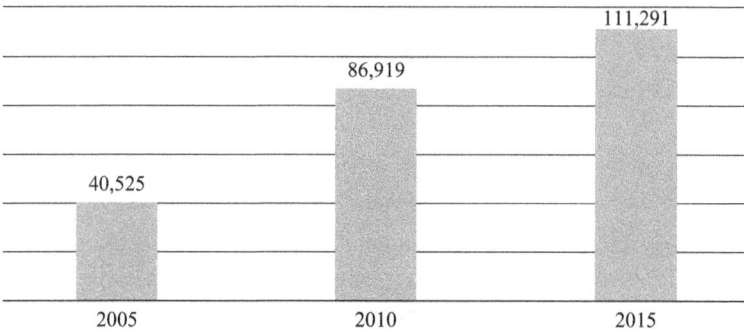

FIGURE 9.11 Malaysia: Total foreign students, 2005–2015.
SOURCE: Data for 2005 and 2010 from Kassim 2014; data for 2015 from UNESCO Institute of Statistics *UIS.Stat* database, at http://data.uis.unesco.org.

In parallel with its 1996 educational reforms, the government has encouraged foreign universities to organize branch campuses in Malaysia. Australia's Monash University and Great Britain's University of Nottingham, for example, both issue degrees taught in English from their Malaysian branch campuses (Arachi 2005). While Malaysia is not primarily an English-speaking country, many universities offer instruction mainly in English, an important key to becoming a top education destination.

At the end of the Cold War, English became the global language of politics and commerce. Throughout Eastern Europe, English replaced Russian as the major second language to learn. Thus, universities in English-speaking countries successfully attract the lion's share of foreign students. Universities in non-English-speaking countries with aspirations to global prestige seriously weigh how much curricula to offer in English to attract foreign students. At the graduate level, for example, German universities are increasing the number of master's and doctoral programs taught in English (Schaefer-Wilke 2018). Between 2011 and 2017, the number of English-language master's programs in Germany increased by 11 percent (Geertz Gonzalez 2017). Similarly, Malaysia's decision to allow and encourage university instruction in English makes it an attractive destination for a larger pool of foreign students.

Surveys of foreign students indicate they are drawn to Malaysia because of the relatively low cost of enrolling in a reputable academic program with good teachers and good facilities (Migin et al. 2015; Zeeshan et al. 2013). Many also look forward to opportunities to work and build careers in Malaysia after graduating. Attracting human capital is an explicit goal of Malaysia's education policy reforms (Kassim 2014). In addition, after the 2001 attacks on the United States, students from Asia and the Middle East faced increasingly restricted visa and university admissions and began to search for other educational centers. Malaysia is a majority Muslim country, which makes it particularly attractive to Muslim students (Zeeshan et al. 2013). Figure 9.12 shows the top twelve countries that sent foreign students to Malaysia in 2015.

Most analyses of soft power and education focus on the United States, the United Kingdom, and France as traditional major destinations; some include Australia and Canada as well. This perspective is based on preconceived images of which countries are the most popular education destination. It turns out to be a limited view. From the research on travel, why people travel to a place depends greatly on the image they have of a destination (Karl, Reintinger, and Schmude 2015). Changing a destination's image requires time and effort; in the travel industry, it is the goal of many tourism promotion boards. The Soft Power Rubric allows us to easily shift perspectives from the host to the sender, from the core to the periphery, and unmasks important country-to-country relationships previously invisible in our usual cognitive frameworks.

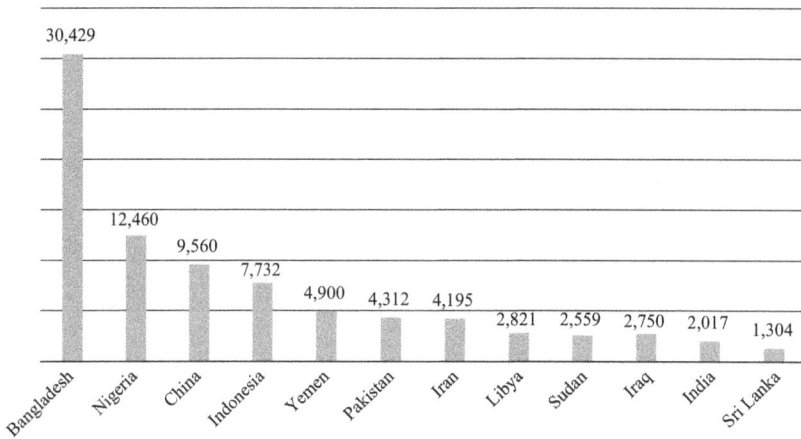

FIGURE 9.12 Malaysia: Top twelve countries sending students, 2015.
SOURCE: Data from UNESCO Institute of Statistics *UIS.Stat* database, at http://data
.uis.unesco.org.

Using the Soft Power Rubric in this case to approach the education data
from the perspective of sending countries from Sub-Saharan Africa highlights Malaysia and South Africa as important. It also places France in
perspective—growing in terms of attracting foreign students but not as rapidly as other leading destinations. The Soft Power Rubric uncovers our blind
spots. The quantitative data are signposts pointing toward undertold stories
of cultural influence.

The Soft Power Rubric's Other Elements:
Migration and Travel

To place the study abroad data in context for the several countries discussed
in this chapter, Figure 9.13 and Table 9.1 also provide data on international
migration and travel. For the fourth element of the soft power rubric—
audiences viewing foreign movies—the data are not complete enough to
make comparisons among this set of countries. In Figure 9.13, the countries
are listed according to the number of foreign students they host; the United
States has the most, at around nine hundred thousand, and South Africa the
least, at forty thousand (see Table 9.1). The graph shows that France, despite
having fewer foreign students than the United Kingdom, has far more foreign visitors. Australia hosts a large number of foreign students compared to

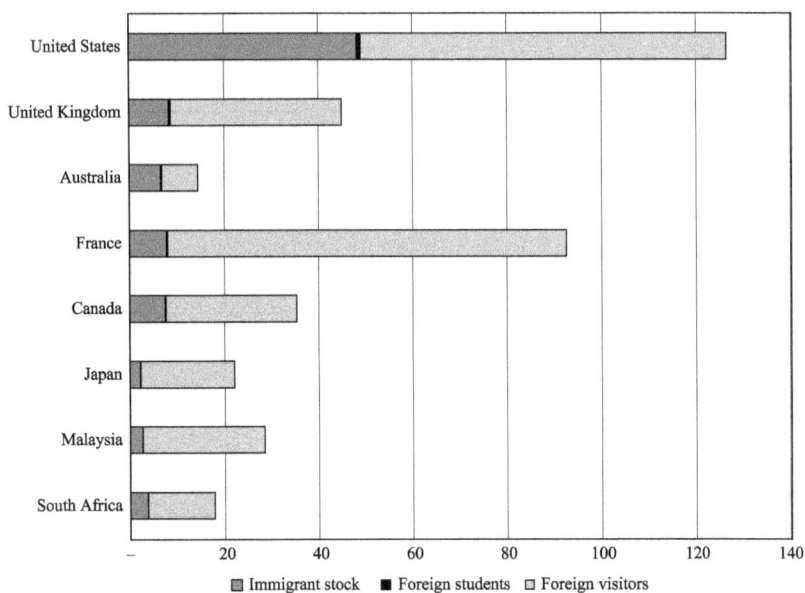

FIGURE 9.13 Immigrants, foreign students, and foreign visitors in selected host countries, 2015 (in millions).

SOURCE: Data from UNESCO Institute of Statistics *UIS.Stat* database, at http://data .uis.unesco.org.

TABLE 9.1 Immigrants, foreign students, and foreign visitors in selected host countries, 2015 (in millions)

Country	Immigrant stock	Foreign students	Foreign visitors
United States	48.18	0.91	77.47
United Kingdom	8.41	0.43	36.11
Australia	6.71	0.29	7.44
France	7.92	0.24	84.45
Canada	7.56	0.17	27.55
Japan	2.23	0.13	19.74
Malaysia	2.65	0.11	25.72
South Africa	3.82	0.04	13.95

SOURCE: Data from UNESCO Institute of Statistics *UIS.Stat* database, at http://data.uis .unesco.org.

other countries but the least foreign visitors of any country in the table. Also apparent is the United States' current overwhelming dominance in attracting foreigners—whether migrants, students, or visitors. In general, Figure 9.13 shows that international education in terms of number of people affected is nearly trivial compared to migration and travel. However, in the narrative of what makes a country a soft power, the experience of foreign students looms large as education and culture are so tightly intertwined.

For all these elements, a successful soft power regime depends on foreign visitors, students, and immigrants having a good experience in the host country. For example, a town interested in attracting tourists will be more successful if the town's businesses and organizations cooperate while competing. If visitors have happy experiences at the coffee shop, on the bus, at the sports arena, and at the visitor center, they will relay their recommendations to their friends. The responsibility for investing in soft power resources—foreigners enjoying their vacation and going home to tell family and friends about it—is the joint responsibility of all those in the host town. If a visitor had a bad day at the park, perhaps a glass of wine on the house will make up for the friction. Individuals taking responsibility only for their own interactions with visitors may not be enough; a collective view is more likely to be successful.

Colonialism, Cold War, and the Knowledge Economy: Push and Pull in International Education

In the literature on international education, the most widely used model to conceptualize students' decision-making process is the push-pull model developed by Tim Mazzarol and Geoffrey Soutar (2002). They describe the dynamics that push a student to go abroad, choosing a particular country and university, and the forces that pull students into that country, including knowledge of the university, personal recommendations from family and friends, whether friends are already studying there, and practical considerations like cost and crime rates. The push-pull model can also be used as a framework to examine the larger world of international education, particularly the historical, global dynamics behind international education over the last two centuries. Colonialism, the Cold War, and the knowledge economy have each influenced the flow of international students.

Colonialism: Pulling foreigners to the center. In terms of pulling students, the nineteenth- and twentieth-century empires used education as a policy tool to shape hearts and minds in their colonies. The British established colleges in India and Africa in the British mold. Ali Mazrui (1992) describes his experience teaching at Makerere College in Uganda in the 1960s. His students' exam questions were sent from and returned to London, passing through the hands of instructors there to ensure conformity with British standards of excellence. Once, Mazrui taught Marx and Lenin in class, but when the exams arrived from London, his question on Marx and Lenin had been deleted and was explained away as a printer's error. When the French established schools in Vietnam, they taught Vietnamese in a Latin script, resulting in the abandonment of the earlier Chinese script and attenuating access to pre-French literary culture and traditions (Kelly 1992). US education goals in the Philippines were to establish democracy and maintain an agricultural economy (Foley 1992), in contrast with neighbors Taiwan and South Korea, where the education goals supported industrialization and economic growth first and democracy later. Colonial education systems further the interest of empires more than the colonies.

Cold War: Pulling students again. During the Cold War, higher education was also an important front. Even prior to World War II, the Soviets invested in supporting students as potential intellectual leaders in their global communist struggle. Many students from developing countries returned home to lead revolutionary movements. The government also sponsored Soviet professors abroad to build academic partnerships with foreign universities (Altbach and de Wit 2016).

The Cold War approach of countries like the United Kingdom and France were extensions of their colonial policies. France continued to sponsor students from its former colonies to study in France and also supported French universities in Africa and other former colonies. The British gave scholarships to students from its former colonies and supported foreign universities as well. The United States' Fulbright program brought foreign students and professors to the United States. Also, funds were available for Americans to train in areas of the world where the United States sought to lead (Altbach and de Wit 2016).

A similar pattern of exchange continues today. Universities make internationalizing the campus an educational goal, another pull for foreign students. Many universities want a diverse campus community to give students a multicultural learning environment. Ross Hudson's (2016) study of a 2013 survey of more than 1,300 higher education institutes in more than 130 countries shows that three-quarters have or are developing a strategy for internationalization. The idea of bringing foreign students and scholars to campus or sending students and professors abroad has become a normal ambition of universities around the world. In a narrower analysis of around 600 European institutions in the survey, Hudson finds that the primary goal of internationalization is to increase cultural understanding and improve the quality of teaching, not commercial considerations.

Knowledge economy: The push abroad. In more recent decades, the rise of the knowledge economy is pushing students to study abroad. The growing importance of information and technology means that for students from developing countries the value of foreign university education is growing.

As educational standards rise throughout the world and more women enroll in universities, the total pool of university students in the world has grown dramatically over the last half-century (Freeman 2010). An increasing fraction of this growing pool enrolls in universities abroad as illustrated in Figure 9.14 (Altbach 2016).

The push for more students to attend universities is great enough to overcome the high cost of a foreign education. In Great Britain, for example, part

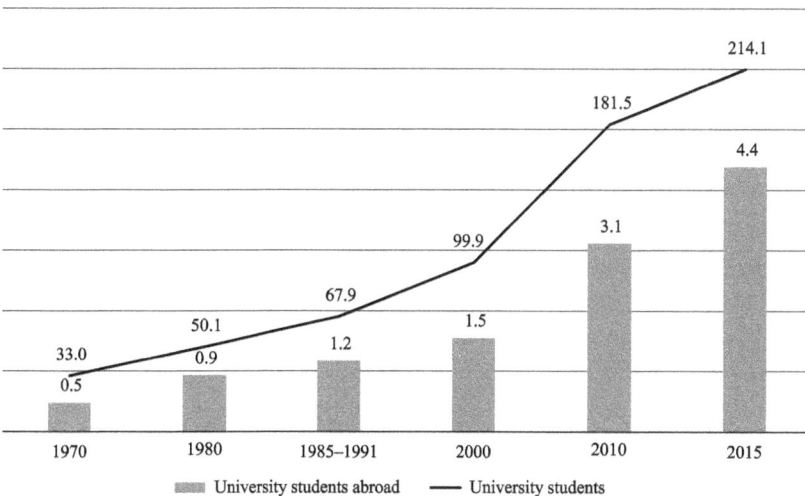

FIGURE 9.14 World total of university students and university students abroad, 1970–2015 (in millions).
SOURCE: Data from UNESCO Institute of Statistics *UIS.Stat* database, at http://data.uis.unesco.org.

of domestic economic reforms in the 1980s included ending full scholarships for overseas students from former colonies. Instead, foreign students paid higher fees than British students, a system that continues today (Williams 1984). British students and EU students pay one level of tuition, while students from other countries pay a higher level. Despite the tuition increase, the foreign demand for British higher education is such that more foreign students enroll now than during the earlier period of scholarships. As of 2015, only the United States hosts more foreign students than Great Britain.

Many countries now compete for foreign students in part because their tuition fees form an important part of university income, a new pull (Altbach and Knight 2011). Sharon Stein and Vanessa Oliveira de Andreotti, in their study of international students in Canada, source their information from local news reports in contrast with Hudson's (2016) surveys of European universities. Stein and Andreotti find a more candid narrative that frames international students as either competition or cash—unwanted competitors against Canadian students or desirable fee-payers that infuse needed funds into the system. For the United States, international students contributed $41 billion to the US economy in 2018–2019 (NAFSA, n.d.). This business aspect of international education incentivizes suppliers to meet the needs of the customer.

The Core-Periphery Structure of the International Education System

For all four elements of the Soft Power Rubric—migration, study abroad, travel, and watching foreign movies—scholars return to the idea of cultural dependence, building on the core-periphery dependency theories of Fernando Henrique Cardoso and Enzo Faletto (1979) and others. In the movie industry, for example, transnational companies headquartered in the United States leverage the structural advantages of access to capital, technology, and large distribution channels to produce programming at a far lower cost than other countries could produce for themselves. A contrasting view put forward by Joseph Straubhaar (1991) and others is that domination of the global movie industry reflects a business cycle that favors the United States now but that will favor others over time. As local producers of programming and content compete, the business-cycle approach predicts that audiences will prefer movies and TV programs that are culturally proximate over US products. Examples include the success of Brazilian and Korean content industries in exporting their programs around the world (Jun 2017; Yang 2012; Straubhaar 1984).

In education, Philip Altbach argues forcefully in a series of coauthored books and articles that the global system is divided between core and periphery countries and that even national systems have similar divisions between core and periphery institutions. At the core are esteemed research universities in prestigious countries with expert faculty, large libraries, and deep research funds. They are the headquarters for publication industries that distribute knowledge. At the periphery are most other universities in most other countries. They depend on the core for innovation and direction (Altbach 2016; Altbach and Kelly 1991; Altbach and de Wit 2016; and Altbach and Knight 2011).

The tragedy of this core-periphery inequality is that the intellectual traditions of many Asian and African countries were jettisoned as the Western model of university education was imposed. The instruction language is often English or another Western language, in effect cutting off students' ability to engage and contribute to intellectual traditions in their native language. The central research questions that consume Western scholars may not be relevant to other societies. Further, research questions that are relevant remain marginalized (Mazrui 1992). Altbach (2016) argues that while developing nations accept foreign educational assistance, the offer is a double-edged sword that simultaneously provides technical help while maintaining dependency.

However, while the legacies of colonialism and the Cold War remain evident in the data on international education, the rise of new educational hubs from more students pushing for university education suggests that a more multipolar system is emerging. Will scholarly work from centers like Malaysia and South Africa challenge the traditional centers of training? More research is necessary to answer this question.

Conclusion

The Soft Power Rubric takes the audience's perspective in uncovering people's social and cultural interactions across borders. The more frequent and intense the interactions between countries, the greater the depth of soft power resources in the relationship. The quantitative data are signposts marking relationships between countries. Changes over time are clues to the historical and cultural shifts between countries.

This chapter focuses on the soft power relationships built through international education. The first starting point is the nations that send the most students abroad to foreign universities: China, India, Germany, Republic of Korea, and Nigeria. Digging deeper into the data shows that the major destinations for these students include the United States and United Kingdom. Other important destinations are Australia, Canada, and Japan. This data set yields some surprising results: Malaysia is an important destination for Nigerian students, and France, generally thought of as a major educational hub, is absent.

A second point of departure is the Sub-Saharan African nations that send students abroad. Here, France is the top destination. Unpacking the countries that send the most students to France, five out of ten are African nations. After France and the United States, South Africa is the third most popular destination for Sub-Saharan students going abroad. South Africa, after many years as an international pariah because of apartheid, is now a regional soft power. In education, South Africa attracts students from many countries across the continent. Malaysia is the fifth most popular destination for Sub-Saharan African university students abroad. Since the 1990s, Malaysia has actively invested in higher education and promoted itself as an international hub. After the 2001 terrorist attacks in the United States, this majority Muslim state benefited from tightened visa regulations. In particular, Malaysia attracted African, Asian, and Middle Eastern students who had more difficulty getting visas and school admissions to some countries.

Finally, the data on study abroad are placed in context with migration and travel data. The number of students crossing borders is nearly negligible compared to the number of migrants and visitors. However, education is a key policy tool for integrating people into society and therefore historically has been an important foreign policy tool.

The Soft Power Rubric is one example of how culture connects with empirical data and conceptual models. International education is an international market trading in services; however, at every level people make choices based not only on financial calculations but on cultural values—as Livingston demonstrates in Chapter 6, bringing both his professional and personal experience to bear. The Soft Power Rubric responds to the challenge posed by Hausman in Chapter 2 to find a way to bring culture into economics and by Throsby in Chapter 3 to find an alternative to financial value to measure culture.

Colonial empires like the United Kingdom, France, and the United States used education to pull colonists into their intellectual orbit; by teaching in the language of the metropole, they actively pushed to the periphery colonists' own intellectual traditions. During the Cold War, the United States and Europe, the Soviet Union and its allies, all used scholarships and academic exchanges to promote their own political ideologies. The traces of these hard power relationships translated into soft power networks and are still visible in the quantitative data today. In France, for example, about half of foreign students hail from former colonies. This affirms the example raised by Singh in Chapter 1 that the paternalistic values of the North have an exploitive effect on trading relations with the South. However, the specifics of the postcolonial international education patterns in France complicate Singh's argument, as they reflect not only this historical exploitation but also a deeply embedded preference for French higher education that resides in the society, families, and individual students of its former colonies and other countries as well.

At the same time, the globalization of markets, the rise of women, and the emergence of the knowledge economy generate a growing, worldwide hunger for university education. As the number of students increases, so does the number who study abroad, pushed by the ambition to enjoy the benefits of globalization. Countries seek to attract foreign students as a matter of prestige and profit. The experience of these hosts countries shows that for foreign students to thrive there needs to be a hospitable community that takes responsibility for the students' well-being. Much like the culture of accountability that Krause uses in Chapter 4 to reframe the cultural values that are necessary to sustain the environment, similarly for foreigners to feel welcome, communities need to go beyond individual responsibility for interactions with these students and consider the whole experience of foreigners. When this is successful, students return to home countries with good skills and stories to share, inspiring the next wave to go abroad.

The Wu Soft Power Rubric uncovers network relationships across countries created by students going abroad. Examining student choices at a global level and regional levels leads to both expected and novel relationships, each of which is a potential research study. This achieves one goal of the Wu Soft Power Rubric, to measure soft power by making cultural relationships among countries tractable to comparisons across countries and across time, and a second, to open new vistas for learning in the process.

Notes

Acknowledgments: This work reflects my views only and not those of the Federal Communications Commission, its members, or staff. I thank the Woodrow Wilson Center for International Scholars for funding the research. J. P. Singh, Henning Schulzrinne, Nanette Levinson, Aynne Kokas, Liz Stanley, Neeti Nair, Monde Muyangwa, Esther Brimmer, and many other colleagues provided much support for this work. Finally, the Kluge Center provided important guidance to the Library of Congress.

1. Note that all the data in this chapter are for "international student mobility in tertiary education," UNESCO's terminology for students enrolled in foreign universities for a degree. While students in less committed study abroad programs are substantively relevant to the question of soft power resources, they are not included in the data set. See http://data.uis.unesco.org/index.aspx?queryid=171.

References

Acemoglu, Daron, David Autor, David Dorn, Gordon H. Hanson, and Brendan Price. 2016. "Import Competition and the Great US Employment Sag of the 2000s." *Journal of Labor Economics* 34 (S1): S141–S198.

Achen, Christopher H., and Larry M. Bartels. 2016. *Democracy for Realists: Why Elections Do Not Produce Responsive Government*. Princeton, NJ: Princeton University Press.

Acheson, Keith, and Christopher Maule. 2006. "Culture in International Trade." In *Handbook of the Economics of Art and Culture*, vol. 1, edited by Victor A. Ginsburgh and David Throsby, 1141–1182. Amsterdam: Elsevier.

Adamy, Janet, and Paul Overberg. 2016. "Counties That Experienced Rapid Diversification Voted Heavily for Donald Trump." *Wall Street Journal*, November 9. http://www.wsj.com/articles/counties-that-experienced-rapid-diversification-voted-heavily-for-donald-trump-1478741076.

Aisch, Gregor, Larry Buchanan, Amanda Cox, and Kevin Quealy. 2017. "Some Colleges Have More Students from the Top 1 Percent than the Bottom 60." *New York Times*, January 18. https://www.nytimes.com/interactive/2017/01/18/upshot/some-colleges-have-more-students-from-the-top-1-percent-than-the-bottom-60.html.

Akerlof, George A., and Rachel E. Kranton. 2010. *Identity Economics: How Identities Shape Our Work, Wages, and Well-Being*. Princeton, NJ: Princeton University Press.

Akhtar, Shayerah Ilias. 2015. "Export-Import Bank: Overview and Reauthorization Issues." Congressional Research Service, March 25. https://www.hsdl.org/?view&did=763640.

Alba, Richard, and Nancy Foner. 2017. "Immigration and the Geography of Polarization." *City and Community* 16 (3): 239–243.

Altbach, Philip G. 2016. *Global Perspectives on Higher Education*. Baltimore: Johns Hopkins University Press.

Altbach, Philip, and Hans de Wit. 2016. "Internationalization and Global Tension: Lessons from History." In *Global Perspectives on Higher Education*, edited by Philip G. Altbach, 73–80. Baltimore: Johns Hopkins University Press.

Altbach, Philip, and Gail Kelly. 1991. *Education and the Colonial Experience*. New York: Advent Books.

Altbach, Philip, and Jane Knight. 2011. "Higher Education's Landscape of Internationalization." In *Leadership for World-Class Universities: Challenges for Developing Countries*, edited by Philip G. Altbach, 108–127. New York: Routledge.

Andolina, Molly W., and Clyde Wilcox. 2000. "Public Opinion: The Paradoxes of Clinton's Popularity." In *The Clinton Scandal and the Future of American Government*, edited by Mark J. Rozell and Clyde Wilcox, 171–194. Washington, DC: Georgetown University Press.

Andrews, Richard N. L. 2016. "The Environmental Protection Agency." In *Environmental Policy: New Directions for the Twenty-First Century*, 9th ed., edited by Norman J. Vig and Michael E. Kraft, 168–192. Los Angeles: Sage.

Ang, Ien. 1982. *Watching Dallas: Soap Opera and the Melodramatic Imagination*. Translated by Della Couling. London: Methuen.

Angelini, Francesco, and Massimiliano Castellani. 2019. "Cultural and Economic Value: A Critical Review." *Journal of Cultural Economics* 43 (2): 173–188.

Appadurai, Arjun. 1989. "Small-Scale Techniques and Large-Scale Objectives." In *Conversations Between Economists and Anthropologists: Methodological Issues in Measuring Economic Change in Rural India*, edited by Pranab Bardhan, 250–282. New York: Oxford University Press.

———. 1996. *Modernity at Large: Cultural Dimensions of Globalization*. Minneapolis: University of Minnesota Press.

———. 2004. "The Capacity to Aspire: Culture and the Terms of Recognition." In *Culture and Public Action*, edited by Vijayendra Rao and Michael Walton, 59–84. Stanford, CA: Stanford University Press.

Appiah, Kwame Anthony. 2006. *Cosmopolitanism: Ethics in a World of Strangers*. New York: Norton.

Arachi, Diana. 2005. "Foreign Branch Campuses in Malaysia: State Action and Consumer Choices Revisited." Master's thesis, Lund University. https://www.researchgate.net/publication/27818731_FOREIGN_BRANCH_CAMPUSES_IN_MALAYSIA_STATE_ACTION_AND_CONSUMER_CHOICES_REVISITED.

Arendt, Hannah. 1958. *The Human Condition*. Chicago: University of Chicago Press.

Aristotle. 1984. *Nicomachean Ethics*. Translated by Hippocrates G. Apostle. Grinnell, IA: Peripatetic.

Ashbee, Edward. 2011. "Bewitched—the Tea Party Movement: Ideas, Interests and Institutions." *Political Quarterly* 82 (2): 157–164.

Atkinson, Carol. 2014. *Military Soft Power: Public Diplomacy Through Military Educational Exchanges*. Lanham, MD: Rowman and Littlefield.

———. 2015. "The Role of U.S. Elite Military Schools in Promoting Intercultural Understanding and Democratic Governance." *All Azimuth* 4 (2): 19–29.

Attridge, Derek. 2004. *The Singularity of Literature.* Abingdon, UK: Routledge.

Auboin, Marc. 2015. "Improving the Availability of Trade Finance in Developing Countries: An Assessment of Remaining Gaps." WTO Staff Working Paper ERSD-2015-06. https://read.wto-ilibrary.org/economic-research-and-trade-policy-analysis/improving-the-availability-of-trade-finance-in-developing-countries-an-assessment-of-remaining-gaps_af342241-en.

Austin, John C. 2017a. "Segregation and Changing Populations Shape Rust Belt's Politics." *The Avenue* (blog), September 14. https://www.brookings.edu/blog/the-avenue/2017/09/14/segregation-and-changing-populations-shape-regions-politics/.

———. 2017b. "A Tale of Two Rust Belts: Diverging Economic Paths Shaping Community Politics." *The Avenue* (blog), June 30. https://www.brookings.edu/blog/the-avenue/2017/06/30/a-tale-of-two-rust-belts-diverging-economic-paths-shaping-community-politics/.

Autor, David H., David Dorn, and Gordon H. Hanson. 2013a. "The China Syndrome: Local Labor Market Effects of Import Competition in the United States." *American Economic Review* 103 (6): 2121–2168.

———. 2013b. "The Geography of Trade and Technology Shocks in the United States." *American Economic Review: Papers and Proceedings* 103 (3): 220–225.

Autor, David H., David Dorn, Gordon H. Hanson, and Kaveh Majlesi. 2016. "A Note on the Effect of Rising Trade Exposure on the 2016 Presidential Election." https://economics.mit.edu/files/12418.

Badkar, Mamta, Sam Fleming, and Joe Rennison. 2018. "US Unemployment Rate Hits Lowest Level Since 1969." *Financial Times*, October 5. https://www.ft.com/content/e77aeobc-c88e-11e8-ba8f-ee390057b8c9.

Bageant, Joe. 2007. *Deer Hunting with Jesus: Dispatches from America's Class War.* New York: Random House.

Bagwell, Kyle, and Robert W. Staiger. 1997. "An Economic Theory of GATT." National Bureau of Economic Research Working Paper 6049. https://www.nber.org/papers/w6049.pdf.

———. 2002. *The Economics of the World Trading System.* Cambridge, MA: MIT Press.

Bailey, Sarah Pulliam. 2016. "The Trump Effect? A Stunning Number of Evangelicals Will Now Accept Politicians' 'Immoral' Acts." *Washington Post*, October 19. https://www.washingtonpost.com/news/acts-of-faith/wp/2016/10/19/the-trump-effect-evangelicals-have-become-much-more-accepting-of-politicians-immoral-acts/.

———. 2017. "'Their Dream President': Trump Just Gave White Evangelicals a Big Boost." *Washington Post*, May 4. https://www.washingtonpost.com/news/acts-of-faith/wp/2017/05/04/their-dream-president-trump-just-gave-white-evangelicals-a-big-boost/.

Bair, Sheila. 2015. "Jeb Hensarling Takes a Swing at Corporate Welfare." *Fortune*, May 18. https://fortune.com/2015/05/18/jeb-hensarling-takes-a-swing-at-corporate-welfare/.

Bardhan, Pranab, and Isha Ray. 2006. "Methodological Approaches in Economics and Anthropology." Q-Squared Working Paper No. 17. https://www.trentu.ca/ids/sites/trentu.ca.ids/files/documents/Q2_WP17_BardhanandRay.pdf.

Barenboim, Daniel. 2008. *Everything Is Connected: The Power of Music*. London: Weidenfeld and Nicolson.

Barnard, Alan. 2000. *History and Theory in Anthropology*. Cambridge: Cambridge University Press.

Barnett, Michael N. 2011. *Empire of Humanity: A History of Humanitarianism*. Ithaca, NY: Cornell University Press.

———. 2012. "International Paternalism and Humanitarian Governance." *Global Constitutionalism* 1 (3): 485–521.

Barnett, Michael, and Raymond Duvall. 2005. *Power in Global Governance*. Cambridge: Cambridge University Press.

Barreto, Matt A., Betsey L. Cooper, Benjamin Gonzalez, Christopher S. Parker, and Christopher Towler. 2011. "The Tea Party in the Age of Obama: Mainstream Conservatism or Out-Group Anxiety?" *Political Power and Social Theory* 22 (1): 1–29.

Barro, Robert J., and Rachel M. McCleary. 2003. "Religion and Economic Growth Across Countries." *American Sociological Review* 68 (5): 760–781.

Baumol, William J., and William G. Bowen. 1966. *Performing Arts: The Economic Dilemma*. New York: Twentieth Century Fund.

Becker, William H., and William M. McClenahan. 2003. *The Market, the State, and the Export-Import Bank of the United States, 1934–2000*. Cambridge: Cambridge University Press.

Benhabib, Seyla. 2006. *Another Cosmopolitanism*. Edited by Robert Post. New York: Oxford University Press.

Bennett, Jane. 2010. *Vibrant Matter: A Political Ecology of Things*. Durham, NC: Duke University Press.

Berger, Peter L., and Thomas Luckmann. 1966. *The Social Construction of Reality*. New York: Doubleday.

Bergsten, C. Fred. 2014. "A Strategy to Bolster the Export-Import Bank." *Washington Post*, September 12. https://www.washingtonpost.com/opinions/c-fred-bergsten-a-strategy-to-bolster-the-export-import-bank/2014/09/12/bfa730dc-390d-11e4-9c9f-ebb47272e40e_story.html.

Blaug, Mark, ed. 1976. *The Economics of the Arts: Selected Readings*. London: Martin Robertson.

———. 2001. "Where Are We Now on Cultural Economics?" *Journal of Economic Surveys* 15 (2): 123–143.

Block, Fred. 2011. "Innovation and the Invisible Hand of Government." In *State of Innovation: The U.S. Government's Role in Technology Development*, edited by F. Block and M. R. Keller, 1–26. Boulder, CO: Paradigm.

Block, Fred, and Matthew R. Keller. 2014. "Can the U.S. Sustain Its Global Position? Dynamism and Stagnation in the U.S. Institutional Model." *Political Power and Social Theory* 26:19–51.

Bomberg, Elizabeth. 2012. "Mind the (Mobilization) Gap: Comparing Climate Activism in the United States and European Union." *Review of Policy Research* 29 (3): 408–430.

Borofsky, Robert. 1998. "Cultural Possibilities." In *World Culture Report: Culture, Creativity and Markets*, 64–75. Paris: UNESCO.

Boston, Rob. 2019. "Falwell Says Nothing Could Lead Him to Drop Support for Trump." *Church and State Magazine*, February. https://www.au.org/church-state/february-2019-church-state-magazine/people-events/falwell-says-nothing-could-lead-him.

Bowen, William G., Martin A. Kurzweil, and Eugene M. Tobin. 2005. *Equity and Excellence in American Higher Education*. Charlottesville: University of Virginia Press.

Bozeman, Adda B. 1960. *Politics and Culture in International History*. Princeton, NJ: Princeton University Press.

Bräutigam, Deborah. 2009. *The Dragon's Gift: The Real Story of China in Africa*. Oxford: Oxford University Press.

Bromwich, David. 2014. *Moral Imagination: Essays*. Princeton, NJ: Princeton University Press.

Buck, Tobias. 2018. "Bavaria Poll Will Shape Germany's Political Future." *Financial Times*, October 12. https://www.ft.com/content/9d004874-cd20-11e8-b276-b9069bde0956.

Buckley, F. H. 2016. "Catholic Surprise: Another Way That Trump Is Remaking the GOP." *New York Post*, December 19. http://nypost.com/2016/12/19/catholic-surprise-another-way-trump-is-remaking-the-gop/.

Burns, Tom R., and Peter Hall, eds. 2013. *The Meta-power Paradigm: Impacts and Transformations of Agents, Institutions, and Social Systems*. New York: Peter Lang.

Cadei, Emily. 2015. "Smackdown: Conservatives vs. Big Business." *Newsweek*, June 8. https://www.newsweek.com/smackdown-conservatives-vs-big-business-340661.

Callon, Michel, Pierre Lascoumes, and Yannick Barthe. 2001. *Acting in an Uncertain World: An Essay on Technical Democracy*. Translated by Graham Burchell. Cambridge, MA: MIT Press.

Calmes, Jackie. 2015. "Ex-Im Bank Is Reopened, but Big Loans Are Stalled." *New York Times*, December 7. https://www.nytimes.com/2015/12/08/business/ex-im-bank-is-reopened-but-big-loans-are-stalled.html.

———. 2016. "A Single Senator Stymies the Export-Import Bank." *New York Times*, June 27. https://www.nytimes.com/2016/06/28/business/international/a-single-senator-stymies-the-export-import-bank.html.

Cardoso, Fernando Henrique, and Enzo Faletto. 1979. *Dependency and Development in Latin America*. Berkeley: University of California Press.

Carey, Kevin. 2015. "How to Raise a University's Profile: Pricing and Packaging." *New York Times*, February 8. https://www.nytimes.com/2015/02/08/education/edlife/how-to-raise-a-universitys-profile-pricing-and-packaging.html.

Carnes, Nicholas, and Noam Lupu. 2017. "It's Time to Bust the Myth: Most Trump Voters Were Not Working Class." *Monkey Cage* (blog), June 5. https://www.washingtonpost.com/news/monkey-cage/wp/2017/06/05/its-time-to-bust-the-myth-most-trump-voters-were-not-working-class.

Carney, Timothy. 2011. "Time for Free-Market Populism from the GOP." *Washington Examiner*, July 10. https://www.washingtonexaminer.com/time-for-free-market-populism-from-the-gop.

Casson, Mark. 2006. "Culture and Economic Performance." In *Handbook of the Economics of Art and Culture*, vol. 1., edited by Victor A. Ginsburgh and David Throsby, 359–397. Amsterdam: Elsevier.

Centers for Disease Control and Prevention. 2018. "Cigarette Smoking Among U.S. Adults Lowest Ever Recorded: 14% in 2017." https://www.cdc.gov/media/releases/2018/p1108-cigarette-smoking-adults.html.

Chamberlain, Edward. 1933. *Monopolistic Competition*. Cambridge, MA: Harvard University Press.

Chang, Ha-Joon. 2002. *Kicking Away the Ladder: Development Strategy in Historical Perspective*. London: Anthem.

Chazan, Guy. 2018. "Bavarians Deliver Stunning Rebuke to Conservative Merkel Allies." *Financial Times*, October 14. https://www.ft.com/content/c095f3f8-cfc1-11e8-a9f2-7574db66bcd5.

Cherlin, Andrew J. 2016. "The Downwardly Mobile for Trump." *New York Times*, August 25. https://www.nytimes.com/2016/08/25/opinion/campaign-stops/the-downwardly-mobile-for-trump.html.

Chin, Gregory, and Kevin P. Gallagher. 2015. "Demise of the US Ex-Im Bank Would Leave the Field to China." *Financial Times*, June 22. https://www.ft.com/content/2322407d-d32a-3f2f-88c6-9d928159bc28.

Chong, Dennis. 2000. *Rational Lives: Norms and Values in Politics and Society*. Chicago: University of Chicago Press.

Chozick, Amy. 2016. "Hillary Clinton Calls Many Trump Backers 'Deplorables,' and G.O.P. Pounces." *New York Times*, September 10. https://www.nytimes.com/2016/09/11/us/politics/hillary-clinton-basket-of-deplorables.html.

Cirilli, Kevin. 2015. "Republican Study Committee Comes Out Against Ex-Im." *The Hill*, May 21. https://thehill.com/business-a-lobbying/242803-republican-study-committee-comes-out-against-ex-im.

Clarke, Harold D., Matthew Goodwin, and Paul Whiteley. 2017. *Brexit: Why Britain Voted to Leave the European Union*. Cambridge: Cambridge University Press.

CNN. 2016. "Trump Speaks at Freedom and Faith Summit." June 10. http://transcripts.cnn.com/TRANSCRIPTS/1606/10/wolf.02.html.

Coase, Ronald H. 1960. "The Problem of Social Cost." *Journal of Law and Economics* 3 (1): 1–69.

Cohen, Jere. May 1980. "Rational Capitalism in Renaissance Italy." *American Journal of Sociology* 85 (6): 1340–1355.

Cohn, Nate. 2017. "A 2016 Review: Why Key State Polls Were Wrong About Trump." *New York Times*, May 31. https://www.nytimes.com/2017/05/31/upshot/a-2016 -review-why-key-state-polls-were-wrong-about-trump.html.

Colantone, Italo, and Piero Stanig. 2018. "Global Competition and Brexit." *American Political Science Review* 112 (2): 201–218.

Coleman, James S. 1988. "Social Capital in the Creation of Human Capital." *American Journal of Sociology* 94:S94–S120.

Congressional Budget Office. 2003. "The Economic Costs of Fuel Economy Standards Versus a Gasoline Tax." December. https://www.cbo.gov/sites/default/files/108th -congress-2003-2004/reports/12-24-03_cafe.pdf.

Coontz, Stephanie. 2017. "Do Millennial Men Want Stay-at-Home Wives?" *New York Times*, March 31. https://www.nytimes.com/2017/03/31/opinion/sunday/do -millennial-men-want-stay-at-home-wives.html.

Costa, Robert, and Jenna Johnson, 2016. "Evangelical Leader Jerry Falwell Jr. Endorses Trump." *Washington Post*, January 26. https://www.washingtonpost.com/news/ post-politics/wp/2016/01/26/evangelical-leader-jerry-falwell-jr-endorses-trump/.

Cox, Daniel, Rachel Lienesch, and Robert P. Jones. 2017. "Beyond Economics: Fears of Cultural Displacement Pushed the White Working Class to Trump." Public Religion Research Institute, May 9. https://www.prri.org/research/white-working -class-attitudes-economy-trade-immigration-election-donald-trump/.

Cramer, Katherine J. 2016. *The Politics of Resentment: Rural Consciousness in Wisconsin and the Rise of Scott Walker.* Chicago: University of Chicago Press.

Cronon, William. 1995. "The Trouble with Wilderness; or, Getting Back to the Wrong Nature." In *Uncommon Ground: Rethinking the Human Place in Nature*, edited by William Cronon, 69–90. New York: Norton.

CSIS (Center for Strategic and International Studies). 2013. *Restoring US Leadership in Nuclear Energy: A National Security Imperative.* Washington, DC: Center for Strategic and International Studies.

Daily Kos. 2016. "Be Happy for Coal Miners Losing Their Health Insurance: They're Getting Exactly What They Voted For." December 12. http://www.dailykos.com/ story/2016/12/12/1610198/-Be-happy-forcoal-miners-losing-their-health-insurance -They-re-getting-exactly-what-they-voted-for.

Dann, Carrie. 2019. "'A Deep and Boiling Anger': NBC/WSJ Poll Finds a Pessimistic America Despite Current Economic Satisfaction." *NBC News*, August 25. https:// www.nbcnews.com/politics/meet-the-press/deep-boiling-anger-nbc-wsj-poll -finds-pessimistic-america-despite-n1045916.

Darchy-Koechlin, Brigitte, and Hugues Draelants. 2010. "'To Belong or Not to Belong?' The French Model of Elite Selection and the Integration of International Students." *French Politics* 8 (4): 429–446.

Davis, Rowenna. 2010. "Working-Class Revolution Not Reaching 'Posh' Universities." *The Guardian*, September 28. https://www.theguardian.com/education/2010/sep/ 28/working-class-students-posh-universities.

Day, Amber. 2011. *Satire and Dissent: Interventions in Contemporary Political Debate.* Bloomington: Indiana University Press.

Deutsch, Karl. 1966. *Nationalism and Social Communication: An Inquiry into the Foundations of Nationality.* Cambridge, MA: MIT Press.

De Vries, Catherine E. 2018. "The Cosmopolitan-Parochial Divide: Changing Patterns of Party and Electoral Competition in the Netherlands and Beyond." *Journal of European Public Policy* 25 (11): 1541–1565.

Dijkstra, Lewis, Hugo Poelman, and Andrés Rodríguez-Pose. 2018. "The Geography of EU Discontent." European Commission Working Paper WP 12/2018. https://ec.europa.eu/regional_policy/sources/docgener/work/2018_02_geog_discontent.pdf.

Douglas, Mary. 1986. *How Institutions Think.* Syracuse, NY: Syracuse University Press.

Douglas, Mary, and Aaron Wildavsky. 1982. *Risk and Culture: An Essay on the Selection of Technical and Environmental Dangers.* Berkeley: University of California Press.

Dryzek, John S. 2016. "Institutions for the Anthropocene: Governance in a Changing Earth System." *British Journal of Political Science* 46 (4): 937–956.

Eagleton, Terry. 2016. *Culture.* New Haven, CT: Yale University Press.

Eckersley, Robyn. 2004. *The Green State: Rethinking Democracy and Sovereignty.* Cambridge, MA: MIT Press.

The Economist. 2017. "Where France's National Front Is on the Rise." March 2. https://www.economist.com/graphic-detail/2017/03/02/where-frances-national-front-is-on-the-rise.

Ehrenberg-Shannon, Billy, and Aleksandra Wisniewska. 2017. "How Education Level Is the Biggest Predictor of Support for Geert Wilders." *Financial Times*, March 2. https://www.ft.com/dutchvoting.

Ehrenreich, Barbara. 2017. "The Future of Work." *New York Times Magazine*, February 23. https://www.nytimes.com/2017/02/23/magazine/american-working-class-future.html.

Eichengreen, Barry. 2018. *The Populist Temptation: Economic Grievance and Political Reaction in the Modern Era.* Oxford: Oxford University Press.

Elster, Jon. 1983. *Sour Grapes: Studies in the Subversion of Rationality.* New York: Cambridge University Press.

———. 1989. *Nuts and Bolts for the Social Sciences.* Cambridge, MA: Cambridge University Press.

Espenshade, Thomas J., and Alexandria Walton Radford. 2013. *No Longer Separate, Not Yet Equal: Race and Class in Elite College Admission and Campus Life.* Princeton, NJ: Princeton University Press.

Eurostat. 2019. "Unemployment Statistics." November. Available at https://ec.europa.eu/eurostat/statistics-explained/index.php/Unemployment_statistics.

Evans, Geoffrey, and Anand Menon. 2017. *Brexit and British Politics.* Cambridge, UK: Polity Press.

EXIM (Export-Import Bank of the United States). 2014. "Annual Report, 2014." https://www.exim.gov/sites/default/files/reports/annual/EXIM-2014-AR.pdf.

———. 2015. "Report to the U.S. Congress on Global Export Credit Competition." https://www.exim.gov/sites/default/files/reports/2015EXIMCompetitive ReportFINAL-v3.3.pdf.

Fahrenhold, David A. 2016. "Trump Recorded Having Extremely Lewd Conversation About Women in 2005." *Washington Post*, October 8. https://www.washingtonpost.com/politics/trump-recorded-having-extremely-lewd-conversation-about-women-in-2005/2016/10/07/3b9ce776-8cb4-11e6-bf8a-3d26847eeed4_story.html.

Faux, Jeff. 2012. "The Myth of the Level Playing Field." *American Prospect* 23 (3): 47–50.

Feeney, Nolan. 2014. "Pentagon: 7 in 10 Youths Would Fail to Qualify for Military Service." *Time*, June 29. http://time.com/2938158/youth-fail-to-qualify-military-service/.

Feinberg, Joel. 1970. *Doing and Deserving: Essays in the Theory of Responsibility*. Princeton, NJ: Princeton University Press.

Financial Times. 2019. "Brexit, German Elections, US Jobs." September 1. https://www.ft.com/content/f28d0aec-ca4b-11e9-a1f4-3669401ba76f.

Fine, Ben. 2000. "Economics Imperialism and Intellectual Progress: The Present as History of Economic Thought?" *History of Economics Review* 32 (1): 10–35.

Fine, Gary Alan. 2012. *Tiny Publics: A Theory of Group Action and Culture*. New York: Russell Sage Foundation.

Finnemore, Martha, and Kathryn Sikkink. 1998. "International Norm Dynamics and Political Change." *International Organization* 52 (4): 887–917.

Fitzgerald, Jennifer. 2018. *Close to Home: Local Ties and Voting Radical Right in Europe*. Cambridge: Cambridge University Press.

Flegenheimer, Matt, and Maggie Haberman. 2016. "Donald Trump, Abortion Foe, Eyes 'Punishment' for Women, Then Recants." *New York Times*, March 30. https://www.nytimes.com/2016/03/31/us/politics/donald-trump-abortion.html.

Focarelli, Carlo. 2012. *International Law as Social Construct: The Struggle for Global Justice*. Oxford: Oxford University Press.

Foley, Douglas. 1992. "Colonialism and Schooling in the Philippines, 1898–1970." In *Education and the Colonial Experience*, edited by Philip Altbach and Gail Kelly, 33–53. New York: Advent Books.

Forbes, Duncan. 1975. *Hume's Philosophical Politics*. Cambridge: Cambridge University Press.

Fordham, Benjamin O., and Katja Kleinberg. 2012. "How Can Economic Interests Influence Support for Free Trade?" *International Organization* 66 (2): 311–328.

Forman-Barzilai, Fonna. 2010. *Adam Smith and the Circles of Sympathy: Cosmopolitanism and Moral Theory*. Cambridge: Cambridge University Press.

Forrest, Adam. 2014. "Naomi Klein: 'A 3-Day Week Will Help to Save Life on Earth.'" *Big Issue*, October 28. http://www.bigissue.com/interviews/naomi-klein-3-day-week-will-help-save-life-earth.

Frank, Robert. 2009. "Would a Carbon Tax Make Higher Gasoline Taxes Unnecessary?" *FiveThirtyEight*, May 21. https://fivethirtyeight.com/features/would-carbon-tax-make-higher-gasoline/.

Frank, Thomas. 2004. *What's the Matter with Kansas?* New York: Henry Holt.

Franz, Christian, Marcel Fratzscher, and Alexander S. Kritikos. 2018. "German Right-Wing Party AfD Finds More Support in Rural Areas with Aging Populations." *DIW Weekly Report* 7–8:69–80. https://www.diw.de/documents/publikationen/73/diw_01.c.578785.de/dwr-18-07-1.pdf.

Frazer, Michael. 2010. *The Enlightenment of Sympathy: Justice and the Moral Sentiments in the Eighteenth Century and Today.* Oxford: Oxford University Press.

Freeman, Richard B. 2010. "What Does Global Expansion of Higher Education Mean for the United States?" In *American Universities in a Global Market*, edited by Charles T. Clotfelter, 373–404. Chicago: University of Chicago Press.

Freund, Caroline. 2016. "Deconstructing Branko Milanovic's 'Elephant Chart': Does It Show What Everyone Thinks?" Peterson Institute for International Economics, November 30. https://piie.com/blogs/realtime-economic-issues-watch/deconstructing-branko-milanovics-elephant-chart-does-it-show.

Freund, Caroline, and Dario Sidhu. 2017. "Manufacturing and the 2016 Election: An Analysis of US Presidential Election Data." Peterson Institute for International Economics Working Paper 17-7. https://www.piie.com/publications/working-papers/manufacturing-and-2016-election.

Frey, William H. 2017. "A Substantial Majority of Americans Live Outside Trump Counties, Census Shows." *The Avenue* (blog), March 23. https://www.brookings.edu/blog/the-avenue/2017/03/23/a-substantial-majority-of-americans-live-outside-trump-counties-census-shows/.

Friedman, Jeffrey, ed. 1996. *The Rational Choice Controversy: Economic Models of Politics Reconsidered.* New Haven, CT: Yale University Press.

Fussell, Paul. 1992. *Class: A Guide Through the American Status System.* New York: Simon and Schuster.

Gabler, Neal. 2016. "The Secret Shame of Middle-Class Americans." *The Atlantic*, May. https://www.theatlantic.com/magazine/archive/2016/05/my-secret-shame/476415/.

Galbraith, John K. 1960. *The Liberal Hour.* London: Hamish Hamilton.

Gallagher, Maggie. 2016. "Four Truths About the Party of Trump." *National Review*, July 22. http://www.nationalreview.com/article/438238/donald-trumps-republican-party-will-move-left-social-issues.

Gans, John A., Jr. 2013. "Did Bruce Springsteen Win the Cold War?" *Survival* 55 (6): 169–178.

Gaventa, John. 1982. *Power and Powerlessness: Quiescence and Rebellion in an Appalachian Valley.* Urbana: University of Illinois Press.

Gayte, Marie, Blandine Chelini-Pont, and Mark J. Rozell, eds. 2018. *Catholics and US Politics After the 2016 Elections: Understanding the "Swing Vote."* New York: Palgrave MacMillan.

Geertz, Clifford. 1973. *The Interpretation of Cultures.* New York: Basic Books.

Geertz Gonzalez, Roger. 2017. "Internationalization at a German University: The Purpose and Paradoxes of English Language." *International Education Journal* 16 (2): 49–62.

Gellner, Ernest. 1983. *Nations and Nationalism.* Ithaca, NY: Cornell University Press.

Gest, Justin. 2016. *The New Minority: White Working Class Politics in an Age of Immigration and Inequality.* New York: Oxford University Press.

Gibson-Graham, J. K. 2006. *Postcapitalist Politics.* Minneapolis: University of Minnesota Press.

Giddens, Anthony. 1984. *The Constitution of Society: Outline of the Theory of Structuration.* Berkeley: University of California Press.

Ginsburgh, Victor A., and Pierre-Michel Menger, eds. 1996. *Economics of the Arts: Selected Essays.* Amsterdam: Elsevier.

Ginsburgh, Victor A., and David Throsby, eds. 2006. *Handbook of the Economics of Art and Culture.* Vol. 1. Amsterdam: Elsevier.

———, eds. 2013. *Handbook of the Economics of Art and Culture.* Vol. 2. Amsterdam: Elsevier.

Goffman, Irving. 1959. *The Presentation of Self in Everyday Life.* New York: Anchor Books.

Golbert, Rebecca. 2001. "Transnational Orientations from Home: Constructions of Israel and Transnational Space Among Ukrainian Jewish Youth." *Journal of Ethnic and Migration Studies* 27 (4): 713–773.

Goldsmith, Benjamin E., and Yusaku Horiuchi. 2012. "In Search of Soft Power: Does Foreign Public Opinion Matter for US Foreign Policy?" *World Politics* 64 (3): 555–585.

Goodhart, David. 2017. *The Road to Somewhere: The New Tribes Shaping British Politics.* New York: Penguin Books.

Goodwin, Craufurd. 2006. "Art and Culture in the History of Economic Thought." In *Handbook of the Economics of Art and Culture,* vol. 1, edited by Victor A. Ginsburgh and David Throsby, 25–68. Amsterdam: Elsevier.

Goodwin, Matthew, and Oliver Heath. 2016. "Brexit Vote Explained: Poverty, Low Skills and Lack of Opportunities." Joseph Rowntree Foundation, August 31. https://www.jrf.org.uk/report/brexit-vote-explained-poverty-low-skills-and-lack -opportunities.

Goodwin, Matthew, and Caitlin Milazzo. 2017. "Taking Back Control? Investigating the Role of Immigration in the 2016 Vote for Brexit." *British Journal of Politics and International Relations* 19 (3): 450–464.

Granovetter, Mark. 1985. "Economic Action and Social Structure: The Problem of Embeddedness." *American Journal of Sociology* 91 (3): 481–510.

———. 2005. "Business Groups and Social Organization." In *Handbook of Economic Sociology,* edited by Neil J. Smelser and Richard Swedberg, 429–450. Princeton, NJ: Princeton University Press.

Gray, Mark M. 2018. "Catholics and the 2016 Elections." In *Catholics and US Politics After the 2016 Elections: Understanding the "Swing Vote,"* edited by Marie Gayte, Blandine Chelini-Pont, and Mark J. Rozell, 209–219. New York: Palgrave MacMillan.

Greif, Avner. 1993. "Contract Enforceability and Economic Institutions in Early Trade: The Maghribi Traders' Coalition." *American Economic Review* 83 (3): 525–548.

Guèvremont, V. 2015. "Promoting the Convention in International Forums." In *Reshaping Cultural Policies: A Decade Promoting the Diversity of Cultural Expressions for Development*, 135–147. Paris: UNESCO.

Guiso, Luigi, Paola Sapienza, and Luigi Zingales. 2006. "Does Culture Affect Economic Outcomes?" *Journal of Economic Perspectives* 20 (2): 23–48.

Gul, Faruk, and Wolfgang Pesendorfer. 2008. "The Case for Mindless Economics." In *The Foundations of Positive and Normative Economics: A Handbook*, edited by Andrew Caplin and Andrew Schotter, 3–39. New York: Oxford University Press.

Haakonssen, Knud. 1996. *Natural Law and Moral Philosophy: From Grotius to the Scottish Enlightenment*. Cambridge: Cambridge University Press.

Hacker, Jacob S., and Paul Pierson. 2016. "Making America Great Again." *Foreign Affairs* 95 (3): 69–90.

Hainmueller, Jens, and Daniel J. Hopkins. 2014. "Public Attitudes Toward Immigration." *Annual Review of Political Science* 17:225–249.

Hakhverdian, Armen, Erika van Elsas, Wouter van der Brug, and Theresa Kuhn. 2013. "Euroscepticism and Education: A Longitudinal Study of 12 EU Member States, 1973–2010." *European Union Politics* 14 (4): 522–541.

Hamper, Ben. 1991. *Rivethead: Tales from the Assembly Line*. New York: Warner Books.

Hannerz, Ulf. 1992. *Cultural Complexity*. New York: Columbia University Press.

Harraway, Donna J. 2008. *When Species Meet*. Minneapolis: University of Minnesota Press.

Harrison, Lawrence E., and Samuel P. Huntington. 2000. *Culture Matters: How Values Shape Human Progress*. New York: Basic Books.

Hart, H. L. A. 2008. *Punishment and Responsibility: Essays in the Philosophy of Law*. New York: Oxford University Press.

Hausman, Daniel M. 2012. *Preference, Value, Choice, and Welfare*. Cambridge: Cambridge University Press.

Hertel-Fernandez, Alexander, and Theda Skocpol. 2016. "Five Myths About the Koch Brothers—and Why It Matters to Set Them Straight." Moyers, March 10. http://billmoyers.com/story/five-myths-about-the-koch-network-and-why-it-matters-to-set-them-straight/.

Heyer, Kristin E., Mark J. Rozell, and Michael A. Genovese, eds. 2008. *Catholics and Politics: The Dynamic Tension Between Faith and Power*. Washington, DC: Georgetown University Press.

Hiebert, Daniel. 2002. "Cosmopolitanism at the Local Level: The Development of Transnational Neighborhoods." In *Conceiving Cosmopolitanism: Theory, Context, and Practice*, edited by Steven Vertovec and Robin Cohen, 209–223. New York: Oxford University Press.

Hochschild, Arlie Russell. 2016. *Strangers in their Own Land: Anger and Mourning on the American Right*. New York: New Press.

Hoffman, Andrew J. 2015. *How Culture Shapes the Climate Change Debate*. Stanford, CA: Stanford University Press.

Hooghe, Marc, and Ruth Dassonneville. 2018. "Explaining the Trump Vote: The Effect of Racist Resentment and Anti-immigrant Sentiments." *PS: Political Science and Politics* 51 (3): 528–534.

Hopewell, Kristen. 2017. "When Market Fundamentalism and Industrial Policy Collide: The Tea Party and the US Export-Import Bank." *Review of International Political Economy* 24 (4): 569–598.

———. 2018. "What Is 'Made in China 2025'—and Why Is It a Threat to Trump's Trade Goals?" *Washington Post*, May 3. https://www.washingtonpost.com/news/monkey-cage/wp/2018/05/03/what-is-made-in-china-2025-and-why-is-it-a-threat-to-trumps-trade-goals/.

———. 2019. "Power Transitions and Global Trade Governance: The Impact of a Rising China on the Export Credit Regime." *Regulation and Governance*, April 23. https://onlinelibrary.wiley.com/doi/abs/10.1111/rego.12253.

Hoxby, Caroline M., and Christopher Avery. 2012. "The Missing 'One-Offs': The Hidden Supply of High-Achieving, Low Income Students." National Bureau of Economic Research Working Paper 18586. https://www.nber.org/papers/w18586.pdf.

Hudson, Deal W. 2008. *Onward Christian Soldiers: The Growing Political Power of Catholics and Evangelicals in the United States.* New York: Threshold Press.

Huang, Jon, Samuel Jacoby, Michael Strickland, and K. K. Rebecca Lai. 2016. "Election 2016: Exit Polls." *New York Times*, November 8. https://www.nytimes.com/interactive/2016/11/08/us/politics/election-exit-polls.html.

Hudson, Ross. 2016. "Dominated by Economics? Evidence of Changing Drivers of Internationalization and Its Funding Within Higher Education Institutions in Europe." *Higher Education Policy* 29:1–19.

Hufbauer, Gary Clyde, Meera Fickling, and Woan Foong Wong. 2011. "Revitalizing the Export-Import Bank." Peterson Institute for International Economics Policy Brief No. PB11-6. https://www.piie.com/sites/default/files/publications/pb/pb11-06.pdf.

Hume, David. 1968. *A Treatise of Human Nature.* Edited by L. A. Selby-Bigge. Oxford, UK: Clarendon Press.

Hutter, Michael, and David Throsby, eds. 2008. *Beyond Price: Value in Culture, Economics, and the Arts.* New York: Cambridge University Press.

Iammarino, Simona, Andrés Rodríguez-Pose, and Michael Storper. 2019. "Regional Inequality in Europe: Evidence, Theory and Policy Implications." *Journal of Economic Geography* 19 (2): 273–298.

Iapadre, P. Lelio. 2013. "Cultural Products in the International Trading System." In *Handbook of the Economics of Art and Culture*, vol. 2, edited by Victor A. Ginsburgh and David Throsby, 381–409. Amsterdam: Elsevier.

Ignatieff, Michael. 2011. *Human Rights as Politics and Idolatry.* Princeton, NJ: Princeton University Press.

Inglehart, Ronald. 1990. *Culture Shift in Advanced Industrial Society.* Princeton, NJ: Princeton University Press.

Inglehart, Ronald, and Wayne E. Baker. 2000. "Modernization, Cultural Change, and the Persistence of Traditional Values." *American Sociological Review* 65 (1): 19–51.

Inglehart, Ronald F., and Pippa Norris. 2016. "Trump, Brexit, and the Rise of Populism: Economic Have-Nots and Cultural Backlash." Harvard Kennedy School Working Paper No. RWP16-026. https://www.hks.harvard.edu/publications/trump-brexit-and-rise-populism-economic-have-nots-and-cultural-backlash.

Isenberg, Nancy. 2016. *White Trash: The 400-Year Untold History of Class in America.* New York: Penguin.

Ivaldi, G., and J. Gombin. 2015. "The Front National and the New Politics of the Rural in France." In *Rural Protest Groups and Populist Political Parties*, edited by Dirk Strijker, Gerrit Voerman, and Ida Terluin, 243–264. Netherlands: Wageningen Academic.

Jaki, Stanley L. 1993. "Medieval Christianity: Its Inventiveness in Technology and Science." In *Technology in the Western Political Tradition*, edited by Arthur M. Melzer, Jerry Weinberger, and M. Richard Zinman, 46–68. Ithaca, NY: Cornell University Press.

Jamieson, Dale W., and Marcello Di Paola. 2016. "Political Theory for the Anthropocene." In *Global Political Theory*, edited by David Held and Pietro Maffettone, 254–280. Cambridge, UK: Polity Press.

Jelen, Ted G. 2018. "'Can We Get the Catholic Vote?': The Effects of Catholic Running Mates in Presidential Elections." In *Catholics and US Politics After the 2016 Elections: Understanding the "Swing Vote,"* edited by Marie Gayte, Blandine Chelini-Pont, and Mark J. Rozell, 193–208. New York: Palgrave MacMillan.

Jennings, Bruce. 2016. *Ecological Governance: Toward a New Social Contract with the Earth.* Morgantown: West Virginia University Press.

Jennings, Will, and Gerry Stoker. 2019. "The Divergent Dynamics of Cities and Towns: Geographical Polarisation and Brexit." *Political Quarterly* 90 (S2): 155–166.

Jennings, Will, Gerry Stoker, and Ian Warren. 2018. "Towns and Cities." In *Brexit and Public Opinion*, 43–46. London: UK in a Changing Europe. https://ukandeu.ac.uk/wp-content/uploads/2018/01/Public-Opinion.pdf.

Johnson, Julian. 2002. *Who Needs Classical Music? Cultural Choice and Musical Value.* New York: Oxford University Press.

Jones, Owen. 2016. *Chavs: The Demonization of the Working Class.* Kindle ed. London: Verso Books.

Jones, Robert P. 2016. "Donald Trump and the Transformation of White Evangelicals." *Time*, November 19. http://time.com/4577752/donald-trump-transformation-white-evangelicals/.

Jun, Hannah. 2017. "*Hallyu* at a Crossroads: The Clash of Korea's Soft Power Success and China's Hard Power Threat in Light of Terminal High Altitude Area Defense (THAAD) System Deployment." *Asian International Studies Review* 18 (1): 153–169.

Kahlenberg, Richard D. 2017. "Harvard's Class Gap: Can the Academy Understand Donald Trump's 'Forgotten' Americans?" *Harvard Magazine*, May–June. http://harvardmagazine.com/2017/05/harvards-class-gap.

Kahler, Miles. 1998. "Rationality in International Relations." *International Organization* 52 (4): 919–941.

Kahn, Herman. 1979. *World Economic Development: 1979 and Beyond*. Boulder, CO: Westview Press.

Kahneman, Daniel. 2011. *Thinking, Fast and Slow*. New York: Farrar, Straus and Giroux.

Kahneman, Daniel, and Amos Tversky. 1984. "Choices, Values, and Frames." *American Psychologist* 39 (4): 341–350.

Kaplan, Alice. 2013. *Dreaming in French: The Paris Years of Jacqueline Bouvier Kennedy, Susan Sontag, and Angela Davis*. Chicago: University of Chicago Press.

Karl, Marion, Christine Reintinger, and Jürgen Schmude. 2015. "Reject or Select: Mapping Destination Choice." *Annals of Tourism Research* 54:48–64.

Kassim, Azizah. 2014. Recent Trends in Transnational Population Inflows into Malaysia: Policy, Issues and Challenges. *Malaysian Journal of Economic Studies* 51 (1): 9–23.

Kaufmann, Eric, and Gareth Harris. 2014. *Changing Places: "Mapping the White British Response to Ethnic Change . . ."* London: Demos. https://www.demos.co.uk/files/Changing_places_-_web.pdf.

Keesing, Roger M., Malcom Crick, Barbara Frankel, Jonathan Friedman, Elvin Hatch, J. G. Osten, Rik Pinxten, Jerome Rousseau, and Marilyn Strathern. 1987. "Anthropology as Interpretive Quest." *Current Anthropology* 28 (2): 161–176.

Kelly, Gail P. 1992. "Colonialism, Indigenous Society, and School Practices: French West Africa and Indochina." In *Education and the Colonial Experience*, edited by Philip Altbach and Gail Kelly, 9–32. New York: Advent Books.

Kendall, Gavin, Ian Woodward, and Zlatko Skrbiš. 2009. *Sociology of Cosmopolitanism: Globalization, Identity, Culture and Government*. New York: Palgrave Macmillan.

Kenny, Charles. 2005. "Does Development Make You Happy? Subjective Wellbeing and Economic Growth in Developing Countries." *Social Indicators Research* 73 (2): 199–219.

Kim, Sung Ho. 2017. "Max Weber." In *Stanford Encyclopedia of Philosophy*, Winter 2017 ed., edited by Edward N. Zalta. https://plato.stanford.edu/archives/win2017/entries/weber.

Kinder, Donald R., and D. Roderick Kiewiet. 1981. "Sociotropic Politics: The American Case." *British Journal of Political Science* 11 (2): 129–161.

King, Gary, Robert O. Keohane, and Sidney Verba. 1994. *Designing Social Inquiry: Scientific Inference in Qualitative Research*. Princeton, NJ: Princeton University Press.

Klein, Naomi. 2014. *This Changes Everything: Capitalism vs. the Climate*. New York: Simon and Schuster.

Klotz, Audie. 1995. "Norms Reconstituting Interests: Global Racial Equality and US Sanctions Against South Africa." *International Organization* 49 (3): 451–478.

Kmiec, Douglas W. 2018. "The Catholic Vote in the Election of Donald J. Trump." In *Catholics and US Politics After the 2016 Elections: Understanding the "Swing Vote,"* edited by Marie Gayte, Blandine Chelini-Pont, and Mark J. Rozell, 129–160. New York: Palgrave MacMillan.

Knight, Frank H. 1921. *Risk, Uncertainty and Profit*. Boston: Houghton Mifflin.

———. 1941. "Anthropology and Economics." *Journal of Political Economy* 49 (2): 247–268.

Kotkin, Joel. 2016. "It Wasn't Rural 'Hicks' Who Elected Trump: The Suburbs Were—and Will Remain—the Real Battle Ground." *Joel Kotkin* (blog), November 29. http://joelkotkin.com/001305-it-wasnt-rural-hicks-who-elected-trump-suburbs -were-and-will-remain-real-battleground/.

Kramer, Lawrence. 2007. *Classical Music Still Matters*. Berkeley: University of California Press.

Krasner, Stephen. 1985. *Structural Conflict: The Third World Against Global Liberalism*. Berkeley: University of California Press.

Krause, Sharon R. 2008. *Civil Passions: Moral Sentiment and Democratic Deliberation*. Princeton, NJ: Princeton University Press.

———. 2015. *Freedom Beyond Sovereignty: Reconstructing Liberal Individualism*. Chicago: University of Chicago Press.

———. 2019. "Environmental Domination." *Political Theory*, December 2. https:// journals.sagepub.com/doi/full/10.1177/0090591719890833.

———. 2020. "Political Respect for Nature." *Philosophy and Social Criticism*, March 26. https://journals.sagepub.com/doi/10.1177/0191453720910441.

Krogstad, Jens Manuel, and Mark Hugo Lopez. 2016. "Hillary Clinton Won Latino Vote but Fell Below 2012 Support for Obama." Pew Research Center, November 29. https://www.pewresearch.org/fact-tank/2016/11/29/hillary-clinton-wins-latino -vote-but-falls-below-2012-support-for-obama/.

Krugman, Paul R. 1987. "Is Free Trade Passé?" *Journal of Economic Perspectives* 1 (2): 131–144.

Kuhn, Theresa. 2012. "Why Educational Exchange Programmes Miss Their Mark: Cross-Border Mobility, Education and European Identity." *Journal of Common Market Studies* 50 (6): 994–1010.

———. 2011. "Individual Transnationalism, Globalisation and Euroscepticism: An Empirical Test of Deutsch's Transactionalist Theory." *European Journal of Political Research* 50:811–837.

Kusisto, Laura. 2016. "Housing Gains Highlight Economic Divide." *Wall Street Journal*, December 27. http://www.wsj.com/articles/housing-gains-highlight -economic-divide-1482881929.

Kutz, Christopher. 2000. *Complicity: Ethics and Law for a Collective Age*. Cambridge: University of Cambridge Press.

Kuznets, Simon. 1959. "The Meaning and Measurement of Economic Growth." In *Six Lectures on Economic Growth*, 13–19. Glencoe, IL: Free Press.

Kymlicka, Will. 1995. *Multicultural Citizenship: A Liberal Theory of Minority Rights*. Oxford, UK: Clarendon Press.

Lake, David A. 2009a. *Hierarchy in International Relations*. Ithaca, NY: Cornell University Press.

———. 2009b. "Open Economy Politics: A Critical Review." *Review of International Organization* 4:219–244.

Lal, Deepak. 1988–1989. *The Hindu Equilibrium*. 2 vols. Oxford: Clarendon Press.

———. 2001. *Unintended Consequences: The Impact of Factor Endowments, Culture, and Politics on Long-Run Economic Performance*. Cambridge, MA: MIT Press.

Lamont, Michèle. 2002. *The Dignity of Working Men Morality and the Boundaries of Race, Class, and Immigration*. Cambridge, MA: Harvard University Press.

Lamont, Michèle, and Sada Aksartova. 2002. "Ordinary Cosmopolitanisms: Strategies for Bridging Racial Boundaries Among Working-Class Men." *Theory, Culture and Society* 19 (4): 1–25.

Land, Richard D. 2017. "The Presidential Election: An Excruciating Choice." *Christian Post*, August 23. http://www.christianpost.com/news/the-presidential-election-an-excruciating-choice-168428/.

Lawder, David. 2015. "GE May Ship $10 Billion in Work Overseas as U.S. Trade Bank Languishes." *Reuters*, July 30. https://www.reuters.com/article/us-usa-eximbank-general-electric/ge-may-ship-10-billion-in-work-overseas-as-u-s-trade-bank-languishes-idUSKCN0Q42J920150730.

Lazonick, William. 2008. "Entrepreneurial Ventures and the Developmental State." United Nations University Discussion Paper No. 2008/01. https://www.wider.unu.edu/sites/default/files/dp2008-01.pdf.

Leatherby, Lauren. 2016. "US Urban-Rural Political Divide Deepened in 2016." *Financial Times*, November 15. https://www.ft.com/content/f7c7dd96-ab65-11e6-ba7d-76378e4fef24.

Lebow, Richard Ned. 2008. *A Cultural Theory of International Relations*. Cambridge: Cambridge University Press.

Legal Information Institute. n.d. "Strict Liability." Accessed January 14, 2020. https://www.law.cornell.edu/wex/strict_liability.

Leonhardt, David. 2017a. "The Assault on Colleges—and the American Dream." *New York Times*, May 25. https://www.nytimes.com/2017/05/25/opinion/sunday/the-assault-on-colleges-and-the-american-dream.html.

———. 2017b. "2017 College Access Index Methodology." *New York Times*, May 26. https://www.nytimes.com/2017/05/26/opinion/2017-college-access-index-methodology.html?action=click&contentCollection=Opinion&module=RelatedCoverage&region=Marginalia&pgtype=article.

Litfin, Karen. 2016. "Ontologies of Sustainability in Ecovillage Culture: Integrating Ecology, Economics, Community, and Consciousness." In *The Greening of Everyday Life: Challenging Practices, Imagining Possibilities*, edited by John M. Meyer and Jens M. Kersten, 249–264. Oxford: Oxford University Press.

Long, Heather. 2017. "Private Prison Stocks Up 100% Since Trump's Win." *CNN*, February 24. http://money.cnn.com/2017/02/24/investing/private-prison-stocks-soar-trump.

Loris, Nicolas D., and Derrick Morgan. 2012. "Cap-and-Trade for Cars Means Higher Prices and Less Choice for Car Buyers." *Backgrounder*, no. 2751. http://thf_media.s3.amazonaws.com/2012/pdf/bg2751.pdf.

Luke, Timothy W. 1997. *Ecocritique: Contesting the Politics of Nature, Economy, and Culture.* Minneapolis: University of Minnesota Press.

Lukes, Steven. 2005. *Power: A Radical View,* 2nd ed. Houndmills, UK: Palgrave Macmillan.

Mackie, J. L. 1980. *Hume's Moral Theory.* London: Routledge.

Mamonova, Natalia. 2019. "Understanding the Silent Majority in Authoritarian Populism: What Can We Learn from Popular Support for Putin in Rural Russia?" *Journal of Peasant Studies* 46 (3): 561–585.

Mansfield, Edward D., and Diana C. Mutz. 2009. "Support for Free Trade: Self-Interest, Sociotropic Politics, and Out-Group Anxiety." *International Organization* 63 (3): 425–457.

———. 2013. "US Versus Them: Mass Attitudes Toward Offshore Outsourcing." *World Politics* 65 (4): 571–608.

Mapes-Martins, Brad. 2016. "Household Maintenance and the Environmental Politics of Tending." In *The Greening of Everyday Life: Challenging Practices, Imagining Possibilities,* edited by John M. Meyer and Jens M. Kersten, 98–112. Oxford: Oxford University Press.

Martínez, Jessica, and Gregory A. Smith. 2016. "How the Faithful Voted: A Preliminary 2016 Analysis." Pew Research Center, November 9. http://www.pewresearch.org/fact-tank/2016/11/09/how-the-faithful-voted-a-preliminary-2016-analysis/.

MarketWatch. 2013. "The 10 Most Dangerous Cities in America." June 24. https://www.marketwatch.com/story/the-10-most-dangerous-cities-in-america-2013-06-22?page=7.

Marx, Karl. (1843) 1970. *Critique of Hegel's "Philosophy of Right."* Translated by Annette Jolin and Joseph O'Malley. Cambridge: Cambridge University Press.

Mascaro, Lisa. 2015. "Export-Import Bank's Expiration a Victory for Billionaire Koch Brothers." *Los Angeles Times,* July 2. https://www.latimes.com/business/la-fi-export-import-bank-20150701-story.html.

Maxwell, Angie, and T. Wayne Parent. 2012. "The Obama Trigger: Presidential Approval and Tea Party Membership." *Social Science Quarterly* 93 (5): 1384–1401.

Mayer, Jane. 2016. *Dark Money: The Hidden History of the Billionaires Behind the Rise of the Radical Right.* New York: Doubleday.

Mazower, Mark. 2009. *No Enchanted Palace: The End of Empire and the Ideological Origins of the United Nations.* Princeton, NJ: Princeton University Press.

Mazrui, Ali A. 1992. "The African University as a Multinational Corporation: Problems of Penetration and Dependency." In *Education and the Colonial Experience,* edited by Philip Altbach and Gail Kelly, 283–291. New York: Advent Books.

Mazzarol, Tim, and Geoffrey N. Soutar. 2002. "'Push-Pull' Factors Influencing International Student Destination Choice." *International Journal of Educational Management* 16 (2): 82–90.

McCarthy, Tom. 2017. "Trump Diehards Dismiss Russia Scandal: 'Show Me the Proof or Get Off His Case.'" *The Guardian,* May 19. https://www.theguardian.com/us-news/2017/may/19/trump-russia-the-promise-scandal-proof.

McClory, Jonathan. 2016. *The Soft Power 30: A Global Ranking of Soft Power*. Portland Communications. https://portland-communications.com/pdf/The-Soft-Power-30-Report-2016.pdf.

McCloskey, Deirdre N. 2010. *Bourgeois Dignity: Why Economics Can't Explain the Modern World*. Chicago: University of Chicago Press.

McKibben, Bill. 1989. *The End of Nature*. New York: Random House.

McNamara, Kathleen R. 2015. *The Politics of Everyday Europe: Constructing Authority in the European Union*. Oxford: Oxford University Press.

———. 2017. "Constructing Economic Interests: Geography, Culture and the Liberal International Order." Paper prepared for "Understanding Challenges to the Contemporary Global Order" conference, Filzbach, Switzerland, October 6–7.

Menon, Anand, and Alan Wager. 2018. "Brexit and British Politics." In *Brexit and Public Opinion*, 6–8. London: UK in a Changing Europe. https://ukandeu.ac.uk/wp-content/uploads/2018/01/Public-Opinion.pdf.

Mercatus Center. 2014. "The Biggest Beneficiaries of the Ex-Im Bank." https://www.mercatus.org/system/files/derugy-exim-exporters-final.pdf.

Merritt, Richard. 1966. "Nation Building in America: The Colonial Years." In *Nation Building in Comparative Contexts*, edited by Karl W. Deutsch and William Foltz, 56–72. New Brunswick, NJ: AdlineTransaction.

Mestre, Abel. 2013. "'Sudiste' et 'nordiste,' les deux électorats du FN" ["Southern" and "northern," the two FN electorates]. *Le Monde*, August 7. https://www.lemonde.fr/politique/article/2013/08/07/face-nord-et-face-sud-les-deux-electorats-du-fn_3458468_823448.html.

Migin, Melissa W., Mohammad Falahat, Mohd Shukri Ab Yajid, and Ali Khatibi. 2015. "Impacts of Institutional Characteristics on International Students' Choice of Private Higher Education Institutions in Malaysia." *Higher Education Studies* 5 (1): 31–42.

Milanović, Branko. 2016. *Global Inequality: A New Approach for the Age of Globalization*. Cambridge, MA: Harvard University Press.

Mishra, Pankaj. 2017. *Age of Anger: A History of the Present*. New York: Farrar, Straus Giroux.

Mitchell, Michael, Michael Leachman, and Kathleen Masterson. 2016. "Funding Down, Tuition Up: State Cuts to Higher Education Threaten Quality and Affordability at Public Colleges." Center on Budget and Policy Priorities, August 15. http://www.cbpp.org/research/state-budget-and-tax/funding-down-tuition-up.

Moen, Matthew. 1992. *The Transformation of the Christian Right*. Tuscaloosa: University of Alabama Press.

Moggridge, Donald E. 2005. "Keynes, the Arts, and the State." *History of Political Economy* 37 (3): 535–555.

Monnat, Shannon M. 2016. "Deaths of Despair and Support for Trump in the 2016 Presidential Election." Pennsylvania State University Department of Agricultural Economics, Sociology, and Education Research Brief 12/04/16. https://aese.psu.edu/directory/smm67/Election16.pdf.

Moravcsik, Andrew M. 1989. "Disciplining Trade Finance: The OECD Export Credit Arrangement." *International Organization* 43 (1): 173–205.

Moretti, Enrico. 2012. *The New Geography of Jobs*. New York: Houghton Mifflin Harcourt.

Muro, Mark, and Sifan Liu. 2016. "Another Clinton-Trump Divide: High-Output America vs. Low-Output America." *The Avenue* (blog), November 29. https://www.brookings.edu/blog/the-avenue/2016/11/29/another-clinton-trump-divide-high-output-america-vs-low-output-america/.

Murray, Charles. 2012. *Coming Apart: The State of White America, 1960–2010*. New York: Random House.

Mutz, Diana C. 2018. "Status Threat, Not Economic Hardship, Explains the 2016 Presidential Vote." *Proceedings of the National Academy of Science in the United States of America* 115 (19). https://www.pnas.org/content/115/19/E4330.short?rss=1.

Naess, Arne. 1986. "The Deep Ecological Movement: Some Philosophical Aspects." *Philosophical Inquiry* 8:10–31.

NAFSA. n.d. "Economic Value Statistics." http://www.nafsa.org/econvalue (accessed February 13, 2020).

Nagel, Thomas 1979. "Moral Luck." In *Mortal Questions*, 24–38. Cambridge: Cambridge University Press.

National Catholic Register. 2016. "Pope on Trump: Person Who Thinks Only About Building Walls, Not Building Bridges, Is Not Christian." February 18. http://www.ncregister.com/daily-news/pope-person-who-thinks-only-about-building-walls-not-building-bridges-is-no.

Navrud, Ståle, and Richard C. Ready, eds. 2002. *Valuing Cultural Heritage: Applying Environmental Valuation Techniques to Historic Buildings, Monuments and Artifacts*. Cheltenham, UK: Edward Elgar.

NBC News. 2016. "Trump: 'I Will Be Appointing Pro-Life Judges.'" October 19. https://www.nbcnews.com/video/trump-i-will-be-appointing-pro-life-judges-789632067780.

Niezen, Ronald. 2004. *A World Beyond Difference: Cultural Identity in the Age of Globalization*. Malden, MA: Blackwell.

Nolan, Riall W. 2001. *Development Anthropology*. London: Routledge.

Norris, Pippa. 2005. *Radical Right: Voters and Parties in the Electoral Market*. New York: Cambridge University Press.

———. 2018. "Understanding Brexit: Cultural Resentment Versus Economic Grievances." Harvard Kennedy School Working Paper No. RWP18-021. https://www.hks.harvard.edu/publications/understanding-brexit-cultural-resentment-versus-economic-grievances.

Norris, Pippa, and Ronald Inglehart. 2009. *Cosmopolitan Communications: Cultural Diversity in a Globalized World*. New York: Cambridge University Press.

North, Douglass C. 1994. "Economic Performance Through Time." *American Economic Review* 84 (3): 359–368.

Norton, David Fate. 1999. "Hume, Human Nature, and the Foundations of Morality." In *The Cambridge Companion to Hume*, edited by D. F. Norton, 148–191. Cambridge: Cambridge University Press.

Nye, Joseph S., Jr. 2004. *Soft Power: The Means to Success in World Politics*. New York: Public Affairs.

OECD (Organization for Economic Co-operation and Development). 2013. *Perspectives on Global Development, 2013: Industrial Policies in a Changing World*. Paris: OECD.

Office of the US Trade Representative. 1986. "Ambassador Yeutter Signs Investment Treaty with Bangladesh." March 12. In the author's possession.

———. 1992. "Bolivia, Colombia Eligible for Andean Trade Preferences." July 6. In the author's possession.

Olmstead, Sheila M. 2016. "Applying Market Principles to Environmental Policy." In *Environmental Policy: New Directions for the Twenty-First Century*, 9th ed., edited by Norman J. Vig and Michael E. Kraft, 215–238. Los Angeles: Sage.

Onuf, Nicholas. 2012. *Making Sense, Making Worlds: Constructivism in Social Theory and International Relations*. London: Routledge.

Ortner, Sherry B. 1984. "Theory in Anthropology Since the Sixties." *Comparative Studies in Society and History* 26 (1): 126–166.

Ostrom, Elinor. 2003. "Toward a Behavioral Theory Linking Trust, Reciprocity, and Reputation." In *Trust and Reciprocity: Interdisciplinary Lessons from Experimental Research*, edited by Elinor Ostrom and James Walker, 19–79. New York: Russell Sage.

Patten, Allen. 2011. "Rethinking Culture: The Social Lineage Account." *American Political Science Review* 105 (4): 735–749.

Pew Research Center. 2016. "Evangelicals Rally to Trump, Religious 'Nones' Back Clinton." July 13. http://www.pewforum.org/2016/07/13/evangelicals-rally-to-trump-religious-nones-back-clinton.

Pitts, Jonathan M. 2016. "Catholic Bishops, in Baltimore, Elect Advocates for Immigrants to Top Posts." *Baltimore Sun*, November 15. https://www.baltimoresun.com/maryland/bs-md-usccb-catholic-bishops-fall-assembly-election-20161115-story.html.

Plato. 1991. *Republic*. Translated by Allan Bloom. New York: Basic Books.

Pollan, Michael. 2006. *The Omnivore's Dilemma: A Natural History of Four Meals*. New York: Penguin.

Porter, Eduardo. 2016. "Where Were Trump's Votes? Where the Jobs Weren't." *New York Times*, December 13. https://www.nytimes.com/2016/12/13/business/economy/jobs-economy-voters.html.

Posner, Daniel N. 2004. "The Political Salience of Cultural Difference: Why Chewas and Tumbukas Are Allies in Zambia and Adversaries in Malawi." *American Political Science Review* 98 (4): 529–545.

Posner, Richard A. 1980. "Anthropology and Economics." *Journal of Political Economy* 88 (3): 608–616.

Prendergast, William B. 1999. *The Catholic Voter in American Politics: The End of the Democratic Monolith.* Washington, DC: Georgetown University Press.

Press, Daniel, and Daniel A. Mazmanian. 2016. "Toward Sustainable Production: Finding Workable Strategies for Government and Industry." In *Environmental Policy: New Directions for the Twenty-First Century*, 9th ed., edited by Norman J. Vig and Michael E. Kraft, 239–264. Los Angeles: Sage.

Puchala, Donald J. 2003. *Theory and History in International Relations.* New York: Routledge.

Purdy, Jedediah. 2015. *After Nature: A Politics for the Anthropocene.* Cambridge, MA: Harvard University Press.

Putnam, Robert D., Robert Leonardi, and Raffaella Y. Nonetti. 1993. *Making Democracy Work: Civic Traditions in Modern Italy.* Princeton, NJ: Princeton University Press.

Raju, Manu, and Burgess Everett. 2015. "Ex-Im Bank Expiration Now 'Inevitable' amid 2016 GOP Fight." *Politico*, June 4. https://www.politico.com/story/2015/06/ex-im-bank-expiration-now-inevitable-amid-2016-gop-fight-118663.

Ranganath, Aditya Narayanan. 2018. "The Politics of Globalization in a World of Global Cities." PhD diss., University of California, San Diego.

Rao, Vijayendra, and Michael Walton, eds. 2004. *Culture and Public Action.* Stanford, CA: Stanford University Press.

Rappeport, Alan. 2016. "Donald Trump Criticizes Pope Francis as 'Very Political' for Mexico Trip." *New York Times*, February 11. https://www.nytimes.com/politics/first-draft/2016/02/11/donald-trump-criticizes-pope-francis-as-very-political-for-mexico-trip/.

Raz, Joseph. 2011. *From Normativity to Responsibility.* Oxford: Oxford University Press.

Reissman, Leonard. 1959. *Class in American Society.* Glencoe, IL: Free Press.

Rich, Frank. 2017. "No Sympathy for the Hillbilly." *New York Magazine*, March 20. http://nymag.com/daily/intelligencer/2017/03/frank-rich-no-sympathy-for-the-hillbilly.html.

Richomme, Olivier. 2018. "A Catholic Latino Vote?" In *Catholics and US Politics After the 2016 Elections: Understanding the "Swing Vote,"* edited by Marie Gayte, Blandine Chelini-Pont, and Mark J. Rozell, 193–208. New York: Palgrave MacMillan.

Risse, Thomas. 2000. "'Let's Argue!': Communicative Action in World Politics." *International Organization* 54 (1): 1–39.

Robins, Kevin, and Asu Aksoy. 2001. "From Spaces of Identity to Mental Spaces: Lessons from Turkish-Cypriot Cultural Experience in Britain." *Journal of Ethnic and Migration Studies* 27 (4): 685–711.

Robinson, James A. 2011. "Industrial Policy and Development: A Political Economy Perspective." In *Annual World Bank Conference on Development Economics*, edited by J. Y. Lin and B. Pleskovic, 61–79. Washington, DC: World Bank.

Rodríguez-Pose, Andrés. 2018. "The Revenge of the Places That Don't Matter (and What to Do About It)." *Cambridge Journal of Regions, Economy and Society* 11 (1): 189–209.

Rodrik, Dani. 2008. "Normalizing Industrial Policy." World Bank Commision on Growth and Development Working Paper No. 3. http://documents.worldbank.org/curated/en/524281468326684286/pdf/577030NWP0Box31UBLIC10gc1wp10031web.pdf.

———. 2018. *Straight Talk on Trade: Ideas for a Sane World Economy.* Princeton, NJ: Princeton University Press.

Rodrik, Dani, and Arvind Subramanian. 2005. "From 'Hindu Growth' to Productivity Surge: The Mystery of the Indian Growth Transition." *IMF Staff Papers* 52 (2): 193–228.

Rommel, Tobias, and Stefanie Walter. 2016. "The Electoral Consequences of Offshoring." Center for Competitive Advantage in the Global Economy Working Paper No. 286. https://ideas.repec.org/p/cge/wacage/286.html.

Rorty, Richard. 1998. "Human Rights, Rationality, and Sentimentality." In *Truth and Progress: Philosophical Papers*, vol. 3, 167–185. Cambridge: Cambridge University Press.

Ross, Marc Howard. 2009. "Culture in Comparative Political Analysis." In *Comparative Politics: Rationality, Culture, and Structure*, 2nd ed., edited by Mark Irving Lichbach and Alan S. Zuckerman, 134–161. New York: Cambridge University Press.

Roth, Andrew. 2015. "Economist Greg Mankiw on the Export-Import Bank." Club for Growth, June 17. https://www.clubforgrowth.org/economist-greg-mankiw-on-the-export-import-bank/.

Rothwell, Jonathan, and Pablo Diego-Rosell. 2016. "Explaining Nationalist Political Views: The Case of Donald Trump." SSRN, November 2. https://papers.ssrn.com/sol3/papers.cfm?abstract_id=2822059.

Rozell, Mark J. 1997. "Growing Up Politically: The New Politics of the New Christian Right." In *Sojourners in the Wilderness: The Christian Right in Comparative Perspective*, edited by Corwin E. Smidt and James M. Penning, 235–248. Lanham, MD: Rowman and Littlefield.

———. 2018. "Introduction: The 'Catholic Vote' in the USA." In *Catholics and US Politics After the 2016 Elections*, edited by Marie Gayte, Blandine Chelini-Pont, and Mark J. Rozell, 1–19. New York: Palgrave Macmillan.

Rozell, Mark J., and Debasree Das Gupta. 2009. "Presidential Direct Action and Policy Continuity: The Case of U.S. International Population Policy." *Social Science Quarterly* 90 (4): 949–959.

Rozell, Mark J., and Clyde Wilcox. 1998. "Pragmatism and Its Discontents: The Evolution of the Christian Right in the United States." In *Religion in a Changing World: Comparative Studies in Sociology*, edited by Madeleine Cousineau, 193–202. Westport, CT: Praeger.

Ryle, Gilbert. 1971. *Collected Papers*, vol. 2, *Collected Essays: 1929–1968.* London: Hutchinson.

Said, Edward. 1994. *Culture and Imperialism.* New York: Vintage Books.

Salatin, Joel. 2007. *Everything I Want to Do Is Illegal: War Stories from the Local Food Front.* Swoope, VA: Polyface.

Sassen, Saskia. 2001. *The Global City*. 2nd ed. Princeton, NJ: Princeton University Press.

Schaefer-Wilke, Ute. 2018. "English Language Policy in German Public Sector Higher Education." Master's diss., St. Mary's University, London. https://doc player.net/90076873-English-language-policy-in-german-public-sector-higher -education-author-ute-schafer-wilke-st-mary-s-university-twickenham-london .html.

Schaffer, Lena Maria, and Gabriele Spilker. 2019. "Self-Interest Versus Sociotropic Considerations: An Information-Based Perspective to Understanding Individuals' Trade Preferences." *Review of International Political Economy* 26 (6): 1266–1292. https://www.tandfonline.com/doi/full/10.1080/09692290.2019.1642232.

Schlosberg, David. 2007. *Defining Environmental Justice*. Oxford: Oxford University Press.

Schlosberg, David, and Romand Coles. 2016. "The New Environmentalism of Everyday Life: Sustainability, Material Flows, and Movements." In *The Greening of Everyday Life: Challenging Practices, Imagining Possibilities*, edited by John M. Meyer and Jens M. Kersten, 13–30. Oxford: Oxford University Press.

Schrank, Andrew, and Josh Whitford. 2009. "Industrial Policy in the United States: A Neo-Polanyian Interpretation." *Politics and Society* 37 (4): 521–553.

Scitovsky, Tibor. 1972. "What's Wrong with the Arts Is What's Wrong with Society." *American Economic Review* 62 (1–2): 62–69.

Sen, Amartya. 1999. *Development as Freedom*. New York: Anchor Books.

———. 2006. *Identity and Violence: The Illusion of Destiny*. New York: Norton.

———. 2008. "Violence, Identity and Poverty." *Journal of Peace Research* 45 (1): 5–15.

Shearer, Chad. 2016. "The Small Town-Big City Split That Elected Donald Trump." *The Avenue* (blog), November 11. https://www.brookings.edu/blog/the-avenue/ 2016/11/11/the-small-town-big-city-split-that-elected-donald-trump/.

Sides, John, and Michael Tesler. 2016. "How Political Science Helps Explain the Rise of Trump (Part 3): It's the Economy, Stupid." *Monkey Cage* (blog), March 4. https:// www.washingtonpost.com/news/monkey-cage/wp/2016/03/04/how-political -science-helps-explain-the-rise-of-trump-part-3-its-the-economy-stupid.

Singh, J. P. 2008. *Negotiation and the Global Information Economy*. Cambridge: Cambridge University Press.

———. 2011. *Globalized Arts: The Entertainment Economy and Cultural Identity*. New York: Columbia University Press.

———. 2013. "Information Technologies, Meta-power, and Transformations in Global Politics." *International Studies Review* 15 (1): 5–29.

———. 2017. *Sweet Talk: Paternalism and Collective Action in North-South Trade Relations*. Stanford, CA: Stanford University Press.

Skocpol, Theda. 2016. "Who Owns the GOP?" *Dissent* 63 (2): 142–148.

Skocpol, Theda, and Alexander Hertel-Fernandez. 2016. "The Koch Network and Republican Party Extremism." *Perspectives on Politics* 14 (03): 681–699.

Skocpol, Theda, and Vanessa Williamson. 2012. *The Tea Party and the Remaking of Republican Conservatism*. New York: Oxford University Press.

Skrbiš, Zlatko, and Ian Woodward. 2007. "The Ambivalence of Ordinary Cosmopolitanism: Investigating the Limits of Cosmopolitan Openness." *Sociological Review* 55 (4): 730–747.

Smelser, Neil J. 2013. *The Sociology of Economic Life*. New Orleans, LA: Quid Pro Quo Books.

Smith, Adam. (1759) 1976. *The Theory of Moral Sentiments*. Edited by Alexander L. Macfie and David D. Rafael. Oxford, UK: Clarendon Press.

———. (1776) 1976. *An Inquiry into the Nature and Causes of the Wealth of Nations*. Edited by Roy Campbell, Andrew Skinner, and William B. Todd. Oxford, UK: Clarendon Press.

Smith, Barbara Herrnstein. 1988. *Contingencies of Value: Alternative Perspectives for Critical Theory*. Cambridge, MA: Harvard University Press.

Smith, Gregory A. 2017. "Most White Evangelicals Approve of Trump Travel Prohibition and Express Concerns About Extremism." Pew Research Center, February 27. http://www.pewresearch.org/fact-tank/2017/02/27/most-white-evangelicals-approve-of-trump-travel-prohibition-and-express-concerns-about-extremism/.

Sobolewska, Maria, and Robert Ford. 2018. "Brexit and Identity Politics." In *Brexit and Public Opinion*, 21–23. London: UK in a Changing Europe. https://ukandeu.ac.uk/wp-content/uploads/2018/01/Public-Opinion.pdf.

Sommers, Tamler. 2009. "The Two Faces of Revenge: Moral Responsibility and the Culture of Honor." *Biology and Philosophy* 24 (1): 35–50.

Stein, Sharon, and Vanessa Oliveira de Andreotti. 2016. "Cash, Competition, or Charity: International Students and the Global Imaginary." *Higher Education* 72 (2): 225–239.

Stengers, Isabelle. 2015. *In Catastrophic Times: Resisting the Coming Barbarism*. Translated by Andrew Goffey. London: Open Humanities Press.

Stewart, Katherine. 2016. "Eighty-One Percent of White Evangelicals Voted for Donald Trump: Why?" *The Nation*, November 17. https://www.thenation.com/article/eighty-one-percent-of-white-evangelicals-voted-for-donald-trump-why/.

Stiglitz, J. E., J. Esteban, and J. Y. Lin, eds. 2013. *The Industrial Policy Revolution I: The Role of Government Beyond Ideology*. New York: Palgrave Macmillan.

Stokols, Eli. 2016. "Trump Says He's 'Fine' with Legalization of Same-Sex Marriage." *Politico*, November 13. https://www.politico.com/story/2016/11/donald-trump-same-sex-marriage-231310.

Stone, Christopher D. 2010. *Should Trees Have Standing? Law, Morality, and the Environment*. Oxford: Oxford University Press.

Storper, Michael. 2018. "Separate Worlds? Explaining the Current Wave of Regional Economic Polarization." *Journal of Economic Geography* 18 (2): 247–270.

Straubhaar, Joseph D. 1984. "Brazilian Television: The Decline of American Influence." *Communication Research* 11 (2): 221–240.

———. 1991. "Beyond Media Imperialism: Asymmetrical Interdependence and Cultural Proximity." *Critical Studies in Mass Communication* 8 (1): 39–59.

Sunstein, Cass R. 2018. *#Republic: Divided Democracy in the Age of Social Media.* Princeton, NJ: Princeton University Press.

Swales, Kirby. 2016. "Understanding the Leave Vote." http://natcen.ac.uk/media/1319222/natcen_brexplanations-report-final-web2.pdf.

Swidler, Ann. 1986. "Culture in Action: Symbols and Strategies." *American Sociological Review* 51 (2): 273–286.

———. 2001. *Talk of Love: How Culture Matters.* Chicago: University of Chicago Press.

Swidler, Ann, and Susan C. Watkins. 2015. "Practices of Deliberation in Rural Malawi." In *Deliberation and Development: Rethinking the Role of Voice and Collective Action in Unequal Societies*, edited by Patrick Heller and Vijayendra Rao, 133–166. Washington, DC: World Bank.

Taxidou, Olga. 2018. "Hypocrite, Actor, Politician. . ." *Arts and International Affairs*, May 14. https://theartsjournal.net/2018/05/14/hypocrite-actor-politician/.

Taylor, Jessica. 2016. "Citing 'Two Corinthians,' Trump Struggles to Make the Sale to Evangelicals." *NPR*, January 18. https://www.npr.org/2016/01/18/463528847/citing-two-corinthians-trump-struggles-to-make-the-sale-to-evangelicals.

Thomas, Cal. 2016. "Cal Thomas Interviews Donald Trump." *Richmond Times-Dispatch*, June 9. https://www.richmond.com/opinion/their-opinion/thomas-cal-thomas-interviews-donald-trump/article_18a91f97-7e3b-5b46-a46d-e7a267957ed9.html.

Throsby, David. 1994. "The Production and Consumption of the Arts: A View of Cultural Economics." *Journal of Economic Literature* 32 (1): 1–29.

———. 2001. *Economics and Culture.* Cambridge: Cambridge University Press.

———. 2006. "Introduction and Overview." In *Handbook of the Economics of Art and Culture*, vol. 1., edited by Victor A. Ginsburgh and David Throsby, 3–22. Amsterdam: Elsevier.

———. 2011. "*The Political Economy of Art*: Ruskin and Contemporary Cultural Economics." *History of Political Economy* 43 (2): 275–294.

———. 2017. "Culturally Sustainable Development: Theoretical Concept or Practical Policy Instrument?" *International Journal of Cultural Policy* 23 (2): 133–147.

Throsby, David, and Anita Zednik. 2013. "The Economic and Cultural Value of Paintings: Some Empirical Evidence." In *Handbook of the Economics of Art and Culture*, vol. 2, edited by Victor A. Ginsburgh and David Throsby, 81–99. Amsterdam: Elsevier.

Throsby, David, Jan Zwar, and Callum Morgan. 2017. "Australian Book Readers: Survey Method and Results." Macquarie University Economics Research Paper 1/2017. https://www.australiacouncil.gov.au/workspace/uploads/files/australian-book-readers-24-05-592762e0c3ade.pdf.

Towse, Ruth, ed. 1997. *Cultural Economics: The Arts, the Heritage and the Media Industries.* 2 vols. Cheltenham, UK: Edward Elgar.

———, ed. 2007. *Recent Developments in Cultural Economics*. Cheltenham, UK: Edward Elgar.

Trump, Donald J. 2016. Letter to pro-life leaders. September. https://www.sba-list.org/wp-content/uploads/2016/09/Trump-Letter-on-ProLife-Coalition.pdf.

Turner, Edith. 2012. *Communitas: The Anthropology of Collective Joy*. New York: Palgrave Macmillan.

Turner, Laura. 2016. "Will Trump's Nomination Be the End of the Religious Right?" *Politico Magazine*, July 11. https://www.politico.com/magazine/story/2016/07/2016-donald-trump-religion-christian-conservatives-republican-party-gop-faith-voters-evangelicals-214037.

UK and a Changing Europe. 2018. *Brexit and Public Opinion*. London: UK and a Changing Europe. https://ukandeu.ac.uk/wp-content/uploads/2018/01/Public-Opinion.pdf.

UNESCO. 2001. "Universal Declaration on Cultural Diversity." November. http://www.unesco.org/new/fileadmin/MULTIMEDIA/HQ/CLT/pdf/5_Cultural_Diversity_EN.pdf.

———. 2015. *Reshaping Cultural Policies: A Decade Promoting the Diversity of Cultural Expressions for Development*. Paris: UNESCO.

US Bureau of Labor Statistics. 2020. "Databases, Tables and Calculators by Subject." https://data.bls.gov/timeseries/LNS14000000.

US Government Accountability Office. 2014. "Export-Import Bank: Information on Export Credit Agency Financing Support for Wide-Body Jets." July 8. https://www.gao.gov/assets/670/664679.pdf.

Van Dyke, N., and D. S. Meyer, eds. 2016. *Understanding the Tea Party Movement*. New York: Routledge.

van Graan, Mike, and Sophia Sanan. 2015. "Minding the Gaps: Promoting Mobility." In *Reshaping Cultural Policies: A Decade Promoting the Diversity of Cultural Expressions for Development*, 105–119. Paris: UNESCO.

Van Oudenaren, John S., and Benjamin E. Fisher. 2016. "Foreign Military Education as PLA Soft Power." *Parameters* 46 (4): 105–118.

Vance, J. D. 2016. *Hillbilly Elegy: A Memoir of a Family and Culture in Crisis*. New York: HarperCollins.

Vanderheiden, Steve. 2009. *Atmospheric Justice: A Political Theory of Climate Change*. Oxford: Oxford University Press.

Vertovec, Steven. 2001. "Transnationalism and Identity." *Journal of Ethnic and Migration Studies* 27 (4): 573–582.

Vertovec, Steven, and Robin Cohen. 2002. "Introduction: Conceiving Cosmopolitanism." In *Conceiving Cosmopolitanism: Theory, Context, and Practice*, 1–22. New York: Oxford University Press.

Vogel, Steven. 2016. *Thinking Like a Mall: Environmental Philosophy After the End of Nature*. Cambridge, MA: MIT Press.

Wagner, John, and Sarah Pulliam Bailey. 2017. "Trump Signs Order Seeking to Allow Churches to Engage in More Political Activity." *Washington Post*, May 4.

https://www.washingtonpost.com/politics/trump-signs-order-aimed-at-allowing
-churches-to-engage-in-more-political-activity/2017/05/04/024ed7c2-30d3-11e7
-9534-00e4656c22aa_story.html.

Walker, Shaun. 2019. "German President Asks Poland for Forgiveness at WW2 Ceremony." *The Guardian*, September 1. https://www.theguardian.com/world/2019/
sep/01/german-president-asks-poland-for-forgiveness-at-ww2-ceremony.

Wang, Hongying. 2001. *Weak State, Strong Networks: The Institutional Dynamics of
Foreign Direct Investment in China*. New York: Oxford University Press.

Warwick, Ken. 2013. "Beyond Industrial Policy: Emerging Issues and New Trends."
OECD Science, Technology and Industry Policy Papers No. 2. https://www
.oecd-ilibrary.org/science-and-technology/beyond-industrial-policy_5k4869clw
0xp-en.

Weber, Max. 1930. *The Protestant Ethic and the Spirit of Capitalism*. London: Allen and
Unwin.

Wedeen, Lisa. 2002. "Conceptualizing Culture: Possibilities for Political Science."
American Political Science Review 96 (4): 713–728.

Weigel, David, and Jose A. Del Real. 2016. "Phyllis Schlafly Endorses Trump in
St. Louis." *Washington Post*, March 11. https://www.washingtonpost.com/news/
post-politics/wp/2016/03/11/phyllis-schlafly-endorses-trump-in-st-louis/.

Weisman, Jonathan. 2015. "Tea Party Divided by Export-Import Bank." *New York
Times*, March 9. https://www.nytimes.com/2015/03/10/business/smallbusiness/
small-business-leaders-wage-counteroffensive-to-save-export-import-bank.html.

Weiss, Linda. 2014. *America Inc.? Innovation and Enterprise in the National Security
State*. Ithaca, NY: Cornell University Press.

Wendt, Alexander. 1999. *Social Theory of International Politics*. Cambridge: Cambridge
University Press.

White, Damian F., Alan P. Rudy, and Brian J. Gareau. 2016. *Environments, Natures and
Social Theory: Towards a Critical Hybridity*. London: Palgrave.

White House. 2017. "Remarks by President Trump at National Prayer Breakfast." February 2. https://www.whitehouse.gov/briefings-statements/remarks-president
-trump-national-prayer-breakfast/.

Whitman, James Q. 2017. *Hitler's American Model: The United States and the Making of
Nazi Race Law*. Princeton, NJ: Princeton University Press.

Wikipedia. 2020. "*Keeping Up Appearances*." February 11. https://en.wikipedia.org/
wiki/Keeping_Up_Appearances.

Wilcox, Clyde, and Carin Larson. 2006. *Onward Christian Soldiers? The Religious
Right in American Politics*. 3rd ed. Boulder, CO: Westview.

Wilkinson, Rorden. 2011. "Measuring the WTO's Performance: An Alternative Account." *Global Policy* 2 (1): 43–52.

Williams, Peter. 1984. "Britain's Full-Cost Policy for Overseas Students." *Comparative
Education Review* 28 (2): 258–278.

Williamson, Kevin D. 2017. "Chaos in the Family, Chaos in the State: The White Working Class's Dysfunction." *National Review*, March 17. http://www.nationalreview

.com/article/432876/donald-trump-white-working-class-dysfunction-real
-opportunity-needed-not-trump.

World Bank. 1993. *The East Asian Miracle: Economic Growth and Public Policy.* Washington, DC: World Bank.

World Commission on Culture and Development (WCCD). 1995. *Our Creative Diversity: Report of the World Commission on Culture and Development.* Paris: WCCD.

World Commission on Environment and Development (WCED). 1987. *Our Common Future: Report of the World Commission on Environment and Development.* Oxford: Oxford University Press.

World Standards. 2019. "Why Do Some Countries Drive on the Left and Others on the Right?" January 13. http://www.worldstandards.eu/cars/driving-on-the-left/.

Wu, Irene S. 2018. "Soft Power Amidst Great Power Competition." Wilson Center, May. https://www.wilsoncenter.org/sites/default/files/2018-05-soft_power_-_wu.pdf.

Wuhs, Steven, and Eric McLaughlin. 2019. "Explaining Germany's Electoral Geography: Evidence from the Eastern States." *German Politics and Society* 37 (1): 1–23.

Yang, Jonghoe. 2012. "The Korean Wave (*Hallyu*) in East Asia: A Comparison of Chinese, Japanese, and Taiwanese Audiences Who Watch Korean TV Dramas." *Development and Society* 41 (1): 103–147.

Young, Iris Marion. 2011. *Responsibility for Justice.* New York: Oxford University Press.

Zeeshan, Muhammad, Sabbar Dahham Sabbar, Shahid Bashir, and Rai Imtiaz Hussain. 2013. Foreign Students' Motivation for Studying in Malaysia. *International Journal of Asian Social Science* 3 (3): 833–846.

Zernike, Kate. 2012. *Boiling Mad: Inside Tea Party America.* New York: St. Martin's.

Zhang, Xiaobo, and Kevin H. Zhang. 2003. "How Does Globalisation Affect Regional Inequality Within a Developing Country? Evidence from China." *Journal of Development Studies* 39 (4): 47–67.

Zito, Salena. 2017. "Why Trump's Approval Ratings Don't Matter." *New York Post,* March 25. http://nypost.com/2017/03/25/dont-believe-trumps-approval-ratings/.

Index

Page numbers in italics indicate material in figures or tables.

The authorized representative in the EU for product safety and compliance is:
Mare Nostrum Group
B.V Doelen 72
4831 GR Breda
The Netherlands

www.ingramcontent.com/pod-product-compliance
Lightning Source LLC
Chambersburg PA
CBHW030353270326
41926CB00009B/1090